3962 9224

110643659

WITHDRAWN
BEAVERTON CITY LIBRARY
Beaverton, OR 97005
Member of Washington County
COOPERATIVE LIBRARY SERVICES

FOREIGN EXCHANGE

AN INTRODUCTION TO THE CORE CONCEPTS

FOREIGN EXCHANGE

AN INTRODUCTION TO THE CORE CONCEPTS

Mark Mobius

John Wiley & Sons (Asia) Pte. Ltd.

Copyright © 2009 by John Wiley & Sons (Asia) Pte Ltd
Published in 2009 by John Wiley & Sons (Asia) Pte Ltd
2 Clementi Loop, #02-01, Singapore 129809

All rights reserved.

No part of this publication may be reproduced, stored in a retrieval system or transmitted in any form
or by any means, electronic, mechanical, photocopying, recording, scanning or otherwise, except as
expressly permitted by law, without either the prior written permission of the Publisher, or authorization
through payment of the appropriate photocopy fee to the Copyright Clearance Center. Requests for
permission should be addressed to the Publisher, John Wiley & Sons (Asia) Pte Ltd, 2 Clementi Loop,
#02-01, Singapore 129809, tel: 65-64632400, fax: 65-64646912, e-mail: enquiry@wiley.com.sg.

This publication is designed to provide accurate and authoritative information in regard to the
subject matter covered. It is sold with the understanding that the publisher is not engaged in rendering
professional services. If professional advice or other expert assistance is required, the services of a
competent professional person should be sought.

Other Wiley Editorial Offices

John Wiley & Sons, Inc., 111 River Street, Hoboken, NJ 07030, USA
John Wiley & Sons Ltd, The Atrium, Southern Gate, Chichester PO19 8SQ, UK
John Wiley & Sons (Canada) Ltd, 5353 Dundas Street West, Suite 400, Toronto, Ontario, M9B 6HB,
    Canada
John Wiley & Sons Australia Ltd, 42 McDougall Street, Milton, Queensland 4064, Australia
Wiley-VCH, Boschstrasse 12, D-69469 Weinheim, Germany

Library of Congress Cataloging-in-Publication Data
978-0-470-82145-9

Typeset in 11points, Galliard by Hot Fusion
Printed in Singapore by Saik Wah Press Ltd
10 9 8 7 6 5 4 3 2 1

CONTENTS

ACKNOWLEDGMENTS

Many commentators and scholars have studied foreign exchange around the world and their concepts have provided the stimulus for many of the ideas discussed in this book. There are too many to mention and to thank individually but I hope that I have been able to accurately reflect the body of knowledge available now about foreign exchange.

Special thanks go to Shalini Dadlani, as well as John Wiley's Janis Soo and Nick Wallwork for their help on this project.

To help us improve future editions of this book, please email your comments to: jmarkmobius@yahoo.com.

THE HISTORY OF MONEY: BARTER AND ANCIENT TRADE

HOW DID MARKETS FUNCTION WITHOUT COINS AND PAPER MONEY?

The concept of barter is familiar to all of us. For instance, a babysitter could exchange her services for a couple of tickets to a rock concert. Or a bachelor might get his elderly neighbor to mend his shirts and trousers in exchange for mowing her lawn. In both cases, no money changes hands. The Oxford English Dictionary defines barter as "to trade by exchanging goods and services for other goods and services, not for money." It is probably the oldest way of conducting business and predates the use of coins and paper money. But as implied by the examples above, bartering is still common in the present day.

Historians trace the origins of barter to the early Stone Age period between 8000 BC and 6000 BC, in settlements in the Middle East, Greece and Turkey, as well as in many parts of Asia and Africa. Before this time, humans mainly subsisted by hunting and gathering food. They had to be self-sufficient to keep from starving and this encouraged a nomadic existence as they sought new areas in which to forage. Sometimes they may not have been compelled to trade, perhaps taking what they wanted from rival groups of hunter-gatherers by force, rather than negotiation, if the situation arose. The hunter-gatherer way of life started to wane during the Neolithic period, when people first learned to cultivate crops and make a variety of basic tools. They began to domesticate animals, such as cattle, sheep, and camels, as sources of food and to work on their farms. As a store of value, these domesticated animals became items for barter. Farming, animal domestication, and trade allowed people to settle in fixed locations and develop greater food productivity. This, in turn, led to accelerated population growth, and consequently, translated into more mouths to feed.

These nascent agrarian communities, faced many problems. Climatic events such as droughts or flooding would have severely damaged or depleted crops. But as communities adapted to a variety of environmental conditions, they may have been able to achieve surpluses of crops and produce. These

"We are neither hunters nor gatherers. We are accountants."

© The New Yorker Collection 1993 Sam Gross from cartoonbank.com. All Rights Reserved.

could have been stored to help sustain those communities over longer periods, such as the winter months, or they could have been exchanged for other goods or produce. In this way, bartering developed as people would trade their surplus goods for items they did not grow or make. Bartering may have started within the communities themselves, gradually expanding to embrace other settlements and cultures.

We can make some inferences about how people bartered in those early days. Let's look at two theoretical communities. One of them was good at rearing cattle while the other became adept at growing wheat. These two communities may have bartered wheat for cattle, if they were able to find each other. The exchange of goods would have been smooth if each community got what it wanted. Therefore, they had to decide what a fair exchange of goods was. This quantum of exchange was hard to determine as it varied with different counterparties and between different regions. For instance, how much would one cow have been worth in terms of bags of wheat? This would have depended on how the two parties valued their own wheat and cattle against the wheat and cattle of other communities, and how badly they needed what the other party had. To make matters worse, communication problems would also have existed between different peoples. Nonetheless, agreements were definitely reached because the barter system started to thrive during the Neolithic period.

THE LIMITS OF BARTER
Indeed, bartering worked as long as people had goods that other people

needed and vice versa. But there were problems with this system. What if a person or a community had something to trade that no one else wanted? Or what if the terms for a fair transaction could not be agreed upon? The limitations of barter trade probably became more evident as communities started to interact over greater distances.

We know that the paths taken by people from one area to another, for trade purposes, were gradually transformed into a network of trade routes connecting larger and more distant areas. These routes, such as the Incense Route stretching from Egypt, through Arabia, to India and the Spice Route from Portugal, around Africa, to India, linked great civilizations. Probably the best known of these ancient trade routes is the Silk Road that connected China with the Mediterranean region. This was not a single road but a series of interconnected routes, especially as it passed through Central Asia. Not only was silk traded on it, but also other goods such as grain, gold, rubies, opium, pearls and jade. The Silk Road was immortalised by Venetian explorer Marco Polo in the book, *The Travels of Marco Polo*, written in the thirteenth century. But by then, barter trade had long been superseded by the use of money for trade. How and why did this happen?

THE DEVELOPMENT OF CURRENCY
There were several reasons for replacing barter trade, some of which we have already alluded to. For barter to successfully take place, there has to be what is termed by economists a "double coincidence of wants"—that is, Mr. A must want what Mr. B has and Mr. B must simultaneously want what Mr. A has. Finding someone else whose immediate needs exactly complement one's own can be costly in terms of time and effort. Imagine transporting your goods to a marketplace miles away from your home only to find that no one is interested in what you have to barter. This may have been the reality for many people during the Neolithic period, who would have had to return to their communities disappointed. In addition, the risk of damage or robbery when traveling beyond your own clan or community would have made barter increasingly unappealing.

To overcome the problems surrounding barter, the great early civilizations, who thrived on trade, gradually developed alternative means of exchange. Common barter commodities, such as wheat, for which there would always be demand, were standardized into weights and measures which, in turn, helped to value other goods and services by using those terms. But, as mediums of exchange, the use of such commodities was still limited since the cost of transporting them was high. Therefore, a "medium of exchange" that could be carried around easily and was broadly recognized as having value was required. Also, once received, people could use these mediums of exchange to buy other goods. This was the origin of what we now call "currency" or "money."

Around 1200 BC, cowrie shells were first used as a medium of exchange or currency, in China. The Chinese character for money originally resembled a cowrie shell since Chinese characters reflected the shape of the physical objects they represented. Over time, these pictograms have evolved from irregular drawings into a definite form—they have been simplified to make them easier to write. Cowrie shells were widely available on the shores of the Pacific and Indian oceans, and were still used as currency in some parts of the world as recently as the middle of the twentieth century.

Cowrie shell

Source: www. calgarycoin.com/ reference/china/ china1.htm

It is unlikely that, in 1200 BC, everyone immediately agreed to use cowrie shells as a form of currency. Indeed, it is widely accepted that the use of currencies did not have a single origin, but developed independently in different parts of the world. For instance, cowrie shells and, later bone, stone and bronze imitations of cowrie shells, were used for trade in China during the period of the Shang dynasty between 1200 BC and 1030 BC. But people in other parts of China, who were often still nomadic, used coins

Chinese character for wealth

shaped like small knives. For shepherds, hunters, and fishermen, the knife was an indispensable object that might be used as barter, and that finally, in a stylized form, had the function of a coin attributed to it. Apart from knife money, a host of other currencies were introduced at different times and in different places. These included amber, beads, drums, feathers, ivory, jade, leather, mats, nails, thimbles, vodka, and yarn. As trade routes opened up and expanded, this variety of currencies became more and more standardized, in order to gain wider acceptance.

WHY WAS BARTER TRADE EVENTUALLY SUPERSEDED?

Some historians hold the view that the disadvantages of barter were not the main factors driving the early development of money. In his book, *A History of Money: From Ancient Times to the Present Day*, Glyn Davies writes that in Neolithic societies, payments were required for many reasons, such as fines for crimes committed, dowries for brides, or taxes and tributes to rulers. In Davies' view, various currencies were already being used for purposes other than trade. He contends that these currencies eventually found further uses in trading activity.

Ancient Chinese spade money

Source: www.calgarycoin.com/ reference/china/china1.htm

Ancient Chinese knife money

Source: www.calgarycoin. com/reference/china /china1.htm

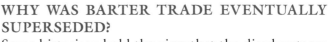

Many questions remain about the exact origins of money. There was a significant period in early human history when barter was the dominant force in trading activities. Furthermore, it is reasonable to say that the shift from barter towards the use of currencies was a gradual one. This shift may have been more seamless in some places than in others. In those transitional times, there would have been haggling as to how much a currency was worth, in terms of goods or services. But is this not unlike the bargaining between buyers and sellers in modern-day street bazaars across the world? The difference is that, initially, our ancestors did not have any fair bases for comparison—that is, agreements on value and price had to be reached without much reference to previous transactions. But as more transactions were executed, this grew the "database" of allocated value to currencies,

OPINION
UNCERTAINTIES ABOUT
THE ORIGINS OF CURRENCIES

Science journalist Heather Pringle delves into the uncertainties about the origins of money in an article she wrote for Discover *magazine in April 2003 titled "The Invention of Money." She writes: "When did humans first arrive at the concept of money? What conditions spawned it? And how did it affect the ancient societies that created it? Until recently, researchers thought they had the answers. They believed that in Europe money was born, as coins, along the coasts of the Mediterranean in the seventh or sixth century BC, a product of the civilization that later gave the world the Parthenon, Plato, and Aristotle. But few see the matter so simply now. With evidence gleaned from such disparate sources as ancient temple paintings, clay tablets, and buried hoards of uncoined metals, researchers have* revealed far more ancient money: Silver scraps and bits of gold, massive rings and gleaming ingots."

Her view that money dates back to an earlier time than has been conventionally believed is shared by Bernard Lietaer who writes in his book, The Future of Money, *that money, "... like certain other essential elements in civilization, is a far more ancient institution than we were taught to believe some few years ago. Its origins are lost in the mists when the ice was melting, and may well stretch into the paradisiac intervals in human history of the inter-glacial periods, when the weather was delightful and the mind free to be fertile of new ideas—in the islands of the Hesperides or Atlantis or some Eden of Central Asia."*

as well as goods and services, resulting in mediums of exchange becoming more standardized and accepted.

THE FUNCTIONS OF CURRENCY

It is useful to map out the key functions of money as we know them now. This will give us a better insight into the motivations governing the development of coins and paper money. Historically, money has had three essential functions:

- **Medium of exchange:** Money is used so that goods and services can be exchanged easily.

- **Measure of value:** Money is used to let people fairly assess the comparative worth of different goods and services.

- **Store of value:** Money can be reliably saved without spoiling and used at a later date with predictability.

On the basis of these three key functions, money developed the following distinct characteristics:

- Convertibility

- Portability

- Divisibility

- Durability

- Stability of value

These characteristics were already evident in the earliest coins recorded in our history. If we look at these functions in terms of a wheat-for-cow barter trade, we can see why a money trade was easier than bartering. Wheat may have been a better medium of exchange than cattle, but it also had its portability limits. As a measure of value, it may have been difficult to consistently assess the comparative worth of wheat and cattle. For instance, some cattle may have been bigger than others, while certain types of wheat may have drawn strong demand from some people, but not from others. As for a store of value, how long could a cow be kept before its value dropped due to ageing? Also, what was the use-by date for wheat before it became mouldy and carried no value at all? Divisibility would be a problem as it would be impossible to divide a cow into equally valued parts. Durability was an issue for both wheat and a cow since one could vanish with a flame while the other would age or die. Coins were an obvious alternative.

THE EARLIEST COINS

What then were the earliest coins? It is generally believed that the Lydians, in Asia Minor, were the first people to have struck metal coins, around 650 BC. This breakthrough was documented by the Greek historian Herodotus in his book *The Histories* in the fifth century BC. The earliest coins were made from electrum, an alloy of gold and silver. Lydia was one of the most important sources of electrum in the ancient world, and its capital city, Sardis, was a major commercial center that linked the Asian kingdoms of the East with cities surrounding the Aegean Sea. From Lydia, electrum coinage spread to the Greek cities of Asia Minor such as Byzantium, Chalcedon and Xanthus (present-day Kinik in western Turkey). From there, it reached the Greek islands and then the mainland. But historians often find it difficult to tell where a particular coin was struck as these early coins were not inscribed with the names of the places where they were made. Still, as coins were produced by states, rather than private individuals, their designs and inscriptions are a very rich source of information about political history, religion, and culture. It helps too that coins are among the most commonly found archaeological objects.

The earliest known hoard of electrum coins was found buried in a pot during the British Museum's 1904–5 excavations of the Temple of Artemis at Ephesus. This was one of the great Ionian Greek cities of Asia Minor that existed in 600 BC, in what is now Turkey. Ancient coins are often found in hoards such as this. It is believed that they were buried due to fear of unrest, such as imminent war, and the levels of destruction often found in the proximity of coin hoard discoveries suggest this to be true.

In the book *Sources of Ancient History*, Michael Crawford writes that a coin hoard can be defined as a "group of coins whose discovery makes it clear that the hoard was deliberately buried in a group." According to Crawford, what the hoard comprises can help us understand why it was put together in the first place. For example, he says that some hoarders chose coins based on how valuable they were, while others selected coins that reflected the contemporary ruler. Another view is that coin hoards could simply have been ancient savings accounts—people dipped into them when funds were needed for payments or trade. The hoarding of coins is in itself revealing as it shows that the people of these times were aware of the value of coins and made provision to keep them safe.

Coins have survived over the centuries for several reasons. Since they were made of sturdy metals like electrum, gold, silver, copper, and its alloys bronze or brass, they lasted longer than other ancient artifacts. Some metal coins, such as those made of gold and silver, have survived longer than bronze coins. The latter tended to corrode more easily, but to archaeologists and historians this corrosion can also be useful as it helps to date the coins. The relatively small size of coins is another property that has helped them to survive over a long periods—unlike metal tools, which disintegrate into smaller pieces. Finally, older coins would have been recognized, by people who found them, as objects of value and they would have been more mindful of keeping them safe.

THE PHYSICAL CHARACTERISTICS OF EARLY COINS

In his essay, *The Production of Ancient Coins,* Jere M. Wickens says that almost all early coins were struck by hand, and the striking process changed little from the beginning of coinage until the sixteenth century, when machines were first used. He describes three stages in the striking of coins:

- Making a blank, or flan—the plain lump or disk of metal

- Making the dies with the letters, numerals, symbols, or reliefs to stamp the blank

- Striking the coin by hammering the die onto the blank

According to Wickens, almost all early coins were issued by the government, either in its own name or in the name of the ruler or some official designated by the state. The issuer determined the weight, type, and purity of the metal for the coins and also the wording or symbols stamped on them. The state would have also specified a nominal value for each coin. Although they were not of standard size, the early electrum coins of ancient Greek or Lydian origin were struck according to strict weights. The British Museum notes that the denominations ranged from one "stater" (about 14.1g) through half-staters, thirds, sixths, twelfths, twenty-fourths, and forty-eighths to ninety-sixth staters (about 0.15g). These early electrum coins were not minted for long and were replaced by coins made out of silver. According to historians, gold coins did not become common until the time of King Philip II of Macedon (382–336 BC), the father of Alexander the Great.

Coins of gold and silver had intrinsic value, and the weight of individual coins of the same denomination was closely monitored. Not all states followed the same weight standard, but each state adhered to its own standard in striking coins. The purity of the metal used for gold and silver coins was also closely monitored. Throughout Greek and Roman times, between 750 BC and 476 AD, gold coins were consistently of a very high purity—often more than 95% pure gold. Silver coins were of an equally high purity until the time of the Emperor Nero of Rome (37–68 AD), who lowered the silver content in the first century AD, but only to about 90%. Silver content in silver coins was progressively lowered in the years that followed, eventually settling at about 2.5%.

THE DEVELOPMENT OF PAPER MONEY

The coinage of the Lydians had been in existence for more than a millennium when paper money first emerged in China under the Tang dynasty (618–907 AD). The early development of paper money continued during the Song dynasty (960–1279 AD). With its capital in present-day Xi'an, in the central region of China (where the famous terracotta soldiers were discovered), the Tang dynasty was considered one of China's most glorious eras, marked by significant social, political, and cultural changes.

According to *A History of World Societies*, by John P. McKay *et al.*, the Chinese economy was prospering during these eras. Peasants in the more densely populated regions were drawn to commerce, selling their food surpluses and buying charcoal, tea, oil, and wine. This created a demand for shipping services for interregional trade, with the Yangtze River a key conduit for transporting goods to settlements along its banks. As the level of activity grew, the demand for money grew in tandem. According to McKay et al., "by 1085 the

Early Chinese paper money
© Garry Saint, Esquire 1999-2008
www.numismondo.com

output of coins had increased tenfold to more than six billion coins a year. To avoid the weight and bulk of coins for large transactions, local merchants in late Tang times started trading receipts from deposit shops where they left money or goods. The early Song dynasty authorities awarded a small set of shops a monopoly on the issuing of these certificates of deposit, and in the 1120s the government took over the system, producing the world's first government-issued paper money." Paper money was originally known as *feiqian* or "flying money" because of its light weight. With the government taking over the issuing of paper money, local taxes and revenues could be more easily forwarded to the capital. Paper exchange certificates issued by the government were also in circulation. These were redeemable, in different locations, for commodities such as salt and tea. With these developments in paper money during the early Song dynasty, Chinese financial institutions were already conducting all major banking functions, including the acceptance of deposits, the making of loans, issuing of notes, money exchange, and the long-distance remittance of money.

Marco Polo was impressed by the use of the paper money in China and mentioned it in his book. This may have helped to carry the idea to the West. He described the issue of paper money in China thus: "All these pieces of paper are issued with as much solemnity and authority as if they were of pure gold or silver; and on every piece, a variety of officials, whose duty it is, have to write their names, and to put their seals. And when all is duly prepared, the chief officer deputed by the Khan smears the Seal entrusted to him with vermilion, and impresses it on the paper, so that the form of the Seal remains printed upon it in red—the Money is then authentic. Anyone forging it would be punished with death." Northern China was ruled by

Kublai Khan during the time that Marco Polo was there. In 1260, Kublai Khan had stepped up as the Great Khan of the vast Mongol Empire and had moved the Mongolian capital to Beijing, showing his intent to conquer the rest of China. Marco Polo became a confidante of Kublai Khan during his time in China.

According to the Silk Road Foundation, a form of paper currency called "flying cash" by the Chinese (since the wind could blow the paper away) was first used in the Tang dynasty (618–907 AD) in China in the form of certificates which could be converted into copper or silver currency on demand at the capital. Since the certificates were transferable, merchants exchanged them amongst themselves and used them almost as currency. Real official paper currency was adopted early in the Song dynasty (960–1279 AD) when it was used in Szechuan Province where printing was first invented. Bank notes issued at that time had pictures of houses, trees and people printed on them. Red and black inks were used with the each bill with various seals and confidential marks which made counterfeiting difficult. The notes could be converted to hard cash at the issuing banks. In 1023 they were withdrawn and only notes printed by the government were allowed. This system was successful because each note was backed by cash in standard interchangeable units and people could use the notes to buy salt and other commodities from government-owned stores. The Chin dynasty (1115–1234 AD) followed the Song system and established a Bureau of Paper Currency in 1154 as the sole agency to issue paper currency with each note exchangeable to standard coins. However, the currency was not fully backed with hard cash and excessive currency printing resulted in inflation. When the Mongols took over China and Kublai Khan established the yuan dynasty (1264–1368 AD) the use of paper currency was continued. Various denominations were printed, ranging from a face value of two standard coins to the highest denomination of two strings of coins. Excessive printing year after year soon flooded the market with depreciated paper money until the face value of each certificate bore no relation whatsoever to its counterpart in silver. In 1272 a series of new issues was put in circulation and the old issues were converted into the new ones at the ratio of five to one. The new issues were of better quality since they were printed with copper plates instead of wood blocks as had been used previously. A number of currency issues were made resulting in massive depreciation so that in the fifty years from 1260 to 1309, the yuan dynasty's paper money was depreciated by 1000 percent.

THE INTRODUCTION OF PAPER MONEY IN EUROPE

Paper money usage on a national scale and on a regular basis fizzled out until it reappeared in Europe around the seventeenth century. Indeed, when the older methods of paper money issuance became known in the West, they probably had a deep influence on banking activity there. While it is unclear exactly how the older, Chinese concept of paper money reached Europe, it can be assumed that the original idea of issuing paper money—to provide a valuable substitute that was redeemable in gold or silver—would have held. Paper money was more convenient, and as long as it was regarded as equivalent to precious metals, people were confident in using it.

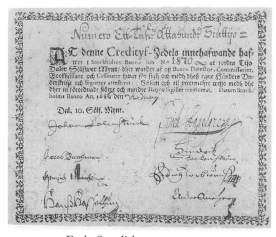

Early Swedish paper money
© Garry Saint, Esquire 1999-2008
www.numismondo.com

Europeans may have viewed paper money as a natural extension of the bills of exchange that had been in use since the fourteenth century. The bill of exchange was a key early instrument for banking and international trade as it covered both the lending and transfer of funds, in different currencies, in the main trading centers of Europe. The bill of exchange could not bear interest given the ban on usury by the medieval church. Nonetheless, a trader, acting as a de facto banker, could make a profit from transactions using bills of exchange via the differences in rates of exchange. North Italian bankers, including the famous Medici family, dominated lending and trade financing throughout Europe and brought the bills of exchange to all major trading centers.

Bankers, such as the Medicis, were known as Lombards, a name that was synonymous with Italians in the Middle Ages (476–1453 AD). As trade expanded across Europe in the late Middle Ages, many merchants found it more convenient to leave their gold and silver with a goldsmith or a moneychanger. The goldsmith issued paper certificates of a preset denomination, which the depositor could spend. The paper would be accepted because of the goldsmith's promise to redeem it in gold or silver. But goldsmiths and moneychangers were not banks. Although they took deposits, they did not make loans.

THE DEVELOPMENT OF BANKING

At the turn of the sixteenth century, probably beginning in Italy, moneychangers and goldsmiths took the necessary step that turned them into banks. They started making loans from their customers' deposits. This simple move released funds that would otherwise sit unused in their coffers and increased the amount of money in circulation. But you can imagine that the lenders had to be careful with how much they lent because depositors could come in at any time and ask for all their money. The more conscientious among them would have had, in modern-day jargon, a reserve requirement on their deposits for just this purpose.

CASE STUDY: FLAWED GENIUS—
JOHAN PALMSTRUCH

It took Johan Palmstruch, a flawed genius as irritating as he was enchanting, five years to fulfil his dream of a freely circulating paper currency. His stubborn determination was, in time, to transform the economies of Europe, and later the world. In the seventeenth century, as before and for a long time after, many deals and debts, if not settled in coin, were paid in kind, in goods or labour. Could a piece of paper represent value? It would be flimsy testament indeed. But it would be convenient—if it worked.

Palmstruch thought it would. In 1656, he founded the Stockholm Banco, a private company that intended to issue paper money, enjoying royal privileges in return for a royal cut. After sustained lobbying and a public-relations effort that would be impressive today, an issue of bank notes followed in 1661. Here was Europe's first paper currency, one that would still be recognizable as such amidst today's state-issued confetti.

From the outset, half of the bank's net profits were claimed by the crown. Sweden's chancellor was chief regulator, an instant example of all governments' instinctive liking for control of paper

finances. Briefly, and amazingly, the new-fangled money worked. But, heady with success, the venture over-reached itself, issued too many notes and crashed disastrously in 1667. Palmstruch was disgraced and sentenced to death, a fate later commuted to a prison term. But the genie was out of the bottle—paper money had arrived. Nothing would ever be the same again.

The Swedish experiment was a glorious failure. Born of necessity as much as of insight, it answered an absurd practical problem. Before Palmstruch's paper, Sweden had one of the most ridiculous currencies. Huge ingots of copper, itself a depreciating asset, were the weighty stores of value and means of exchange. Merchants and citizens struggled to fulfil their obligations with unwieldy piles of metal. The need for something better was clear. And paper had a merit, especially in Sweden—it was not only lighter than copper, it was also easier to come by than silver or gold. Easier to print too, and that was the problem. Would anyone trust it? His implementation may have been flawed, but Palmstruch had done plenty of thinking, and central to it was the need for credibility. He worked hard to ensure it. His notes were the genuine article. Signed by no fewer than eight local dignitaries, they bore watermarks, personal seals and a fancy border. No one could question their authenticity. The bigger question was whether they represented real money.

Here, he fell down. Once the supply of paper became too great, doubt set in and the venture was doomed. With paper, confidence is everything, as many a central bank has since discovered.

Source: "Paper Gains," *The Economist*, Millennium Issue, December 23, 1999

Banks developed at a faster pace following the innovation of lending from deposits. Two types of banks emerged around this time. The first type, exchange banks, were established to deal with foreign exchange and facilitate trade with other countries. Examples of exchange banks were the Bank of Hamburg and the Bank of Amsterdam. The second type, banks of deposits, would make loans from their deposits and facilitate trade and industrial activity within a country.

With banking innovations gathering pace, the idea of European banks using paper money emerged in the West around the middle of the seventeenth century. The first European to introduce this concept was Johan Palmstruch. Some accounts have him as a Dutch merchant, while others say he was Swedish banker. Perhaps the latter description stuck because he is credited with being the first general manager of Stockholm Banco, which was founded in Sweden in 1656. Palmstruch's key innovation was the introduction of the *Kreditivsedlar*, or credit paper, in 1661, and Stockholm Banco is now regarded as the world's oldest note-issuing bank. Each Kreditivsedlar was exchangeable for metal coins at any time, but so much paper was issued without the necessary collateral that the bank eventually collapsed—not unlike the situation that led to paper money being abandoned in China. In his despair, Palmstruch called on the authorities for financial help, but was put on trial for mismanagement instead. Despite its eventual collapse, Stockholm Banco is regarded as the world's first central bank and the precursor to Sweden's current central bank, the Sveriges Riksbank.

In the years that followed, other countries adopted paper money too. The history of the Bank of England provides an illustration: "In 1694, the Bank of England was established in order to raise money for King William III's war against France. Almost immediately the Bank started to issue notes in return for deposits. Like the goldsmiths' notes, the crucial feature that made Bank of England notes a means of exchange was the promise to pay the bearer the sum of the note on demand. This meant that the note could be redeemed at the Bank for gold or coinage by anyone presenting it for payment—if it was not redeemed in full, it was endorsed with the amount withdrawn. These notes were initially handwritten on Bank paper and signed by one of the Bank's cashiers. They were made out for the precise sum deposited in pounds, shillings and pence. However, after the recoinage of 1696 reduced the need for small denomination notes, it was decided not to issue any notes for sums of less than £50. Since the average income in this period was less than £20 a year, most people went through life without ever coming into contact with banknotes."

Across the Atlantic Ocean, in 1690, the Massachusetts Bay Colony issued the first paper money in the American colonies. Other colonies soon followed suit, to meet the high demand for money fueled by trade between the colonies and the scarcity of coins. Some of this early money was readily accepted, but some was not redeemed in gold or silver as promised and thus depreciated rapidly. In France, the Banque Royale was established in 1718, on the promptings of John Law, the Scottish economist, and issued paper money. It was highly successful at first, but when people realised that the bank had issued twice as much paper money as France's total supply of gold and silver, confidence in it declined and the bank collapsed.

CREDIT AND USURY

In ancient times, temples regularly functioned as banks. They were viewed as the safest places to store gold as their sacred status reduced the risk of theft and looting. Though no one can say for certain where and when loans began, there are records of loans being made by temple priests, to merchants in Babylon, as far back as 1800 BC. The main Mesopotamian temples were not only religious centers, law courts, schools, and archive depositories, they were also banks and mercantile establishments. In financial and monetary transactions, the position of Babylonian temples was not unlike that of state banks—they conducted their banking business with all the weight of official authority. The shrine of the sun-god, the temple of Shamash in Babylon, was considered the most important of these early banks. Forms of lending were also evident in Roman times and monetary loans are mentioned in *The Bible*.

The early days of credit, and of charging interest for money borrowed, found resistance in many of the ancient cultures. This resistance was generally based on religious and moral issues, underscored by mentions of the negatives of usury in documents like the *Old Testament*, *The Koran*, as well as in the works of Plato and Aristotle. In *The Laws*, Plato wrote "there must be no lending at interest because it will be quite in order for the borrower to refuse absolutely to return both interest and principal." Aristotle highlighted moral virtues when he wrote in *The Nicomachean Ethics* that the trade of the usurer is "hated with most reason: It makes a profit from currency itself, instead of making it from the process itself which the currency was meant to serve." As we will find out later in this book, the bulk of modern-day

OPINION
SOME WARNINGS ABOUT USURY

"Take thou no usury of him: but fear God…Thou shalt not give him thy money upon usury, nor lend him thy victuals for increase." (Leviticus 25:36–37)
The Holy Bible, Old Testament

"Believers, do not live on usury, doubling your wealth many times over." (The Imrans 3:130)
The Koran

"To take interest for money lent is unjust in itself, because this is to sell what does not exist, and this evidently leads to inequality, which is contrary to justice. Now, money…was invented chiefly for the purpose of exchange, and, consequently, the proper and principal use of money is its consumption or alienation, whereby it is sunk in exchange. Hence, it is by its very nature unlawful to take payment for the use of money lent, which payment is known as interest, and just as a man is bound to restore other ill-gotten goods, so is he bound to restore the money which he has taken in interest."
Thomas Aquinas (1225–74)

"(As) an instrument in the struggle among powers, the credit system— the ingenious invention of a commercial people during this century—of endlessly growing debts that remain safe against immediate demand (since the demand for payment is not made by all creditors at the same time) is a dangerous financial power. It is a war chest exceeding the treasure of all other nations taken together…This ease in making war, combined with the inclination of those in power to do so…is a great obstacle to perpetual peace. Thus, forbidding foreign debt must be a preliminary article for perpetual peace."
Immanuel Kant (1724–1804)

foreign exchange trading consists of speculating on, and making profit from, currency movements. This situation would surely have Aristotle turning in his grave. In his book, *An Annotated Bibliography on the History of Usury and Interest from the Earliest Times Through the Eighteenth Century*, John M. Houkes notes that in the *Old Testament,* and in India, the attitude was that the poor should not be exploited. He points out that China was an early exception—it didn't have a problem with charging a fee for lending money.

An early form of lending was the indentured loan, which started in the Middle Ages and carried on through to the nineteenth century. Indentured loans allowed the poor to borrow money for major expenses like paying for property or traveling. The indentured individual would then have to work off his debt over several years, but often ended up never totally free of his obligations. Lenders frequently abused the system and would inflate the debt or add new conditions to the loans, even after the debt was fully repaid. Indentured servants often had few rights, and were seen by some wealthy individuals as a way to maintain slave labor.

Moneylenders also played a significant role during the Middle Ages. Italian moneylenders would place benches in marketplaces and charge interest for loans to customers at rates that they had set. Some moneylenders were highly successful while others weren't, possibly because of the resistance to usury that still existed in those times. Unsuccessful moneylenders were said to break their benches and look for other locations to conduct their activities. The words bank and bankrupt are derived from the Italian for bench—*banca,* and breaking up a bench—*banca rupta.*

THE DEVELOPMENT OF CREDIT CARDS AND ELECTRONIC MONEY

More recently, we have seen the development of credit cards and electronic money as fundamental components of international trade, as well as cross-border banking. The International Monetary Fund (IMF) has defined electronic money as follows:

> "Electronic money is a payment instrument whereby monetary value is electronically stored on a technical device in the possession of the customer. The amount of stored monetary value is decreased or increased, as appropriate, whenever the owner of the device uses it to make purchase, sale, loading or unloading transactions."

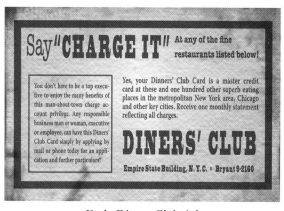

Early Diners Club Ad

The IMF states that to qualify as electronic money, the payment instrument must represent generalized purchasing power, that is, it must be usable for purchases of goods and services from a wide range of vendors. The use of credit cards as a form of electronic money has grown spectacularly since the early 1950s when the Diners Club charge card was invented by

CASE STUDY: DINERS CLUB

The Diners Club was going to be a middleman. Instead of individual companies offering credit to their own customers (whom they would bill later), the Diners Club was going to offer credit to individuals for many companies (then bill the customers and pay the companies). Previously, stores would make money with their credit cards by keeping customers loyal to their particular store, thus maintaining a high level of sales. However, the Diners Club needed a different way to make money since they weren't actually selling anything. To make a profit without charging interest (interest bearing credit cards came much later), the companies who accepted the Diners Club credit card were charged 7% for each transaction while the subscribers to the credit card were charged a US$3 annual fee. McNamara's new credit company focused on salesmen. Since salesmen often need to dine (hence the new company's name) at multiple restaurants to entertain

their clients, the Diners Club needed both to convince a large number of restaurants to accept the new card and to get salesmen to subscribe. The first Diners Club credit cards were given out in 1950 to 200 people (most were friends and acquaintances of McNamara) and accepted by 14 restaurants in New York. The cards were not made of plastic; instead, the first Diners Club credit cards were made of a paper stock with the accepting locations printed on the back. In the beginning, progress was difficult. Merchants didn't want to pay the Diners Club's fee and didn't want competition for their own store cards, while customers didn't want to sign up unless there were a large number of merchants that accepted the card. However, the concept of the card grew and by the end of 1950, 20,000 people were using the Diners Club credit card.

Source: Jennifer Rosenberg, "The First Credit Card (Part 2)" *About.com*

Frank McNamara, who was head of Hamilton Credit Corporation. The story goes that McNamara was having dinner with some friends in New York but forgot his wallet and couldn't pay the bill. It embarrassed him and he had to get his wife to bring some cash from home to pay for the dinner. Consequently, he invented a card that could address such a situation. The charge card thus started out as a tool for rich people, such as McNamara, to enable them to carry less cash when they went out for dinner, but its use

"Do you take MasterCard?"

© The New Yorker Collection 1990 Robert Weber from cartoonbank.com. All Rights Reserved.

eventually spread to cover a larger demographic and a wider range of uses. American Express introduced a more general card in 1958, and its success immediately caught the eye of the banks. Bank of America introduced the Bank Americard that same year, and the popularity of charge cards took off. However, there were many teething problems with charge cards, such as the administration of payments, fraudulent use, and delinquencies. Indeed, the charge card business is said to have been out of control by 1973, when the then Bank Americard CEO, Dee Hock, implemented the first electronic system to handle charge card transactions. It proved an astute move, cutting down on fraud and administrative costs and thereby boosting the charge card issuer's profitability. Bank Americard became VISA in 1976. The shift towards electronic transactions was complemented by the U.S. government's implementation of electronic funds transfers or EFTs. The growth of electronic transactions was next fueled by the advent of the

Internet in the 1990s, which has seen the development of purely online financial transaction systems. It has also contributed to the birth of Internet-based digital currency schemes.

Today, a lot of the money circulating around the globe is electronic, with the use of cash becoming less frequent. Paper money and coins are being superseded by the introduction of online banking, debit cards and online bill payments. For instance, debit cards and online bill payments facilitate the immediate transfer of funds from an individual's account to a business's account without the actual transfer of any physical money. This suggests we may be in the midst of a new trend, which eventually sees paper money and coins becoming obsolete.

● SUMMARY

Trade originally functioned without money in the form of coins and paper, with many different forms of currency being used ranging from cattle to cowries shells to beads and jade. Historians trace the origins of barter to the Neolithic period in the settlements between 8000 BC and 6000 BC in the Middle East, Greece and Turkey, as well as in many parts of Asia and Africa. The popularity of barter trade was eventually superseded by transactions involving coins and paper money. For barter trade to successfully take place, there has to be what is termed by economists a "double coincidence of wants"—that is, Mr. A must want what Mr. B has and Mr. B must simultaneously want what party A has. Thus, a key motivation for this shift was that people needed mediums of exchange that were easier to transport and more widely accepted. Coins first struck in the region of Lydia, now in modern-day Turkey. From Lydia, electrum coinage spread to the cities of coastal Asia Minor like Byzantium, Chalcedon and present-day Kinik in southwestern Turkey. From there, it reached the Greeks of the islands and the mainland. The coinage of the Lydians had been in existence for more than a millennium when paper money first emerged in China under the Tang Dynasty (618 AD–907 AD). The early development of paper money continued during the Song Dynasty (960 AD–1279 AD). It was further developed in Europe in the centuries that followed. Still, the early history of money remains cloudy with new views about the origins of money regularly being put forward by historians.

QUICK QUIZ

1. During which period in human history is barter believed to have started?

2. What does the "double coincidence of wants" refer to?

3. What items were generally believed to be the first mediums of exchange or currencies?

4. Money is broadly described as having three essential functions. What are these functions?

5. Which place is believed to have struck the earliest coins, around 650 BC?

6. How long had coins been in existence before paper money first appeared in China?

7. Why did paper money fail in China, during the Ming dynasty?

8. Which temple in Babylon was considered one of the most important early banks?

THE HISTORY OF FOREIGN EXCHANGE MARKETS

THE ORIGINS OF MODERN FINANCIAL MARKETS

Everyone has heard of the U.S. coffee chain Starbucks. Since its first outlet opened at Pike Place Market in Seattle, in 1971, it has become one of the most ubiquitous symbols of globalization. But not as many people are likely to know that, during the sixteenth century, coffee houses in London contributed to shaping the financial markets of today. Many of these coffee houses were located close to the Royal Exchange, a mercantile hub founded by English merchant and financier Sir Thomas Gresham late in 1565. The Royal Exchange was inspired by Antwerp's famous market or "bourse." Antwerp, now part of Belgium and in the so-called "Low Countries" region, was regarded as the main financial center of Europe at that time. As local aristocratic bankers were forbidden to engage in trade, many foreigners controlled the trading activities with merchants from England, Venice, Spain and Portugal, as well as a large orthodox Jewish community, operating in the city. English appointed a "king's merchant" for conducting currency exchange and obtaining loans. In 1551, when Sir William Dansell, the king's merchant in Antwerp, mismanaged the crown's affairs, Gresham was called on for advice. He made a number of proposals for raising the value of the pound sterling on the Antwerp bourse. These proposals turned out to be successful, so that within a few years King Edward VI was able to pay back almost all his debt.

Gresham continued to serve under Mary I (1553–58), and Elizabeth I who reigned from 1558 to 1603. He died in 1579 during Queen Elizabeth's reign. Gresham had built the Royal Exchange at his own expense. Modeled on the bourse in Antwerp, he made money by renting the shops in the upper parts of the building. The functions of these early mercantile centers, such as the Royal Exchange, were not especially different from what we see now. They were, initially, places for brokers of all sorts of goods and services to meet. As bourses developed, the differentiation amongst brokers increased, followed by a differentiation in their locations within a single bourse. Later on, different types of brokers operated in different buildings.

Apart from his association with the Royal Exchange, Gresham is also known for an economic theory called Gresham's Law, though he is not believed to have put forward the theory himself. It was more an observation he had made. The basic premise of the theory was that bad money drives good money out of monetary systems. Gresham observed that people faced with a choice of two currencies of the same nominal value—one of which is preferable to the other for various reasons, including the proportion of its silver content or resistance to mutilation—will hoard the good money and spend the bad money. In doing so, they drive the good money out of circulation. Gresham's Law is often used to explain the difficulties of maintaining a stable money supply in a coinage based on both gold and silver. But the law also applied to coinage based on one metal, provided that the relative ratio between the face value of a coin and its metal value differed. Furthermore, Gresham's Law had a cross-border dimension: When foreign coins with a high silver content entered, via trade, a country whose coins had low silver content, the foreign coins were then often taken out of circulation as they were either hoarded or melted down to create domestic coins with a low silver content.

COFFEE HOUSES

Coffee houses became more attractive to the business community when stock dealers

NEWS CLIP
THE ROYAL
EXCHANGE

Thomas Gresham's bourse, Flemish in character, was a long four-storeyed building, with a high double balcony. A bell-tower, crowned by a huge grasshopper, stood on one side of the chief entrance. The bell in this tower summoned merchants to the spot at twelve o'clock at noon and six o'clock in the evening. Within the bourse there were covered walks adorned with statues of English kings. The bourse also had about 100 small shops. Many of the shops in the bourse remained unlet until a visit by Queen Elizabeth in 1570, which gave them a lustre that tended to make the new building fashionable. In 1631, the editor of John Stow's surveys about London said, "Unto which place, on January 23, 1570, Queen Elizabeth came from Somerset House through Fleet Street past the north side of the Bourse to Sir Thomas Gresham's house in Bishopsgate Street, and there dined. After the banquet she entered the Bourse on the south side, viewed every part; especially she caused the building, by herald's trumpet, to be proclaimed 'the Royal Exchange,' so to be called from henceforth, and not otherwise."

Source: "The Royal Exchange," *Old and New London*, Volume 1 (1878), 494–513. www.british-history.ac.uk

Early image of Royal Exchange

Source: Getty Images

were expelled from the Royal Exchange in 1698 for rowdiness. The dealers had to look for new places to conduct their business and turned to coffee houses. In his book *A History of the World in 6 Glasses*, Tom Standage writes that coffee houses were places where men gathered to exchange news, and where social differences were left at the door. Governments tried to suppress these institutions, since coffee houses promoted freedom of speech and an open atmosphere for discussion among different classes of people—governments viewed this sort of social interaction as threatening.

In the book *The First Crash: Lessons from the South Sea Bubble* by Richard Dale, the author notes that by 1700, there were over 2,000 coffee houses in London. He affirms that London's coffee houses fulfilled several important functions, including being sources of political, economic, and financial information. Each coffee house is said to have had a particular clientele, such as marine underwriters, insurance agents, regional traders, and stock jobbers, who were people involved in the secondary markets for debt and equities. However, there is, no concrete evidence that foreign exchange trading took place as a business activity in itself, though we know that moneylenders were already aware that profits could be made from capitalising on exchange rate differentials between the currencies of different countries. In any case, any cross-border activity related to the businesses of regional brokers and traders would have definitely involved foreign exchange components.

Against this backdrop, coffee-house proprietors, like the publicans and bartenders of today, had daily access to a diverse range of information and before long they were making up their own lists on matters such as share prices, ship arrivals and departures, and shipping sales. Dale writes that before the liberation of the press through the expiry of the Licensing Act in 1695, coffee-house lists were possibly the main source of such news. "Several coffee houses made their own news sheets available to patrons, much to the chagrin of the government which tried to suppress even this restricted form of publication," he notes. It is known that the *Lloyd's List* contained information about exchange rates, as did lists compiled by other coffee-house proprietors that were geared toward stocks. This suggests that there may have been some foreign exchange trading taking place already, especially if foreigners wanted to invest in British equities.

According to John J. McCusker, in an article about the origins of the information revolution called "The Demise of Distance" in *The American*

NOTE
COFFEE HOUSES AND COMMERCE

The importance of coffee houses in London was highlighted in a
ditty composed in 1675 by actor and poet Thomas Jordan and called
"Triumphs of London." Here are the first two stanzas:

You that delight in wit and mirth,
And love to hear such news
That come from all parts of the earth,
Turks, Dutch, and Danes, and Jews:
I'll send ye to the rendezvous,
Where it is smoaking new;
Go hear it at a coffee-house,
It cannot but be true.

There battails and sea-fights are fought,
And bloudy plots displaid;
They know more things than e'er was thought,
Or ever was bewray'd:
No money in the minting-house
Is half so bright and new;
And coming from the Coffee-House,
It cannot but be true.

Source: *Sunday Tribune* (South Africa) May 25, 2008

Historical Review, in April 2005, the development of coffee houses as sources
of information for business came in tandem with a shift in thinking amongst
merchants. He writes that around the sixteenth century, the business press
came into being when a group of merchants decided that their comparative
advantage improved significantly by printing and selling information rather
than keeping such information confined to themselves. McCusker notes:
"Up to that point, keeping things a secret, the better to gain the upper
hand over one's competitors, was standard business practice. The prices of
commodities, the availability of goods, the location of customers, the arrival
and departure of cargoes, the sailing of ships, the vagaries of the sea, the
winds, and the tides: There was, and is, a great value to all this information.
Developing private sources of information to the benefit of one's own firm
was fundamental to success. These same notions continue to have currency
in the business world today."

THE BRITISH EMPIRE AND THE GROWTH OF INTERNATIONAL MONEY TRANSFERS

Around the time that these developments in the dissemination of business and commercial information were gathering pace, the British Empire was starting to make its mark. The Empire was made up of territories scattered across the globe, conquered or colonized from about 1600. The Empire lasted more than 300 years and was a truly worldwide empire which comprised, at different times, the American colonies, several West Indian islands, the Indian subcontinent and other parts of Asia, Australia and New Zealand, Canada, and much of Africa. The history of the British Empire is often divided in two parts—the First Empire and the Second Empire. The First Empire comprised territories in North America and the Caribbean, which were colonized by British immigrants. Much of this empire was lost with the American Declaration of Independence in 1776. The Second Empire rose as the first was on its last legs and was developed mainly for the purpose of foreign trade. The voyages of Captain James Cook to Australia and New Zealand in the 1770s, and new conquests in India after 1763, opened this second phase of territorial expansion.

Sir Walter Raleigh, the famous writer and explorer who served under Queen Elizabeth of England in the 1500s said: "Whoever commands the sea commands the trade, whoever commands the trade commands the riches of the world, and consequently the world itself." England thus became a dominant participant in the expansion of trade with countries around the world. Its advocacy of a strong navy provided England with a platform for overseas trade and commerce but a strong navy was not the only factor leading to its development as a world power. Historians attribute the creation of the British Empire to the collective activities of an assortment of characters, including pirates, traders, soldiers, explorers, financial speculators, missionaries, convicts, and refugees. Still, private individuals, or companies, often provided the initial impetus for the exploration of foreign lands and the subsequent development of commercial activities there that would enhance the Empire. The British government was initially reluctant to take part in the commercial boom but was eventually drawn in, most likely due to the enormous revenues it was able to garner from the growing overseas trade activity and the goods that were brought back home.

TEA, THE BRITISH EMPIRE, AND SILVER

If coffee houses helped to pave the way for the birth of modern financial markets in London, tea was viewed as a key driver for the expansion of the British Empire. You could probably have ordered tea at the same public establishments that served coffee during the seventeenth century, but tea was initially more expensive than coffee, and thus less popular.

In the book *Tea: Addiction, Exploitation, and Empire*, author Roy Moxham attributes the introduction of tea in England to Catherine of

Braganza, the Portugese wife of Charles II. She was said to be a tea addict and is believed to have brought a chest of tea with her to England. From that early catalyst, drinking tea became the center of a national domestic ritual, largely presided over by women. It was regarded as a genteel beverage and was served with scones, buns, and jam tarts at, for example, afternoon parties in country cottages. England's tradition of afternoon tea was to catch on in many of its colonies across the globe—it is still evident today in countries such as Sri Lanka and India.

The British taste for tea resulted in the invention of new utensils for tea brewing, serving, and drinking. The setting of the tea table might include teapots, tea caddies, sugar bowls, creamers, strainers, and other elaborate accoutrements. Some of these items, or the raw materials to make them, would have had to have been imported into England, while finished goods would have been exported to countries such as India, establishing more trade flows in and out of England. All this, of course, involved foreign exchange and particularly silver as currency.

Uploading tea at East India Docks
© National Maritime Museum, Greenwich, London.
All Rights Reserved.

Tea was initially imported into England by the powerful East India Company, which acted as the vehicle for British commercial and imperial expansion in Asia. Many hold the view that without this company, there would have been no British Empire. The company was chartered by Elizabeth I for trade in Asia, and started operating in 1600. Its demise came about more than two hundred and fifty years later, in the aftermath of the Indian Mutiny of 1857.

The original objective of the company was to break the Dutch monopoly of the spice trade with the East Indies, but after 1623 it concentrated its activities in India. The Company soon realised that it needed to secure and protect trading posts in the subcontinent from its French and Dutch trade rivals. It started to buy land from Indian rulers to build trading posts, and established its own army and navy to defend them.

Though India was at the heart of the British Empire, it was the East India Company that initially controlled it, not the British government. The

Company established offices throughout Asia, securing port access in regions such as Malaya and Aden where its goods-laden vessels, plying between Britain, India, and China, could dock safely. To pay for the commodities, such as spices, that it was shipping from Asia, the Company used gold and silver, mainly from Spanish South American mining concessions.

Trade was often subject to the exchange rate between gold and silver, as well as the fashion and prejudice for particular currencies at different times and in different regions. The East India Company tried to stabilize the currency fluctuations by licensing private trade. This gave its own staff and officials an incentive to avoid currency speculation.

Initially, the British depended on trade with China for their tea supply. China had restrictions on such foreign trade and insisted on being paid in silver. As the popularity of the beverage grew in the eighteenth century, more and more tea had to be imported into Britain from China. But, by the end of that century, the strain on the British economy from the outflow of silver, to pay for China's tea, was becoming too difficult to bear. The British solution was to produce opium in India, trading it for silver in China, and using some of this silver to pay for tea. Britain invested heavily in the manufacture and distribution of opium, and the revenues amassed were essential to Britain's balance of payments.

The East India Company distributed ever-increasing quantities of opium in China because of the drug's inherently addictive nature and the high tolerance levels of addicts. Such a large amount of opium entered China that its own balance of trade was ultimately reversed, and the massive payments of silver caused a change in the exchange rate between silver and the copper coinage used in the country at that time.

In the book, *China Upside Down: Currency, Society and Ideologies 1808–1856*, Man-houng Lin describes the relationship between copper and silver coins in early nineteenth century China: "In one respect, the relation between silver and copper coins was like that between quarters and the hundred-dollar bill in the American currency system. An exchange worth US$100 would involve too much inconvenience if transacted in quarters. Hence, quarters and hundred dollar bills circulate side by side, as did copper coins and silver in China, for both small- and large-scale exchanges. The difference is that the American government fixed the exchange rate between quarters and hundred-dollar bills. In early nineteenth-century China, the market determined the exchange rate between silver and copper coins, and the rate fluctuated."

According to Lin, silver and copper coins were used for different levels of transactions, which meant that individuals held different currencies or different combinations of these two currencies. "If the copper coin earners— such as peasants who remained in their local area most of the time—had used copper coins exclusively, their real incomes would not have been affected by variations in the exchange rate. The problem was that they had to use silver on many occasions. In addition to paying taxes in silver, these holders of copper coins sometimes had to buy household necessities (salt, clothes, cooking implements, ritual paper, coffins, and the like) produced in distant markets. These commodities could be bought with copper coins in the local market, but their real prices were affected by the silver-copper coin conversion ratio, because merchants generally purchased these products from distant places with silver."

The pegging of taxes to silver was the most critical factor affecting the budgets of ordinary people. Taxes could be paid either in silver, or in copper coins calculated with the market exchange rate. "Given the high transportation costs of copper coins, local officials converted taxes paid in copper coins into silver at the bank shops and forwarded taxes in silver to the provincial financial commissioner, who passed the payments on to the Board of Revenue in silver as well. Whether the peasant obtained silver himself or relied on the local magistrate to exchange copper coins, he was subject to the market silver price," says Lin. Thus, the scarcity of silver and the increased value relative to copper meant that the poorer Chinese workers were paying higher taxes. This led to massive civil unrest within China. To make matters worse, in 1833, the monopoly that the East India Company enjoyed in the opium trade was ended by the British government, opening up a market for free trade in the drug. As a result, there was a substantial increase in opium sales, furthering drug addiction and increasing demand.

China was not pleased with these developments and in 1839 enforced prohibitions on the import of opium, destroying a large quantity of the drug, confiscated from British merchants in Guangzhou port, in the process. The act precipitated the First Opium War between the British and the Chinese, when the British responded by attacking several Chinese coastal cities. Unable to deal with modern gunboats, the Chinese were defeated and forced to sign the Treaty of Nanjing in 1842, which was supplemented by the Treaty of the Bogue in 1843. These treaties provided for an indemnity on Spanish silver to the British and for ports like Guangzhou, Ningbo, and Shanghai to be open to British trade. In addition, Hong Kong was ceded to British control, adding to the growing empire.

Revenue During the British Empire

How vast was commercial activity during the British Empire and how much money was actually involved? There appears to be very little reliable data offering a true global perspective of the empire's commercial activities, but the *Atlas of the British Empire,* by Christopher Bayly, provides some useful clues to answering these questions. Bayly presents a breakdown of British trade in 1900, when Britain was operating with a trade deficit, which means it was importing more goods than it was exporting. While running a trade deficit in an economic downturn, or during a recession, can be a negative signal for any economy, it is likely that the British Empire and its economy were still expanding during at this time. Indeed, according to Bayly, in 1909 the British Empire comprised as much as one fifth of the Earth's land area and about one quarter of its population.

THE SILVER STANDARD

We've seen how the British traded silver, obtained from opium sales, for Chinese tea to meet rapidly growing demand for the tea leaves back home. The use of silver, however, has a history that preceded this development by hundreds of years. Silver has been very important throughout the ages, from the ancient Greek empire to the Roman civilization in Europe, and the Inca civilization in South America. It has often held a value above material and economic considerations. For instance, silver was described by the Inca as "tears of the moon" and the civilization's sacrificial victims were laden with silver and gold jewelry. When the Spanish conquistadores, under Francisco Pizarro, arrived to loot the empire for Spain in the sixteenth century, they couldn't believe the amount of silver and gold the Inca had accumulated.

The earliest known mining of significant amounts of silver was conducted in eastern Anatolia (modern-day Turkey) more than 3,000 years before the rise of the Inca empire. Silver is generally found in a combined state in nature, usually in copper or lead ores, and by 2000 BC, mining and smelting of silver-bearing lead ores was being carried out. Anatolia supplied silver to craftsmen throughout Asia Minor. From the sixth century BC, silver was mined in increasing quantities in Laurion (also known as Laurium), now a suburb of Athens. Although these mines had been worked since the Bronze Age (3500–1200 BC), the Athenians increased production, with silver being used both industrially, and as money. The Laurion mines were fundamental to Athens' rise in the region. Initially, trade simply entailed the exchange of goods, such as grain for metal. But early in the sixth century BC, the Athenians minted their first silver coin, the famous Athenian drachma—drachma is the Greek word for "handful" and is said to have originally referred to a handful of nails.

For the next four centuries, until the absorption of Greece into the Roman Empire, the drachma had an almost constant silver content and became the standard coin of trade in Greece, as well as in many parts of Asia and Europe. Even after the Roman conquest, the drachma continued to be minted and widely used. Production in the Laurion mines dominated silver supply until around the first century AD. One estimate suggests that Laurion produced a total of 160 million ounces of silver. After Laurion, the next important source of silver was Spain. Spanish mines provided a substantial portion of the domestic needs of the Roman Empire until 476 AD and also served as a key source of silver for the Asian spice trade. In the sixteenth century, the Spanish conquistadores developed mines in Mexico, Bolivia, and Peru. These New World mines, much richer in silver, heralded the rise of Central and South America as the regions of greatest silver production in the world.

The significance of silver to modern-day foreign exchange markets is manifested in our currency lexicon. Many currencies have obtained their names from their weight in silver. For instance, the pound sterling originally signified a pound of silver. The dollar began as the generally applied term for an ounce of silver, as named by a Bohemian count, Stefan Schlick, in the sixteenth century. His coins earned a great reputation for their uniformity and fineness. They were widely referred to as "thalers" and the word "dollar" eventually emerged from thaler. peso, lira, and ruble were also originally terms for metallic weights, with the first silver peso introduced by Ferdinand II and Isabella I of Spain. Isabella was the daughter of John II, King of Castille, while Ferdinand was the son of John II, King of Aragon. They were heirs to their respective kingdoms and married in 1469 when both were still in their teens. They jointly ruled a united Spain from 1479 until 1504. During their reign, the Spanish peso became the dominant currency through all the Americas and also in the Far East. English-speaking peoples in the Americas called the coins "dollars" rather than "pesos."

A 16th century thaler from Austria

Source: www.vcoins.com/ world/monarchy

In his book, *Fountain of Fortune: Money and Monetary Policy in China, 1000–1700*, Richard von Glahn suggests that during the sixteenth century "the first truly global economy came into being. Spain's plunder of Peru and Mexico unleashed torrents of gold and silver that cascaded around the globe, joining together, however imperfectly, its disparate economies."

Initially, in colonial North America, many different currencies from different countries were in use, with English, Spanish, Portuguese, French, and German coins predominant. The coins fluctuated in value in different colonies and there was no general standard. The Spanish silver dollar was probably the closest thing to a common currency. It came in via trade across the frontier from Louisiana, which Spain had ceded to France in the late seventeenth century, and from the Spanish territories in the West Indies. The silver dollar circulated in all the colonies, usually at a value of between four and seven shillings. Although the English pound and shilling were desirable to Americans before the Revolution of the late eighteenth century, the British hindered their use by prohibiting anyone going into the colonies from taking British coins with them. They also forbade the colonists from coining, and later printing, their own money.

U.S. silver dollar

Source: Photos courtesy of Steven L. Contursi and Rare Coin Wholesalers

Spanish pesos remained legal tender in the U.S. through most of the nineteenth century, despite the fact that the United States minted its own silver coins from 1794, following the passage of the U.S. Coinage Act in Congress in 1792. Debasing the money was punishable by death and the Act also provided for a U.S. Mint. A dollar was defined as a specific weight of gold or silver coined under the direction of the elected representatives in Congress. It is estimated that nearly 900,000,000 silver dollars were coined from 1794 to 1935.

CHINA AND SILVER

Trading in silver drove the Chinese economy, and indirectly fueled the rise of Europe, by sustaining the Europeans' long sought-after access to Chinese trade. As we have seen, selling opium to the Chinese was part of this trade. While the huge flow of silver to Europe from the Americas led to its rapid devaluation there and the consequent phenomenon of inflation, the enormous demand for silver in the Chinese economy meant that its value in the Chinese market was always much higher. Europeans could thus obtain valuable Chinese goods at relatively low cost to themselves, then sell these for a profit back home.

Earlier, in the fifteenth century, the Ming-dynasty Chinese had been grappling with the negative impact of overprinting paper money. This had undermined public confidence in paper money and fueled a preference for silver as a currency. Just at the point when the official shift to silver was finally being made, China's silver mines started running dry, after a short-lived boom, and many had to be closed. The steady growth of the economy during the latter half of the fifteenth century then created an insatiable demand for silver, which the Japanese were well placed to supply. The conversion of China's monetary and fiscal systems to a silver standard led to a doubling in the value of silver in China, in relation to the rest of the world, by the early sixteenth century. Heightened profit opportunities induced an unprecedented surge in silver production by the Spanish, as well as the Japanese. Destined ultimately for China, tens of thousands of tons of silver passed through Europe via long-distance maritime and land trade routes. Fifty tons of silver also reached China, annually, via the Pacific Ocean route. This route had opened up after the founding of the city of Manila, in 1571, in the Spanish colony of the Philippines, named after Philip II of Spain. Japan exported huge quantities of silver to China until the late seventeenth century. Silver demand grew along with China's population, which in turn led to a lofty silver price premium in China. Largely in response to buoyant demand, more Mexican silver was produced during the eighteenth century than had been produced by all of Spanish America during the sixteenth and seventeenth centuries combined. The Mexican silver dollar circulated throughout Asia, finding its way to the Philippines and, eventually, to China and other parts of Asia.

CHINESE WARLORDS AND SILVER

An interesting episode in the history of silver coins took place early in the twentieth century in Manchuria, at that time a place of complex politics. Although formally a region of China, even Manchuria's Chinese officials challenged the authority of the Chinese national government. In his book, *Civil Government in Warlord China: Tradition, Modernization and Manchuria*, Ronald Suleski offers a study of Manchuria and its most famous son, the warlord Zhang Zuolin. Zhang became a good administrator even though he was a warlord. Though it was conventional wisdom that no

CASE STUDY: CHINESE CHOPS ON SPANISH AND MEXICAN COINS

"Back in the 18th and early 19th century, Spanish Mexican silver coins, including Pillar dollars (1732–1772), and King Carolus III, IV and Ferdinand VII portraited dollars (1773–1821) were widely used in China as one of its major silver currencies, alongside local silver sycees, until the declaration of independence by Mexico in 1821, when the minting of Spanish colonial coins ceased. The new Mexico relaunched its silver coin minting business by introducing a newly designed silver "Real" coin, with its famous national emblem of an eagle on the obverse, and a design of "Cap and Rays" on the reverse, into China and other Asian countries. Chinese people used to call it the "Eagle dollar." Before long, it took over the vacancy left by the former Spanish colonial coins, and became the most popularly traded silver dollars worldwide at that time, and for decades after.

However, the Eagle dollar, in China, needed more than 30 years to gain people's trust and recognition, and then it overwhelmed the markets. It was not until the 1850s, that the monetary and bankers' association in Shanghai rendered their formal approval in accepting the Eagle dollar to supersede the Spanish colonial dollars, in their transactions, exchanges, and bookkeeping, as the base currency.

When accepting this new kind of Mexican silver coin, the Chinese people restarted their authentication procedure, as they had done with the Spanish coins a century before, but even more severely. They chopped and chiseled the coins to make sure of their purity. Even though a silver coin was trusted, its payer would still be requested to put his chop on the coin, by the payee, as evidence of conveyance and guarantee. Under such circumstances, many of the coins were repeatedly chopped and their designs became illegible."

Source: Stephen Tai, "Chopmarks on 5 Mexican Silver dollars Circulated in China," *www.charm.ru*, December 18, 1999

Mexican Eagle dollar
Source: www.vcoins.com/world/monarchy

decent Chinese ever worked for a warlord, Suleski says Chinese government offices all over the country were filled with men who worked for regional warlords. He notes that some of them were very effective. In the 1920s and 1930s, several of the regions of China enjoyed better government than those under the direct rule of national government, for example Shanxi under Yan Xishan, Guangxi under the "Guangxi Clique," and Manchuria under Zhang.

The latter ruled Manchuria from 1916 to 1928, and helped lay the foundations of a healthy industrial economy. One of his henchmen, chief of finance Wang Yongjiang, initiated moves that helped bring financial and administrative stability to the region.

Chinese warlord Zhang Zuolin
Source: Getty Images

At the time, Manchuria was inundated with a number of currencies, and Wang decided to switch to a silver currency. He set the initial value of the new silver dollar, or yuan, against the Japanese yen, which was backed by gold. He also introduced the Fengtian dollar or "Feng Piao." In a 2004 paper entitled *Currencies, Identities, Free Banking, and Growth in Early Twentieth Century Manchuria*, Thomas Gottschang described the Fengtian dollar: "The best-known of the Chinese paper currencies in Manchuria was the Fengtian dollar. These were yuan notes first issued in 1917 by the Three Eastern Provinces Bank on behalf of the Fengtian Provincial Government in a well-planned effort to stabilise the currency situation. In the early years of their existence, when around 20 million yuan were believed to be in circulation, the feng piao were securely supported by reserves and became the most widely accepted notes throughout Manchuria. Beginning in 1922, however, as Zhang's armies engaged in military conflicts with his rivals in China, the number of notes issued rose exponentially, reaching an estimated total of over three billion yuan by the end of 1929. Since the notes printed after the early issues had no real backing, their value rose and fell with Zhang's fortunes."

Gottschang noted that the history of the Fengtian dollar serves as a metaphor for the civil administrations of Chinese warlord governors. Like several warlords, Zhang employed competent civil administrators and made serious efforts to promote economic development in Manchuria, including the carefully and realistically planned introduction of the Feng Piao as a means of monetary stabilisation. "Ultimately, however, just as the overall effect of warlord rule in China was to stifle economic growth, so Zhang's military ambitions took precedence over prudent monetary policy, causing the feng piao to plummet in value, disrupting financial markets all over Manchuria and exacerbating the currency chaos it had been introduced to resolve," he added.

Aureus, a Roman coin minted in 193 AD
Source: www.wildwinds.com
Courtesy of Classical Numismatic Group, www.cngcoms.com

THE GOLD STANDARD

The haphazard history of money across the globe, and through the ages, began to display some semblance of clarity and global homogeneity with the advent of the gold standard in the eighteenth century. Foreign exchange as we know it today has its roots in this standard. As we've already seen, the use of gold and silver had been popular across the centuries and dates as far back as the Lydians, in the seventh century BC. An example of an ancient gold coin is the Aureus, struck by the Romans, between the first century BC and the fourth century AD. The Romans, for whom the gold coin became a crucial way of paying their legions, also adopted the custom of striking the Emperor's head on their gold Aureus coins. Nonetheless, silver was the major monetary metal for much of early currency history with gold used as a store of value, and as a means of payment when portability was at a premium, particularly for the payment of armies. Gold's density, resistance to corrosion, uniformity, and easy divisibility made it useful both as a store of value and as a unit of account.

It was the gold that Spain brought back to Europe, from the New World, that raised its supply five-fold in the sixteenth century. Gold coins and bullion dominated the monetary system of Europe until the eighteenth century, when paper money became the leading medium of currency. The resulting conflict between advocates of paper money and those of gold eventually led to the introduction of the gold standard. It was a monetary system in which paper money was convertible into a fixed amount of gold. Under the gold exchange, currencies gained stability. The gold standard abolished the age-old practice of kings and rulers arbitrarily debasing money and triggering inflation—in other words, the gold standard was designed to instill some discipline into economies. Britain adopted a formal gold standard in 1821 after the Napoleonic Wars, following the reintroduction of the gold sovereign as the main coin in circulation. It is still in production today and generally has a value of one pound sterling. The sovereign had first been issued in 1489 by Henry VII, but was discontinued early in the seventeenth century. It is believed that sovereigns got their name from the majestic size of the coin and what it depicted on its faces. Early sovereigns showed the king sitting on a throne on one side and the royal coat of arms, on a shield surrounded by a Tudor double rose, on the other.

Queen Victoria gold sovereign (1869)
Source: www.vcoins.com/world/monarchy

The rest of Europe stuck to a silver standard until the 1870s, when gold discoveries in the U.S. and Australia made it practical for the yellow metal to be adopted as the main standard. According to Harold Glenn Moulton in his book, *Financial Organization and the Financial System*, Germany switched to a gold standard in 1871, Scandinavia in 1873, the Netherlands in 1875, France and Spain in 1876, and Russia in 1893. The U.S. remained on a bimetallic system of gold and silver until 1900 when the Gold Standard Act confirmed the supremacy of gold. Eventually, more than 50 countries were unified under the gold standard. China was the main exception with silver and many other regional currencies in circulation, such as the feng piao of warlord Zhang Zuolin in Manchuria.

The dominance of the gold standard as a monetary system did not last long, but the era was known as the "Gilded Age" in the U.S. There it marked the growth of industry and the arrival of waves of immigrants. Production of iron and steel rose and resources like lumber, gold, and silver increased the demand for improved transportation. Railroads developed quickly as trains were needed to move goods from the resource-rich west of the U.S. to the east. The period produced great wealth for some businessmen, including John D. Rockefeller in oil and Andrew Carnegie in steel.

The Gilded Age was exemplified by the many great fortunes created and the way of life this wealth supported. But in the end, it was not a particularly auspicious period, as it was tainted by several depressions and many runs on U.S. banks. Because gold had to be used to cover trade deficits between two countries, people would panic if they heard that gold was being moved out of their country. They would rush to banks to withdraw their gold before the banks ran out of it.

When World War I broke out in 1914, most countries stopped gold payments, directing their gold reserves to war needs instead. But reverting to the gold standard became one of their top priorities after the war ended. By 1928, all the major currencies, and most of the minor ones, had returned

"That will be the gold standard by which all other naps are judged."

© The New Yorker Collection 2006 Frank Cotham from cartoonbank.com. All Rights Reserved.

to the standard. Nonetheless, its fallibility was all too apparent with the onset of the Great Depression that followed on the heels of the U.S. stock market crash in 1929. No country could completely protect itself from the problems in the U.S. and its economic woes spread across the Atlantic Ocean to Europe, and elsewhere, as global trade collapsed. One of the reasons for this was that countries began implementing tariff increases on imported goods to boost their own sagging economies. Industrial production fell significantly, not only in the U.S. but also in the other major economies of the time such as Germany, France, and Britain.

On May 11, 1931, in the midst of this downturn, Austria's largest bank, Creditanstalt, collapsed, precipitating worries over the financial health of other banks in Europe. This quickly led to depositors rushing to banks to retrieve their money. Even banks that were doing well couldn't escape the panic and the run on banks included the failure of several German institutions by June that year. This disastrous state of affairs led to Germany reneging on its war reparations from World War I, in turn causing problems for other European countries, and the U.S., which relied on the debt repayments to fund their own government spending.

The combined effects of excessive debt (as evidenced by an increase in money supply), speculative prices and higher than required industrial expansion are seen as the causes of the Great Depression. In the 1920s, American consumers relied on banks' lax lending standards and cheap credit to purchase consumer goods while businesses relied on cheap credit for capital investment to increase production to meet the higher consumer demand. Prices were pushed up initially as a result of the excessive demand and industrialists expanded to unrealistic levels to meet the demand. When prices fell people and businesses deeply in debt cut spending to keep up with high time payments. The debt burden became heavier as prices and incomes fell while the debts remained the same amount in dollars. Businesses began to fail when factory orders declined. This led to massive layoffs. Banks who had financed the debt began to fail as debtors defaulted. Bank depositors, worried about their deposits, began massive withdrawals and bank runs were common. Bank failures snowballed as desperate bankers called in loans which the borrowers did not have time or money to repay. With poor profit expectations, capital investment and construction slowed or ceased. There were many bank failures but those that survived became very conservative in their lending, thus starving businesses of loans. As a result of the domestic economic problems, politicians in Washington searched for a scapegoat and the easy one was foreigners. They blamed foreign imports on the fall in prices. The protectionist Smoot-Hawley Tariff Act was enacted in June of 1930 raising import tariffs and restricting imports. Of course, other countries retaliated with restrictions of their own. This further exacerbated the depression since companies who previously were able to import inexpensive parts and materials were burdened with higher costs while companies able to export found that their export markets were drying up. The final nail in the depression coffin was the actions taken by the Federal Reserve Bank. At that time the amount of credit that the Federal Reserve could issue was limited by laws which required partial gold backing of any money they issued and by the late 1920s the Federal Reserve had almost hit the limit of allowable credit that could be backed by the gold it had in its vaults. The credit that the Federal Reserve issued was in the form of demand notes backed by gold. Holders of such notes could and did demand gold when presenting those notes thus reducing the amount of gold possessed by the Federal Reserve and, in turn, reducing the amount of money (credit) the Federal Reserve could issue. As the Great Depression got worse, the private ownership of gold was declared illegal thus reducing the pressure on Federal Reserve gold.

Britain resorted to major cuts in its budget as well as a change of government. By September 1931, Britain had run out of options to stabilize its economy and decided to free itself from the gold standard to pursue other monetary strategies. With this move, British banks were no longer required to back their money with gold. Other nations followed Britain's lead in abandoning the gold standard, and in 1933 newly installed U.S. President, Franklin Delano Roosevelt, devalued the U.S. dollar against gold and made it illegal for U.S. citizens to own gold bullion. By 1937, not a single country remained on the gold standard. The Great Depression ultimately contributed to a destabilization of the political landscape in Europe, fueling nationalism at the expense of cooperation with neighbors. This heralded the rise of Adolf Hitler in Germany, as he fed on the nationalistic emotions of those troubled times. Ironically, the end of the Great Depression in the U.S. was marked by Germany's invasion of Poland in September 1939, the opening conflict of World War II.

During the 1930s, in an environment of severe global depression and lack of confidence, the international monetary system had disintegrated into rival currency blocs, competitive devaluations, discriminatory trade restrictions and exchange controls, high tariffs, and barter trade arrangements. Against a background of widespread international monetary disorder, bordering on chaos, there were several failed efforts to reestablish order. According to the Federal Reserve Bank of New York, "the collapse of international trade and finance left a profound impression on those who lived through it and on subsequent generations. Unlike the heyday of the gold standard, there was never any nostalgia for a return of the financial conditions of the 1930s. Quite the contrary, it was the experience of conflict, rivalry, and nationalism in the 1930s that created much of the support for international monetary cooperation after the Second World War."

CASE STUDY: BECKONING FRONTIERS

As mass production had to be accompanied by mass consumption, mass consumption, in turn, implies a distribution of wealth—not of existing wealth, but of wealth as it is currently produced—to provide men with buying power equal to the amount of goods and services offered by the nation's economic machinery. Instead of achieving that kind of distribution, a giant suction pump had by 1929–30, drawn into a few hands, an increasing portion of currently produced wealth. This served them as capital accumulations. But by taking purchasing power out of the hands of mass consumers, the savers denied themselves the kind of effective demand for their products that would justify a reinvestment of their capital accumulations in new plants. As a result, as in a poker game where the chips are concentrated in fewer and fewer hands, the other fellows could stay in the game only by borrowing. When their credit ran out, the game stopped. That is what happened to us in the 1920s. We sustained high levels of employment in that period with the aid of an exceptional expansion of debt outside of the banking system. This debt was provided by the large growth of business savings as well as savings by individuals, particularly in the upper-income groups where taxes were relatively low. Private debt outside of the banking system increased about fifty per cent. This debt, which was at high interest rates, largely took the form of mortgage debt on housing, office, and hotel structures, consumer installment debt, brokers' loans, and foreign debt. The stimulation to spending by debt-creation of this sort was short-lived and could not be counted on to sustain high levels of employment for long periods of time. Had there been a better distribution of the current income from the national product —in other words, had there been less savings by businesses and the higher-income groups and more income in the lower groups— we should have had far greater stability in our economy. Had the six billion dollars, for instance, that were loaned by corporations and wealthy individuals for stock-market speculation been distributed to the public as lower prices or higher wages and with less profits to the corporations and the well-to-do, it would have prevented or greatly moderated the economic collapse that began at the end of 1929. The time came when there were no more poker chips to be loaned on credit. Debtors thereupon were forced to curtail their consumption in an effort to create a margin that could be applied to the reduction of outstanding debts. This naturally reduced the demand for goods of all kinds and brought on what seemed to be overproduction, but was in reality under consumption when judged in terms of the real world instead of the money world. This, in turn, brought about a fall in prices and employment. Unemployment further decreased the consumption of goods, which further increased unemployment, thus closing the circle in a continuing decline of prices. Earnings began to disappear, requiring economies of all kinds in the wages, salaries, and time of those employed. Thus, again the vicious circle of deflation was closed until one third of the entire working population was unemployed, with our national income reduced by fifty per cent, and with the aggregate debt burden greater than ever before, not in dollars, but measured by current values and income that represented the ability to pay. Fixed charges, such as taxes, railroad and other utility rates, insurance and interest charges, clung close to the 1929 level and required such a portion of the national income to meet them that the amount left for consumption of goods was not sufficient to support the population. This then, was my reading of what brought on the depression.

Source: *"Marriner S. Eccles who was Chairman of the Federal Reserve Bank from November 1934 to February 1948 detailed what he believed caused the Depression in his memoirs, "Beckoning Frontiers", (New York, Alfred A. Knopf, 1951)*

BRETTON WOODS AGREEMENT

As we have mentioned, toward the end of the World War II, a post-war international monetary system of convertible currencies, fixed exchange rates and free trade was established. The 1944 Bretton Woods agreement established at the ski resort town of Bretton Woods in New Hampshire was designed to establish monetary stability. The new rules called for a system based on the U.S. dollar with a system of fixing exchange rates that partially reinstated the gold standard by fixing the U.S. dollar to US$35 per ounce of gold and fixing the other main currencies to the U.S. dollar. All participating countries agreed to maintain their currency values within a narrow exchange margin against the U.S. dollar and the corresponding rate of gold. Countries agreed not to devalue their currencies in order to obtain a trade advantage. Devaluations of not more than 10% were allowed. Although the delegates attending the Bretton Woods conference believed that stable exchange rates would benefit economies all over the world by expanding international trade, in fact the fixed rates were bound to be challenged by currency speculators. Traders began to bet on the value at which the fixed exchange rates would be reset and currency speculation eventually doomed the fixed rate system.

Although advocates of the Bretton Woods system believed that stable exchange rates would benefit economies around the world by expanding international trade, in practice the fixed rates and infrequent parity changes became ineffectual. Speculation was not discouraged since traders bet on the value at which the fixed exchange rate would be reset.

MODERN FOREIGN EXCHANGE MARKETS

By the start of the 1970s, the Bretton Woods system was about to break down. The effects of speculation and the persistent U.S. balance of payments deficit were viewed as the immediate causes of the demise. With the U.S. dollar as the key reserve currency, the U.S. was reluctant to devalue despite

NEWS CLIP
THE END OF A GAMBLE

The Nixon Administration has deliberately stalled for nearly two months in seeking the necessary congressional approval of the dollar devaluation that it agreed to last December. Reason: the President, and Treasury Secretary John Connally, believed that they could use the delay to wring a few further trade concessions from Japan and the Common Market nations. It was a high-stakes gamble, since their plan ran the risk of undermining confidence in the entire new system of currency exchange rates worked out in the Smithsonian agreement. Last week that system began to teeter, and the Administration decided to take what it could get and end the suspense. In Brussels, U.S. negotiators reached agreement with Common Market officials on several key trade issues. In Washington, Connally promised to send to Congress this week the long-awaited bill raising the price of gold and thus officially lowering the value of the dollar.

The monetary flurry was far short of an outright crisis, but it was nonetheless an uncomfortable reminder that not even the sweeping Smithsonian agreement had ended the world's money jitters. At one point, the dollar's trading value in West Germany sank so close to its allowable minimum that the Bundesbank spent some US$90 million worth of marks to support it, the first time such intervention has been necessary under the new rates. At the same time, the price of gold on Europe's free markets soared to record heights of nearly US$50 per ounce (vs the post-devaluation official rate of US$38). After the U.S.–Common Market agreement was announced, the two courses reversed, with dollars gaining and gold losing in value.

The mini-panic was caused by a combination of wild rumor and hard economic fact. European speculators have been trading bits of unfounded hearsay that the Italian central bank was secretly selling some of its dollars for gold on the free market and that the U.S. Congress was somehow planning to double the price of gold. More sensible investors were troubled by the huge U.S. budget deficit that Nixon disclosed two weeks ago—which they feared would lead to further dollar-weakening American inflation—and by the gap between Europe's relatively high interest rates and the current low cost of money in the U.S. That disparity has at least temporarily prevented the large-scale return of dollars held abroad to U.S. securities, one of the expected results of devaluation. As a result, some dollar holders were convinced that devaluation was not working and sold out for other currencies.

Europeans were most disturbed by Connally's calculatedly slowpoke handling of the gold bill. They regarded the delay as a polite form of blackmail, aimed at forcing trade concessions from them as the price of monetary stability. Then, as time dragged on, some believed that Nixon might try to gain trade advantages on his own by seeking approval of a devaluation larger than the 8.57% level agreed to in December. After all, London's Financial Times noted icily, the Nixon Administration "has been known before now to reverse itself suddenly."

Source: "The End of a Gamble," *Time*, February 14, 1972

persistent deficits. At the same time, countries in surplus chose to add to their U.S. dollar holdings rather than revalue their currencies. As U.S. deficits persisted, the stock of U.S. dollars held abroad ballooned relative to the need for a reserve currency. Some countries viewed the U.S. as abusing its privilege to issue the reserve currency and also as forcing other countries to finance U.S. deficits. The fundamental flaw in the system was that international liquidity considerations encouraged foreign central banks to hold U.S. dollars, but also hindered other nations from revaluing their currencies to eliminate their balance of payments surpluses. Ultimately, confidence in the U.S. dollar as a reserve currency suffered.

On August 15, 1971, without prior warning, U.S. President, Richard Nixon, announced that the U.S. was removing the gold backing from the dollar. In an instant, the commitment by the U.S. to redeem international U.S. dollar holdings at the rate of US$35 per ounce was gone. Nixon's unilateral announcement dealt the Bretton Woods Agreement its fatal blow. Chalmers Johnson criticises Nixon's move in his book *Blowback: The Costs and Consequences of American Empire.* He writes that Nixon decided to end the Bretton Woods system because the Vietnam War had imposed excessive expenditure on the U.S. and he concluded that the government could no longer afford to exchange its currency for a fixed value of gold. In December, 1971, in the wake of Nixon's move, a decision was taken, at the Smithsonian Institution in Washington, D.C., by the Group of Ten countries to devalue the U.S. dollar against gold and most other currencies. The Smithsonian Agreement superseded the Bretton Woods Agreement. It was similar to its predecessor, but allowed for greater fluctuation bands for currencies. The official value of gold was raised to US$38 per ounce. The agreement was hailed by Nixon as the "greatest monetary agreement in the history of the world," but it turned out to be nothing of the sort.

Wary of Nixon's policies, the European Economic Community (EEC) tried to move away from its dependency on the U.S. dollar in 1972. The European Joint Float, popularly called the "snake," was established by West Germany, France, Italy, the Netherlands, Belgium, and Luxembourg. It was an agreement between these countries to manage their currencies so that their exchange rates moved in tandem. The agreement comprised the Exchange Rate Mechanism (ERM) in which countries had to hold their currencies within a band relative to agreed rates, with central banks acting if necessary, by buying or selling their local currencies, to keep them within the preset trading bands.

The theory was similar to the Bretton Woods Agreement, except that it also allowed for wider trading bands. Still, by 1973, both the Smithsonian Agreement and European Joint Float failed as currencies could not be regulated in the way that the architects of the accords intended. The collapse led to the birth of the "free float system," which prevails today. The free float system started by default as there were no new agreements to replace the Smithsonian Agreement or the European Joint Float. Governments were free to peg their currencies, or allow them to freely float. In 1978, the

NOTE
THE GOLD STANDARD

The idea of a "gold standard" is based on the premise that by fixing currencies to a specific amount of gold and exchangeable into that amount of gold, governments are prevented from printing too much paper money, devaluing their currency and creating inflation. It is based on the assumption that if the supply of paper money rises too fast people will exchange the paper money for gold and the gold in the country's treasury will be reduced, thus restricting the ability of governments or central banks to further print more paper money. Many economists criticize this system since they say it prevents governments from increasing the supply of money to stimulate the economy in times of recession or depression and even preventing such economic downturns. They say that when exchange rates are rigid and can't respond to changing conditions in various countries central banks are prevented from increasing money supply thus exacerbating economic downturns. On the other side, the gold standard proponents argue that having a gold standard prevents long-term inflation by placing a strict discipline on government and central banks preventing them from printing too much paper money. Of course one key factor with a gold standard is the credibility of the central bank and the government under which it operates. This is why the so-called "independence" of central bank in often emphasized. The idea is that central banks should not be swayed by populist and political sentiment so that they can implement rigid monetary standards to prevent inflation. As a result of political pressure there have been instances where central banks succumbed to demands by politicians to print more money. They thus lied about how much gold they actually had in their vaults and issued currency in excess of what was allowed. One argument made against the gold standard is that if central banks can't be trusted to keep inflation low by limiting the supply of money then they should not be trusted to keep the gold standard.

free-floating system was officially mandated. Since then, there have been a number of different currency regimes in addition to the free-float system. Governments have changed from one currency regime to another, often in response to financial crises.

The gold standard is no longer used in any country today, having been replaced completely by fiat currency—that is, currency that is not backed by a commodity like gold or silver. What gives money value today is its relative scarcity, and its role as a medium of exchange is generally accepted in good faith by the populace which uses it.

 SUMMARY ——————————————————————

The origins of modern-day financial centers were the late 17th century humble coffee houses of London, where people of all commercial persuasions would meet and information would be exchanged on areas of commerce, finance and shipping. Many of these coffee shops were located close to the Royal Exchange, a mercantile hub set up by English merchant and financier Sir Thomas Gresham late in the 16th century. Apart from his association with the Royal Exchange, Gresham is also known for an economic theory called Gresham's Law, though he is not believed to have put forward the theory himself. It was more an observation he had made. Meanwhile, early information lists supplied by publicans helped to develop a thirst for more of such information. It is known that the Lloyd's List contained information about exchange rates as did lists made by coffee house proprietors that were geared toward stocks. Against this backdrop, one of the longest-surviving companies of all time, the East India Company, was at the heart of the expansion of global trade from the 17th century. It is said that without this company, there would have been no British empire. The money that helped fuel global trade had been backed against different standards like silver and gold through the ages. The advent of the foreign exchange markets as we know them today came soon after the gold standard was finally abandoned by U.S. President Nixon in 1971. This precipitated the collapse of the Bretton Woods agreement signed in July 1944.

 QUICK QUIZ

1. Who set up the Royal Exchange in London, in 1565, and what is the law associated with him?

2. Into which establishments did London's seventeenth century stock dealers move after being expelled from the Royal Exchange?

3. What commodity did the British produce to help pay for their purchases of tea in China?

4. From which European coin is the word "dollar" believed to have originated?

5. Which country in the Americas was a major source of silver for China in the eighteenth century?

6. In which year did Britain formally adopt the gold standard?

7. Against which country's currency were other member countries' currencies pegged under the Bretton Woods Agreement?

8. Which international monetary agreement superseded the Bretton Woods Agreement in 1971?

3
WHO USES FOREIGN EXCHANGE?

INTRODUCTION

In the past, the foreign exchange market was solely the domain of large institutions such as commercial and investment banks. They traded foreign exchange for their customers and among themselves. Currency traders employed by these institutions operated in loose and informal networks. Before the invention of fax machines and the Internet they initially conducted business via telex and dedicated telephone lines. These channels were augmented by electronic communication networks (ECNs) set up by information service providers such as Reuters and EBS (Electronic Broking Services). The advent of these ECNs fueled explosive growth in global foreign exchange trading. Figure 3.1 shows the growing impact of ECNs in foreign exchange trading from 1989 through to 2004.

Figure 3.1 — Market Share of ECNs in Foreign Exchange Transactions

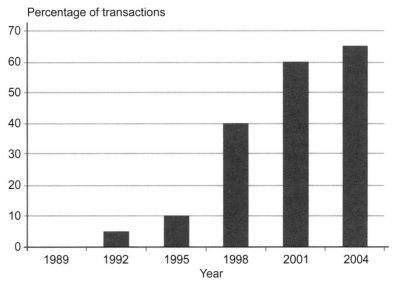

Source: Estimates for 1989-2001 are from Chaboud and Weinberg (2002). The BIS provides the 2004 number.

Growth was further driven by the emergence of the Internet in the 1990s. It lowered the cost of handling and processing information, and brought foreign exchange trading services online. Now, the network of participants in foreign exchange markets has expanded to include multinational corporations, pension funds, asset managers, hedge funds, and individual investors. Nevertheless, trading between banks, via domestic and international interbank transactions, still accounts for the vast majority of the foreign exchange business.

CASE STUDY: REUTERS

Paul Julius Reuter (© Reuters)

The history of Reuters, the information agency, frequently reflects innovation and the use of leading edge technology. In 1851, German-born Reuters founder, Paul Julius Reuter, used the electric telegraph—a new invention, which he augmented with carrier pigeons—to launch the world's first paid news service. The pigeons covered a gap in the telegraph line network between Aachen, where German telegraph lines ended, and Belgium. His core customers were business houses in England, France, and Belgium to whom he supplied news from the European markets, faster than any one could then conceive. On April 26, 1865, Reuters was the first agency to bring the news of President Abraham Lincoln's assassination in the U.S. to the European public. On the back of scoops such as this, Reuters became a respected name for the dissemination of news. It also broke new ground with the use of radio to send news internationally, in 1923. In the early 1980s, Reuters pioneered the electronic marketplace in foreign exchange trading. Until then, trading was conducted over the telephone or by telex. Reuters' innovation allowed foreign exchange trading to be conducted on screens in seconds. The company now offers both a conversational trading application and a matching service that enables traders to match bids and offers anonymously and automatically.

Source: *Reuters.com*

CASE STUDY: EBS

Electronic Broking Services (EBS) was formed in 1990 by some of the largest banks marking markets in foreign exchange in order to break the monopoly held by Reuters in the interbank spot foreign exchange market. EBS was the first organization to facilitate "black box" or algorithmic trading in spot FX through an application programming interface (API). In 2006 EBS was acquired by ICAP, the world's largest interdealer broker. That acquisition combined EBS's strengths in electronic spot foreign exchange with ICAP's electronic broking business to create a single global multi-product business with further growth potential and significant economies of scale. Currently each day the EBS Spot Dealing System handles USD 145 billion in spot foreign exchange transactions, 700,000 oz in gold and 7 million oz in silver. EBS's closest competitor is Reuters.

Source: *www.ebs.com*

BANKS

The world's largest commercial and investment banks are the most active players in foreign exchange trade. These banks participate in the interbank market, which encompasses both the majority of commercial turnover in foreign exchange trade and large amounts of speculative trading every day. The interbank market initially kicked off in the 1980s when large commercial banks began viewing foreign exchange trading as a business activity in itself. Rather than just buying and selling currencies for their customers as a standard banking service, they started to trade on their own account with other commercial banks. As time passed, more commercial banks engaged in interbank trading, with larger investment banks also joining in. Today, banks such as Deutsche Bank, UBS, Citigroup, HSBC, Barclays, Merrill Lynch, JP Morgan Chase, Goldman Sachs, ABN AMRO, and Morgan Stanley trade hundreds of millions of dollars daily. The impact of interbank trading on broader financial markets is highly significant. For example, central banks actively intervene in interbank markets to guide their policy interest rates. Interbank markets also allow banks to trade among themselves—that is, banks with surplus funds can lend to other banks that need liquidity to, for instance, maintain their reserve requirements. Due to the large transaction sizes, the difference between buying and selling prices for currencies is at its most competitive in interbank trading. Participants in this market are regarded as the top tier of currency trading.

BID-ASK SPREADS

It is a characteristic of the foreign exchange market that differences between buying and selling prices (known in financial markets as bid-ask spreads) tend to get wider the smaller the transaction size. This is similar to retail and wholesale prices in other commodities. If individuals are exchanging small amounts of currency, then the difference between the bid and ask prices will be wider because the expenses involved in doing the smaller transaction will be higher than for larger transactions. Thus, an informal hierarchy is embedded into foreign exchange markets, with players in the interbank market on the top tier. The rest of the foreign exchange market has to accept the higher cost of doing business and look to the interbank market for directional cues on currencies. Indeed, dealers at big commercial banks regularly act as market makers, providing liquidity for currencies and, of course, profiting from the wider spreads they charge the retail trade.

NOTE
MARKET MAKERS

A market maker is a dealer who quotes buying and selling prices for one or more currencies to his customers, seeking to make a profit from the difference between the buying and selling prices. As in stock and commodities markets, market makers are viewed as useful to the functioning of currency markets. They contribute to liquidity and price stability in the short term, and provide useful price information.

It must be stressed that the foreign exchange market is primarily an "over-the-counter" market where foreign exchange contracts are agreed upon bilaterally between participants. Thus, the users of foreign exchange can enter into currency contracts directly with banks. The risk of holding a particular currency which may weaken is managed by banks in the interbank market, where the bank traders buy and sell currencies in line with their retail client orders—so, in effect, they transfer the risk among themselves. They are able to work easily together, rapidly buying and selling large amounts of currency by establishing credit relationships. Reflecting these needs, foreign exchange desks at the big banks are typically made up of two sets of traders—corporate traders, who make offers to buy and sell foreign currencies at specific prices to clients, and interbank traders, who then cover these positions by buying the currency from, or selling it to, other large commercial banks.

Technological advances in the last 20 years have transformed the foreign exchange market. Electronic systems enable traders to quickly communicate their foreign exchange needs to other players and match buyers of currencies

Figure 3.2 — Trading floor of a brokerage company

Source: Getty Images

with sellers. This has led to greater transparency, which has helped to level the playing field among different types of market participants. Differences between buying and selling prices have narrowed and the market has become more efficient. Online trading platforms have appeared and are used by a broader range of participants, even opening up the foreign exchange market to individual investors.

ONLINE TRADING PLATFORMS

There are two types of online trading platforms or portals:

- Proprietary or single-bank
- Multi-bank

In proprietary or single-bank systems, a bank makes available its own online trading platform to its customers. Single-bank platforms allow banks to extend existing services to clients, helping to save costs and time in processing trades. The bank and the client are directly linked electronically. Typically, no dual-entry is necessary to record transactions. The bank offers liquidity to its clients, who are limited to exchange rates offered by the bank. Single-bank portals do not give customers much of a choice in terms

OPINION
LIQUIDITY ISSUES

"In the 1990s, the structural changes in the foreign exchange markets had a major impact on price behavior. Early in the decade, market liquidity during extremely volatile price movements was with few exceptions— almost continuous. Today, this has changed. Market liquidity is discontinuous, that is, only small price shocks are required to make market liquidity disappear. When the price movements stabilize again, liquidity reappears and markets return to normal working order.

This behavior pattern is highly disturbing. It increases the risk of exceptionally large price shocks such as the collapse of the Japanese yen in 1998. In this event, market making in the yen was discontinuous whenever there was an above-average price movement, with market liquidity disappearing. As soon as external circumstances led to large sell orders, the orders could not be accommodated due to the lack of liquidity. This, in turn, triggered additional sale orders, which further undermined the currency. Thus, the meltdown.

In our view, today's foreign exchange markets are extremely fragile. The reason for this is quite simple. The mergers between banks, and the closing of smaller dealing rooms within banks, have led to a reduction of overall risk capital allocated to market making. Simultaneously, there has been a dramatic increase in the volume of fundamentally-driven foreign exchange transactions as a result of the rapid growth of international trade and global investing. To absorb the impact of these transactions, a high level of market liquidity is required. In the absence of this, the markets are extremely sensitive to small changes of supply and demand, leading to erratic price swings with intermittent market liquidity."

Richard Olsen
Olsen and Associates

of exchange rates, but one of the main advantages is that trades can be uploaded directly to customers' front-end systems for processing.

Multi-bank platforms, on the other hand, offer exchange rates for currency pairs from different banks. They typically quote exchange rates from various banks that compete on the multi-bank portals. This results in bid-ask spreads tending to be narrower than in single-bank platforms. Thus, customers of multi-bank portals tend to have greater access to the best prices available.

NEWS CLIP
FOREX GIANTS HEAD FOR THE NET

The three largest players in the global currency market are teaming up with Reuters to offer foreign exchange services over the internet to major clients, according to a report in the Wall Street Journal. The report said U.S. banks Chase Manhattan and Citigroup, and Germany's Deutsche Bank were creating a new company together with the news and financial information provider. The move is the latest and most significant sign that big players in currency markets are turning to the internet to answer their clients' demands for faster services at lower prices. Chase, Citigroup and Deutsche Bank together have a market share in world foreign exchange trading of almost 30%.

The Wall Street Journal reported sources familiar with the deal as saying that the four founders were now seeking to include a further 50 or 60 international banks in the venture before publicly announcing its creation. The new venture is set to compete directly with FXall, an internet-based currency venture recently established by 13 other major international banks. They include Credit Suisse First Boston, Goldman Sachs Group, HSBC Holdings, J.P. Morgan, Morgan Stanley Dean Witter and UBS Warburg—all of whom are among the world's top 10 foreign exchange traders. "There is room for two companies—EBS and Reuters—on the interbank matching system so I don't see why there might not be room for two here," said one banker in London. "They could end up specialising in different things but if they don't differentiate themselves like this, it will come down to prices. In the short term, Citi, Deutsche, and Chase could be very aggressive on the pricing." Both services aim to offer their customers—expected to be mainly multinational corporations, institutional investors and hedge funds—a one-stop shop for currency services.

Source: *BBC News,* August 14, 2000

Recent developments related to online trading platforms include the introduction of value-added services such as prime brokerage, white-labelling, and algorithmic trading, all of which are touted to give the bank's clients more flexibility in managing the risks associated with exchange rate fluctuations.

NOTE
FOREIGN EXCHANGE SERVICES

Prime Brokerage: The term "prime broker" describes an investment bank's package of services for clients, mostly hedge fund clients. The advantage of such a bundled service is that it centralizes a number of tasks such as securities clearing, financing leverage, custody, securities lending, and foreign exchange trading. The prime broker can source currency quotes from several banks while maintaining credit relationships with those banks so that clients only need to place collateral with a single bank, the prime broker. By doing this, customers ostensibly have access to better liquidity conditions and more competitive pricing. The prime broker, meanwhile, mainly benefits from garnering new fee-based revenues from the customer. Typically, prime brokers would have links to banks across the world so that, at any time, they should know which bank has the highest buying rate for a currency, and which has the lowest selling rate.

White Labelling: This allows smaller banks and financial institutions to outsource their currency pricing to providers with large liquidity bases, such as HSBC, ABN AMRO, and Citigroup, while promoting these services under their own name. Consequently, they can offer their own clients a broader array of foreign exchange services, without the costs of independently developing those services. The white labelling service provider typically supplies the smaller firm with technology for currency trading. The liquidity provider benefits from the development of additional revenue streams, and from having additional distribution channels, which potentially result in bigger deal volumes.

Algorithmic Trading: Also known as "automatic," "black-box," or "robo" trading where computer programs decided the timing, price, or quantity of the trade. The investor places an order to buy or sell and the computer automatically generates the timing of orders and the size of orders based on goals specified by algorithmic parameters and constraints.

Typically, the best trading systems offered by banks will work with their clients' existing infrastructure to provide direct access to a range of foreign exchange services. In the last decade, banks have realised the value of investing in technologically advanced trading systems to capture a bigger share of the foreign exchange market. UBS, Deutsche Bank and Citigroup have poured money into sophisticated trading platforms incorporating new

ONLINE FOREIGN EXCHANGE TRADING PLATFORMS

FX Connect

FX Connect, owned by State Street Corporation, is a multi-bank foreign exchange trading network that provides secure, real-time trade execution with multiple counterparties 24 hours a day. Launched in 1996, FX Connect is a market leader in electronic foreign exchange trading and became the first multi-bank network in March 2000. Through FX Connect, users can access liquidity from 55 providers and execute spot, forward, and swap transactions across an unlimited number of accounts.

FX Connect also offers Quick FX, a competitive pricing feature that allows investors to transact single or block trades with multiple banks. FX Connect's direct connectivity extends to users' in-house accounting, portfolio management, and custody systems. Trades can be entered manually into the trade blotter or downloaded from existing systems, enabling investors to integrate foreign exchange trading into their portfolio execution process more effectively. FX Connect's live interactive pricing and netting capability across multiple funds and currencies helps manage risk and maximize efficiency throughout the trade execution process.

Source: *www.globallink.com*

FXall

FXall is integrated to more than 60 of the world's leading foreign exchange banks. Between them, these market makers and service providers offer clients comprehensive research and post-trade services, as well as a source of liquidity on the market. FXall's network enables its provider banks to offer clients streaming spot and forward prices across more than 300 currency pairs, with minimum latency. As FXall is relationship-based, banks have more incentive to provide deep liquidity to the platform—meaning that it is faster and easier to execute even the largest transactions. More than 700 institutions have joined the FXall platform and its trading volumes continue to grow rapidly. Annual volumes exceeded US$6.7 trillion in 2005, up from US$4.9 trillion in 2004 and US$2.4 trillion in 2003.

Source: *www.fxall.com*

Currenex

Founded in 1999, Currenex's trading platform connects more than 70 banks, which help provide a deep liquidity pool. It was one of the first companies to provide online foreign currency exchange trading systems with both buy-side and sell-side members that included multinationals and financial institutions. Currenex is now a leading provider of foreign exchange and money market trading services. It uses patented technology for executable streaming prices, and benchmark pricing and prime-brokerage functions. State Street Corporation announced the acquisition of Currenex for approximately US$564 million in January 2007.

Source: *www.currenex.com*

technology. This has seen them emerge as the leading players in the global foreign exchange market. As mentioned, banks also conduct a large amount of trading on their own accounts. As such, they are at an advantage because they have insight into trade and investment flows through their dealings with customers. Consequently, they are able to predict more accurately where the exchange rates they deal with are headed, at least in the short term. Traders across foreign exchange markets will try to assess what banks are doing, and this will help them make their own trading decisions.

COMPANIES

With international trade and investment expanding in this age of globalization, companies often need foreign exchange when they engage in cross-border transactions. They are involved in many different types of activities, both domestically and overseas. Many of them would be described as multinational corporations—simply, companies that operate in two or more countries. Some of the activities that require cross-border transactions include:

- Importing or exporting raw materials, finished products, machinery
- Buying assets like property and buildings
- Participating in joint venture projects
- Buying or selling stocks or bonds
- Opening retail outlets
- Capacity expansions
- Goodwill payments
- Dividend payments
- International payroll payments
- Charitable activities

HOW FOREIGN EXCHANGE CAN IMPACT COMPANIES
FICTITIOUS EXAMPLES

"No problem, B.J. I can talk and baste at the same time."

© The New Yorker Collection 2006 Charles Barsotti from cartoonbank.com. All Rights Reserved.

Bangkok BBQ

Bangkok BBQ is a Thailand-based manufacturer and exporter of portable barbecue pits. It is exposed to different currencies when the company imports various parts and equipment from New Zealand, China, and the U.S. Bangkok BBQ's foreign currency payables are thus in New Zealand dollars, Chinese renminbi and U.S. dollars. Conversely, a good portion of its sales revenue is not in the Thai currency, the baht, but in U.S. dollars and other currencies because it competes with other makers of portable barbecue pits in markets all over the world.

With sales and costs denominated in currencies other than the Thai baht, Bangkok BBQ must keep a close watch on the different currencies that have an impact on it. Changes in these currencies relative to the baht can have a significant impact on its revenue, which the company has to report in its local currency.

Singabooks

Singabooks is a Singapore-based publishing company. It publishes an array of popular children's magazines in Singapore but has recently found that the cost of publishing in Singapore is becoming harder to accommodate, mainly due to escalating printing costs. It has decided to look for a printing company elsewhere in the region to help reduce these costs. In considering this strategic move for its business, Singabooks has to factor in issues such as the cost of logistics and bringing forward editorial deadlines to meet earlier printing schedules. Another important consideration is the exchange rate between the currency where it will print its magazines and the Singapore currency. The chief concern is that Singabooks may need more of its local currency to pay for printing costs in the printer's home currency if an exchange rate movement is unfavorable. An immediate solution could be to negotiate a deal denominated in the Singapore dollar. This will take away exchange rate worries. However, it could also result in Singabooks losing an opportunity to make higher profits. For example, if Singabooks negotiates a printing deal with a Japanese printer denominated in Japanese yen and the Singapore dollar gets stronger against the yen after the deal is signed, Singabooks' profit picture will be enhanced. Since it sells its magazines in Singapore dollars it will profit from the exchange rate differences since the amount of Singapore dollars the company will need to purchase yen will go down.

- Legal proceedings
- Receiving and paying royalties
- Receiving and paying rent

All these activities can involve currencies different from the one in which corporations report their revenues and earnings at their home office, and this difference could have an impact on their financial results. For instance, when a company buys an asset overseas, it will have to factor in the exchange rate at which its home currency is converted to the currency of the country where the asset is located. Alternatively, if a legal proceeding in a foreign country results in a company being sued, the associated legal costs and any subsequent payment are likely to have to be accounted for in terms of the company's home currency. Furthermore, if companies derive revenues and profits different from their home currency, there will be a foreign exchange impact when they repatriate the funds back home.

Among the companies most commonly involved in foreign exchange transactions are import and export firms. Importers must buy foreign exchange to pay for goods they import from overseas, while exporters are paid in foreign currencies and need to exchange this money back to their local currency. Even companies that are not involved in international trade of any form will be concerned about foreign exchange as they may have to buy raw materials for their products from local importers. The costs of these inputs can be influenced by changes in exchange rates which may have had an impact on what the importer had to pay for them. This, in turn, may influence how much users of these products have to pay, as importers may decide to pass on foreign exchange-related costs to them.

CENTRAL BANKS

Central banks like the Federal Reserve System in the U.S., the European Central Bank (ECB), the Bank of Japan (BOJ), and the People's Bank of China have access to huge foreign exchange reserves and play an important role in currency markets.

In recent years one of the main tasks of the central banks has been to control money supply in their respective countries. Their access to extensive

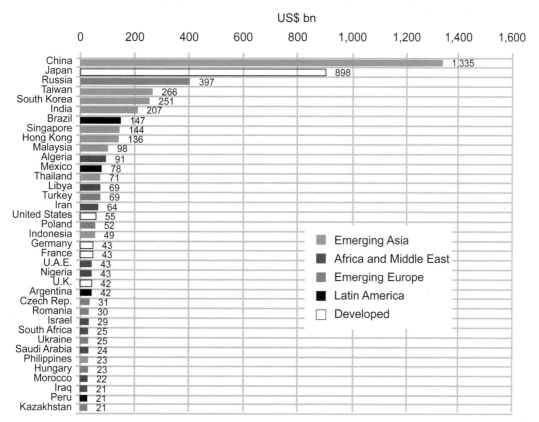

Figure 3.3 — Emerging vs Developed Markets: Foreign Reserves, June 2007

Source: *Economist Intelligence Unit; International Monetary Fund*

CASE STUDY: WORKINGS OF A CENTRAL BANK: BANK OF JAPAN

Bank of Japan building in Tokyo
Source: Getty Images

The Bank of Japan (BOJ) says its missions are to: Maintain price stability and; to ensure the stability of the financial system in Japan, thereby laying the foundations for sound economic development. To fulfil these two missions, the BOJ conducts the following activities:

1. Issuance and management of banknotes:

The Bank of Japan issues banknotes (officially referred to as Bank of Japan notes) as the nation's sole issuing bank. It employs a wide range of measures to prevent counterfeiting, including watermarks, special inks, and micro-lettering. Because banknotes are used in all kinds of transactions, BOJ pays close attention to the control of the physical quality of banknotes so that the public is able to use the notes with confidence.

2. The conduct of monetary policy:

BOJ's mission is to pursue price stability—that is, to maintain an economic environment in which there is neither inflation nor deflation. The bank controls the overall volume of money in the economy and interest rates on a daily basis through money market operations, for example, through its sales or purchases of money market instruments, such as Japanese government securities, to or from private financial institutions. BOJ's policy to stabilize prices in order to contribute to the sound development of the national economy, is called its monetary policy. It believes that price stability is a prerequisite for stability in the daily lives of the Japanese people, and for realizing sustainable and balanced economic growth.

3. **Providing settlement services and ensuring the stability of the financial system:**

The term financial system refers to the collective mechanisms through which financial institutions intermediate funds between depositors and investors, and provide payment and settlement services, such as funds transfers between accounts. The financial system constitutes a fundamental social infrastructure that supports the daily lives of the Japanese people, as does the provision of electric power, water, and gas. BOJ conducts various activities to maintain this particular infrastructure. This includes functioning as the lender of last resort to provide emergency liquidity in the event of a financial institution becoming insolvent.

4. **Treasury and government securities-related operations:**

As the "government's bank," BOJ handles receipts and disbursements of treasury funds, including acceptance of tax monies and payment of public works expenditures and public pensions. It also conducts accounting and bookkeeping for government agencies.

5. **International activities:**

BOJ provides Japanese yen accounts to central banks and governmental institutions overseas. It also makes capital subscriptions and loan extensions to international organizations such as the Bank for International Settlements (BIS) and the IMF. It closely monitors exchange rate developments. It intervenes in foreign exchange markets as an agent of Japan's Minister of Finance, when necessary.

6. **Data compilation, economic analyses and research activities:**

To ensure appropriate implementation of monetary policy, BOJ must have an accurate understanding of the overall economic and financial conditions in Japan. To this end, the bank compiles various statistics, including the wholesale price indexes and the corporate service price index. It also conducts a regular business survey known as the *tankan*—a short-term economic survey of enterprises in Japan. The bank explains its view mainly through the publication of the results of these analyses.

Source: Bank of Japan

NEWS CLIP
THE MAN WHO BROKE THE BANK OF ENGLAND

This week sees the arrival in Britain of George Soros—the international speculator who now aims to reform global capitalism. He will be addressing the House of Commons Treasury Select Committee, and giving a number of press interviews, on the dangers of unregulated free markets. Mr Soros, who operates one of the world's biggest private investment funds, is famous for having made US$1 billion by betting on the devaluation of the pound sterling in 1992.

His Quantum Investment Fund claims to be the world's most profitable. This year, an article he wrote in the *Financial Times* newspaper on the need for Russia to devalue its currency precipitated the fall of the Russian Government, a massive default on its debts, and widespread financial panic. But Mr Soros has aspirations to be more than a speculator. He has donated millions to charitable foundations, most notably to help Eastern Europe. And now he has surprised his critics by calling for more international regulation of markets—a surprising admission perhaps from someone worth US$5 billion.

The 67-year-old financier was born in Hungary, but emigrated to England when he was 17, after the communists took power. He studied philosophy at the London School of Economics with Karl Popper, whose views on the need for open and tolerant societies as a precursor of economic growth, he adopted as his own. After selling souvenirs in Wales, he joined London stockbrokers Singer & Friendlander before moving to Wall Street in 1956.

He set up the Quantum Fund in 1969. Registered in Curacao in the Caribbean, but run from Manhattan, the fund took money from rich individuals and invested in risky, but potential highly profitable international deals. The fund profited hugely from the collapse of fixed exchange rates in the 1970s and the deregulation of global capital markets.

Soros is part of a group of international private investors with an estimated US$100 billion in assets who can significantly affect global markets. In September, another hedge fund, Long Term Capital Management, had to be rescued by the world's major banks for $3 billion—at the behest of the Federal Reserve—because of the risk to the whole world's financial system if that fund were to fail. In October, Mr

Soros had to restructure his own investment companies. He closed the Quantum Emerging Growth Fund, which lost one-third of its value after taking a big loss on its Russian investments, and merged another, after disclosing losses of US$2 billion.

Source: *BBC News,* December 6, 1998

foreign exchange reserves allows them intervene in currency markets if they think their local currency is getting too weak or too strong. They also intervene to smoothen any excessive volatility associated with their local currencies. Often they don't have to act, as verbal warnings of possible intervention are enough to get currency traders worried and curtail speculative trading, helping to stabilize the local currencies.

Central banks closely monitor economic activity, and have many options available to them to regulate their national economies. These options often relate to specific policies that have a big impact on foreign exchange markets. Conversely, currency traders will closely monitor monetary policy statements from central banks to assess their thinking on the strength of the domestic economy and inflation. This allows the foreign exchange market to anticipate what sort of action the central bank will take in the months ahead—whether it will raise or lower benchmark interest rates, or do nothing at all—when it holds its regular monetary policy committee meetings.

INVESTMENT FUNDS

The expanding global economy has helped to service the appetite of investors for foreign equities and fixed-income instruments as they seek to diversify their assets. International investment, pension, and mutual funds, insurance companies, and trusts, recognize the importance of diversification. They constantly adjust their global equity and fixed-income portfolios, moving funds in and out of countries. These adjustments can have an impact on exchange rate movements.

U.S. investors are among the world's leaders in overseas asset investment. According to a joint study by the U.S. Department of the Treasury, Federal Reserve Bank of New York, and the Board of Governors of the Federal Reserve System, total U.S. holdings of long-term foreign securities, from March 1994 to December 2005, jumped almost five times—from US$870.1 billion to US$4.3 trillion (see Figure 3.4).

The bulk of U.S. portfolio investments abroad are in equities and long-term debt instruments issued in developed markets. In recent years, the U.K. was the top destination, with U.S. investors owning long-term U.K. securities worth US$815 billion in December 2005 (see Figure 3.5). Japanese long-term securities (US$531 billion) comprised the next biggest U.S. holding, followed by Canadian securities (US$419 billion). Of the total U.S. foreign holdings of long-term securities in December 2004, about US$3.3 trillion

FUND SPY: HOW MUTUAL FUNDS HANDLE THE FALLING (RISING?) DOLLAR

To put it simply, when a U.S.-based fund buys stocks on a foreign stock exchange, the fund pays for it in that country's currency. The stock moves up or down in that currency. But when the fund calculates its return, it must do so in dollars. So, if the foreign currency is worth more in dollar terms than it had been when the fund bought the stock, the fund—and its shareholders—get a bonus. The reverse is true when the foreign currency falls against the dollar. In 2006, this phenomenon had a tremendous impact on fund performance. In fact, much of the well-publicised outperformance of foreign markets and international funds in 2006 owed to the rise in the euro, pound, and many other currencies. The euro gained about 10% against the dollar and the pound 12%; among the major currencies, only the yen, which was roughly flat against the dollar, failed to join the party.

Different ways to play

The simplest approaches to take are being fully unhedged and being fully hedged. Most international funds take the first approach, with Fidelity's funds serving as a prominent example. They just buy the stocks and let the currency do what it may. Of course, such portfolio managers do typically take into account currency effects when evaluating stocks; for example, a company that relies heavily on exports to the U.S. might find its prospects damped when the dollar is weak. But these managers don't actively try to alter the resulting currency exposure.

Very few funds take the opposite approach. Tweedy, Browne Global Value is one that does, hedging virtually all its foreign-currency exposure back into the dollar. Longleaf Partners International essentially does the same thing, though rather than simply counting up the assets it has in foreign stocks and hedging that amount, it makes a calculation to determine the true economic exposure of its holdings to currency movements. The result is technically less than a 100% hedge, but in essence it removes nearly all of the fund's exposure to foreign currencies. Similarly, the Mutual Series funds, though not always completely hedged into the dollar, tend in that direction.

A third approach is for a manager—or an associated currency team—to make active currency plays in an effort to bolster returns simply through currency trading. Very few stock funds do that. Among the few that do is Oppenheimer Global Opportunities—although even in that case, the extent of its activity is far below the level of a hedge fund-like currency speculator.

Hedging to the benchmark

The variety doesn't end there. Putnam's international funds go in another direction—"hedging to the benchmark." The firm tries to separate a fund's stock picks from its currency exposure, but rather than thinking of an all-dollar position as meeting that goal, it prefers to have currency weightings that match the fund's benchmark. For example, a manager may like a number of Japanese stocks and therefore have a portfolio weighting of 30% in Japan—far above the MSCI EAFE Index's weighting of about 21%. But why, Putnam reasons, should the fund be so overweighted in the yen if its managers have no view on the yen? So, a separate Putnam currency team uses derivative securities to adjust the fund's yen exposure to about 21%. (Some Putnam funds allow the currency team to also make small "bets" above or below that benchmark number, but you get the idea.)

Yet another approach is more common than it may seem, because managers and fund companies tend to downplay it. That's the tendency to not hedge currency exposure, except in certain cases when they do hedge some currency exposure. Often (but not always) this takes place with emerging market currencies, because of the added potential of extreme volatility in such currencies. For example, at one point the managers of Julius Baer International Equity had a (relatively) quite large five percent stake in Turkish stocks but felt that the Turkish lira, for various reasons, was vulnerable. They didn't want to sell the stocks, which they liked and which aren't all that easy to buy and sell quickly. But they didn't want all that exposure to the lira either. So, they hedged that particular currency exposure into the U.S. dollar.

Meanwhile, at Oakmark International, lead manager David Herro rarely hedges—but that doesn't mean he never does. In what he considers extreme cases when currencies are not fairly valued, he'll take action by adjusting currency exposure. When pressed, other managers who say they don't hedge will, after a moment, mention a time or three in the past when they have done so.

Staying out of the dark

Knowing your fund's currency policy can help you better evaluate its performance. For example, one reason Longleaf Partners International had such a lackluster 2006 return in comparison to rival funds is that it had so little exposure to the foreign currency gains that were bolstering the returns of those rivals. It also can help you decide which fund to own. If you're looking for a foreign fund specifically to diversify your U.S.-heavy portfolio, you might prefer an unhedged fund in order to get currency diversification as well (although a "hedged to the benchmark" fund would also provide that).

In short, we don't think you should pick a fund based on where you think the dollar is going. Such predictions are too tough to make accurately with any consistency. But we do think that, as with other areas of investing, knowing what you own and how it is likely to perform under different conditions is preferable to being in the dark.

Source: Gregg Wolper, "Fund Spy: How Mutual Funds Handle the Falling (Rising?) dollar," *Morningstar*, February 6, 2007

Figure 3.4 — Market Value of U.S. Holdings of Foreign Securities, by Type of Security

US$ bn	March 1994	December 1997	December 2001	December 2003	December 2004	December 2005
Long-term securities[1]	870	1,755	2,170	2,954	3,553	4,346
Equity	567	1,208	1,613	2,079	2,560	3,318
Long-term debt	304	547	557	874	993	1,028
Short-term debt	n.a.	n.a.	147	199	233	263
Total	**n.a.**	**n.a.**	**2,317**	**3,152**	**3,787**	**4,609**

n.a.   Not available
1.   Long-term securities are defined as those without a stated maturity date (such as equities) or with an original term-to-maturity in excess of one year.

Source: *U.S. Department of the Treasury*

were in equities. Other leading investors, such as the Europeans and the Japanese, showed a preference for debt securities.

This data demonstrates the variety of countries and foreign currencies that are involved when investment funds scour the globe for returns. There is likely to be more cross-border activity by pension funds and other institutional investors as restrictions on foreign holdings are removed and as the investors become less conservative.

Pension funds around the world are faced with aging populations requiring increased requirements for pension payouts. As a result, the ability of these pension funds to meet the demands of their clients is coming under pressure hence the need for higher returns on their investments. Since investments in equities have been found to offer higher returns than bonds

Figure 3.5— Value of U.S. Holdings of Foreign Securities, by Country and Type of Security as of December 31, 2005

US$ bn		Total	Equities	Debt securities	
				Long-term	Short-term
1	United Kingdom	815	538	185	92
2	Japan	531	493	35	2
3	Canada	419	248	158	14
4	France	274	205	48	21
5	Cayman Islands	249	103	118	28
6	Germany	217	158	49	10
7	Switzerland	196	192	2	2
8	Netherlands	192	133	52	7
9	Bermuda	187	174	11	2
10	Australia	128	71	49	9
11	South Korea	119	110	8	0
12	Brazil	90	69	22	0
13	Mexico	86	58	28	0
14	Italy	79	64	12	3
15	Ireland	75	33	17	25
16	Sweden	75	41	16	18
17	Spain	70	64	6	1
18	Taiwan	58	57	1	0
19	Finland	49	44	4	0
20	Netherlands	47	45	2	0
21	Luxembourg	46	11	29	6
22	Hong Kong	46	44	2	0
23	Israel	44	29	15	0
24	Singapore	36	29	7	0
25	Norway	36	22	9	5
	Rest of the world	445	283	143	19
Total value of investment		**4,609**	**3,318**	**1,028**	**263**

Source: *U.S. Department of the Treasury*

or bank deposits, there has been a move into equities. Additionally the need for diversification and the opportunity for higher returns via international investment means that these funds have increased their foreign exchange exposure. For example, a recent study of 280 Canadian pension funds by financial consultants Greenwich Associates found that most pension funds in Canada still don't have enough money to cover their pension promises. This means that Canadian pension fund managers must embrace new investing strategies to increase their investment returns and make up for underfunded retirement plans. Since good investment management requires that funds be diversified internationally for best returns, these managers are changing their investment behavior. The Canadian markets, like all other markets, will not always be the best performing. Indeed, Greenwich also found that Canadian pension funds planned to boost their foreign fixed-income holdings by 70%, and foreign stock holdings by 30%. Money for new strategies is expected to come from withdrawal from Canadian stocks, as 35% of the managers surveyed said they were cutting back on domestic equity holdings and looking for investments overseas.

INDIVIDUAL INVESTORS

The Internet has opened the foreign exchange market to individual investors who are flocking to trading platforms offered by online foreign exchange brokers like FX Connect, FXall, and Currenex. Indeed, Internet space is inundated by a plethora of online foreign exchange brokers, the numbers of which appear to be growing ever larger. So much so, that there are concerns about the reliability of many online platforms in executing trades fairly. Accusations often fly in online foreign exchange trader blogs about one scam or another perpetrated by dishonest parties offering online broking

"This isn't for me—it's for the economy."

© The New Yorker Collection 2001 Marisa Acocella Marchetto from cartoonbank.com.
All Rights Reserved.

services. Typical services offered by reputable online brokers include fully-automated trading platforms, a wide range of currencies to trade in, price transparency, instant confirmation of orders, settlement with real-time account management, leverage, and analysis tools.

It should be noted that individual investors who trade foreign exchange online are also likely to have had some experience of trading equities online, and will use similar tools to trade in this market. There was a surge of day trading by retail investors during the height of the dot.com craze in 2000. Indeed, the phrase "day trading" is probably most apt when applied

NEWS CLIP
REFCO SHOULD EASE ONLINE CURRENCY WOES

Forex Capital Markets LLC's deal to take over the foreign exchange business of futures brokerage giant Refco Inc. should help shore up the flagging reputation of the online retail currency industry, FXCM's chief executive officer Drew Niv told Reuters in an interview.

Refco on Friday agreed to sell some of its retail foreign exchange assets to online currency broker, Forex Capital Markets, in a deal worth US$110 million. Forex Capital Markets is registered with the Commodities Futures Trading Commission (CFTC) and is a member of the National Futures Association. It has about 500 employees and had posted US$154 million in gross revenue last year, said Niv. Refco, a brokerage that filed for bankruptcy last month amid a financial scandal, said it was selling 15,000 retail client accounts of its foreign exchange

arm, Refco FX, as well as Refco's 35% share in Forex Capital Markets.

The additional 15,000 clients would make FXCM the largest retail currency broker with about 80,000 customers and a notional daily trading volume of between US$10–15 billion.

"The Refco collapse has put a black eye on the (online retail foreign exchange) industry. There's just a lot less trust in the big players. That's an unfortunate thing," Niv said.

He noted that by doing this deal, FXCM is protecting the reputation of the online foreign exchange industry by "demonstrating that there are strong, responsible forex firms able to stabilise the industry in difficult times."

Source: Gertrude Chavez-Dreyfuss, *Reuters*, November 12, 2005

EXAMPLES
CONSUMERS AND FOREIGN EXCHANGE

1. Paying for a child's education overseas

With more children being sent to overseas universities by affluent parents, the issue of foreign exchange frequently surfaces when they have to pay tuition fees and provide for the daily living expenses of their children. For example, if a Malaysian student goes to study in Sydney, the expenses generated during the period of study will be in Australian currency. So, the parents of the student will have to exchange their Malaysian currency for Australian currency to support their child. Normally, the child will set up a bank account in Australia and her parents will transfer money to that account via their bank in Malaysia. They will deposit their money in the local currency in Malaysia. But they will know how much of the Australian currency this will be exchanged for because the Malaysian bank will tell them the exchange rate and the bank charges associated with making such transfers. Their child can then withdraw Australian currency from her bank in Sydney.

2. Shopping across a border and moneychangers

Many Mexicans with visas cross the U.S. border to do their shopping. Mexicans find some U.S. goods cheaper than back home for a variety of reasons. For example, lower productivity levels in Mexico can drive prices higher. Mexico also has higher tariffs than the U.S. for imported goods from countries such as China, as well as higher sales taxes. But before Mexicans can shop in the U.S., they have to change their Mexican pesos into U.S. dollars. Money can be exchanged at banks or moneychangers in either Mexico or the U.S., or both, but rates are not likely to be the same across the board—there will be slight differences. People exchange their money at moneychangers because their rates are better than banks, and also because of the absence of formalities and queues. You don't need to show your ID if you go to a moneychanger—all you need is cash. Moneychangers often operate in a loose network. At their booths, they display the prices at which they will buy and sell currencies against the local currency. In order to make a profit, their buying prices for each currency are always lower than their selling prices, and these prices change frequently as word is passed across the network. They also have the flexibility to offer better rates if amounts to be exchanged are large or if they value a repeat customer highly enough.

to the online foreign exchange market as it is open 24 hours a day. Almost exclusively, individual investors would be in the market to make trading profits and are not generally expected to keep their positions open for more than a few days, especially if they trade on leverage.

A key attraction of the foreign exchange market is that traders can obtain much more leverage than that available in stock markets. With such high leverage and an awareness of the risks of holding a position too long, online investors are likely to open and close trading positions quickly. The foreign exchange market is also attractive to individual investors because there are not as many currencies to analyze as there are equities. Retail participation is thus regarded as the new frontier for foreign exchange trading.

CONSUMERS

Since foreign exchange has such a huge influence on the global economy, affecting the trading of goods, services, and raw materials, it pervades our daily lives to such an extent that we are often unaware of its impact. For example, just consider your simple daily routine of going to work. You may wear a shirt that is made in the U.K. and a pair of trousers sewn in China. You may drink a cup of Ceylon tea. You then drive to work in a Japanese car, assembled in Thailand, with its leather upholstery made in Singapore. These items were likely to have been bought in your local currency but, at some point along the supply chain for each component, transactions occurred in the currency where they originated—the U.K., China, Sri Lanka, Thailand, Japan, and Singapore.

NOTE
REMITTANCES—A FINANCIAL SERVICE IN HIGH DEMAND

As the foreign-born population in the U.S. continues to rise, so does the need for access to safe and affordable financial services—including remittances. Over the past few years there has been a tremendous growth in money transfers, especially to Latin America and the Caribbean (LAC). According to the Inter-American Development Bank, remittances totaling US$45.8 billion were sent to LAC in 2004 of which US$16.6 billion went to Mexico alone.

For many countries, remittances have become a highly important source of household income and often a significant percentage of the country's Gross National Product. For the family and friends back home, these funds are vital to help cover the costs of food, housing, education, new businesses, and to save for the future.

NEWS CLIP
CAN WESTERN UNION KEEP ON DELIVERING?

Once a month, Viktor Murashko, a Ukrainian living and working illegally in Germany, heads to the Western Union outlet in Frankfurt's main railway station. From there, he sends about half of the US$1,300 he earns monthly doing odd jobs at construction sites to his wife, Ludmila, who's raising their three teenage children in Kharkov. The process takes just minutes. By the time Murashko—not his real name—has telephoned his wife with the code needed to identify the transfer, the cash is waiting for her at a local Western Union agent. "It's quick, easy, and reliable," she says. "There's no messing about, and they never lose the money." Murashko is a member of a worldwide army of some 80 million who work in one country and support dependents in another. Together they will send more than US$150 billion in cross-border remittances this year, US$100 billion of which goes anonymously to families in developing countries. Talk about hot money. To put the amount in perspective, that's more cash than international investors invest in those countries' bonds and equities each year. "We're talking about a flood of money from rich to poor countries," says Dilip Ratha, senior economist at the

World Bank in Washington. "And it is growing dramatically."

Indeed, remittances are such a hot business that Western Union Financial Services Inc., long dominant, suddenly has a lot more rivals. Commercial banks, credit unions, even supermarkets are trying to wrest share from the Greenwood Village (Colo.) company. To safeguard its 12 per cent share of world remittances, Western Union is fighting back with a US$300 million global advertising campaign, use of a single logo to bolster brand recognition, and a move into untapped markets such as China and India. "The marketplace is very diversified, and consumers have many choices when sending money," company President Christina A. Gold said in a statement to *BusinessWeek*. "Western Union sees great opportunity as it relates to competition—both in the long and short terms."

It's no secret why Western Union, which started life in 1851 as a telegraph company, is coming under pressure. Commissions on most transactions run 10% or higher, making Western Union a most reliable profit generator for its Denver parent, First Data Corp., which acquired it in 1995.

Analysts expect the wholly owned unit, which almost collapsed a decade ago after fax machines undercut its Telex business, to make more than US$1 billion in operating profits on revenues of more than US$3.5 billion this year. Although Western Union controls 80% of the market in regions such as Latin America, it can no longer take its position for granted. "This is a real high-margin business," says Jeffrey J. Slowik, executive vice-president of PayQuik, a Philadelphia supplier of money-transfer technology to banks. "It's hardly surprising rivals are moving in."

Source: By David Fairlamb in Frankfurt, with Geri Smith in Mexico City and Frederik Balfour in Hong Kong, *BusinessWeek*, December 22, 2003

Let us say you are in France and you bought a British-made shirt in a department store in Paris, for which you paid with euros. The department store, in turn, would have bought the shirt as part of a larger order from a wholesaler or importer also in France, and also paying in euros. But the wholesaler or importer who bought the shirts from the British manufacturer would have had to pay for them in pounds sterling. To do this the company would have had to exchange euros into pounds sterling, probably at the local bank. The company would have to use the exchange rate prevailing at the time—unless they entered a forward agreement (the example is very simplistic).

We can see how companies need foreign exchange to import goods from overseas. We can also see how banks can help these importers with their foreign exchange needs.

But the uses of foreign exchange get more basic than that—consumers themselves often use foreign exchange, especially when they travel overseas on holidays or business trips. The simple reason for this is that, in most cases, they can't use their home currency to pay for items, such as meals, books, or souvenirs, that they buy overseas. Therefore, they will need to exchange their money when they travel. There are many other examples of why consumers would deal in foreign exchange: to pay for their children's education in overseas universities; to pay for care in a foreign hospital; to remit money home if they are working overseas; to buy a wristwatch on an auction site on the Internet; to deliver a present to a friend who is getting married in another country. Each of these examples requires an exchange rate to convert one currency to another.

Such transactions are everyday occurrences and, together with many others, are replicated many times over each day, adding depth to the global foreign exchange market. But consumers do not set exchange rates between currencies. Instead, they respond to exchange rates that have been set in the foreign exchange market, which are passed down to them through the agents that change their currencies, such as banks and moneychangers. Ultimately though, foreign exchange customers are the arbiters of exchange rates. In a free market, if their demand for a particular currency goes up, the exchange rate will change accordingly and if their demand goes down, the rate will change again.

SUMMARY

The advent of foreign exchange markets in the 1970s led to the development of interbank markets, which remain the foundation for foreign exchange trading today. The foreign exchange market used to be solely the domain of large institutions like commercial banks and investment banks. They traded foreign exchange for their customers and among themselves. But the number of participants in interbank markets has expanded from just the large commercial banks to other financial institutions such as finance companies, investment banks and central banks. Electronic communication capabilities such as those provided by Reuters and EBS, followed by the internet, have helped trading volumes in the foreign exchange market soar. Services such as prime brokerage and "white-labelling" are growing in these markets amid intense competition between the different liquidity providers to capture market share in foreign exchange trading. As the interbank markets have grown, a concurrent development in the growth of global portfolio investment has resulted in even more new players engaging in foreign exchange markets. Such organizations include insurance companies, pension funds, mutual funds and hedge funds. The impact of interbank trading on broader financial markets is highly significant. For example, central banks actively intervene in interbank markets to guide their policy interest rates. Interbank markets also allow banks to trade liquidity among themselves—that is, banks with surplus liquidity can channel funds to other banks that need liquidity to, for instance, maintain their reserve requirements. Meanwhile, consumers are also exposed to foreign exchange on a daily basis—sometimes directly when they travel to different countries and often indirectly such as when they use or consume an imported product.

QUICK QUIZ

1. What did newsman Paul Julius Reuter use to cover a gap in the telegraph line network between Aachen, in Germany, and Belgium when he transmitted stories?

2. How do market makers contribute to the proper functioning of foreign exchange markets?

3. How can white-labelling benefit smaller companies?

4. Name five cross-border transactions, that multinational companies might undertake, on which foreign exchange rates can have an impact.

5. What does the Bank of Japan say are its two basic missions?

6. What kind of asset do the majority of U.S. overseas investors put their money into?

7. For how long do individual investors typically keep their trading positions open in the online foreign exchange markets?

8. Name five things that people do where foreign exchange is needed.

THE INTERNATIONAL MONETARY SYSTEM

INTRODUCTION

The world has operated an international monetary system for as long as there have been national currencies and trade across borders. From antiquity, gold was used as money and silver also had an important monetary role. The Federal Reserve Bank of New York describes the international monetary system as "the legal and institutional framework—the laws, rules, customs, instruments, and organizations—within which the foreign exchange market operates." Such a system is designed to have a stabilizing influence on global currencies which, in turn, helps to foster economic cooperation and facilitate international trade.

As we have mentioned, the Bretton Woods Agreement of July 1944 was held by the U.S. to reach international monetary stability by restricting currency speculation and discouraging money from moving from one country to another. A number of difference proposals were considered including one proposal by the famous economist John Maynard Keynes to create a new world reserve currency. Instead U.S. influence prevailed and the U.S. dollar was selected as the currency system around which other currencies would be built. The system approved at the conference included fixed exchange rates partly based on the gold standard but fixing the U.S. dollar at US$35.00 per ounce of gold and then fixing the other currencies to the dollar. The participants agreed to try to maintain the exchange rates of their currencies against the U.S. dollar within a narrow range against the dollar. The important conclusion was that countries were not allowed to devalue their currencies by more than 10% against the U.S. dollar in order to obtain a trade advantage.

At the end of World War II, U.S. President Franklin Delano Roosevelt told Congress about the Bretton Woods proposals for setting up an international monetary system. He said: "It is time for the United States to take the lead in establishing the principles of economic cooperation as the foundation for expanded world trade. We propose to do this, not by setting up a super-government, but by international negotiation and agreement, directed to the improvement of the monetary institutions of the world and

Figure 4.1 — Mount Washington Hotel, New Hampshire, U.S., 1944

Source: International Monetary Fund, Bretton Woods Conference Collection Photographs (www.imf.org)

Towards the end of World War II, in July 1944, a post-war international monetary system of convertible currencies, fixed exchange rates and free trade was established at the Mount Washington Hotel near the ski resort town of Bretton Woods, New Hampshire.

A workforce of 250 craftsmen built the Mount Washington Hotel in a Spanish Renaissance style for industrial magnate Joseph Stickney. It was opened in 1902 and became a favorite summer resort for the rich and famous. Bretton Woods was actually part of a land grant made by Royal Governor John Wentworth (1737–1820). It was named after Wentworth's ancestral home in Yorkshire, England.

of the laws that govern trade … the conference submitted a plan to create an International Monetary Fund, which will put an end to monetary chaos. The Fund is a financial institution to preserve stability and order in the exchange rates between different moneys. It does not create single money for the world—neither we nor anyone else is ready to do that. There will still be different money in each country, but with the Fund in operation the value of each currency in international trade will remain comparatively stable. Changes in the value of foreign currencies will be made only after careful consideration by the Fund of the factors involved."

Supporters of the Bretton Woods system believed that stable exchange rates would improve the world's national economies through the expansion

Figure 4.2 — Bretton Woods conference delegates, July 1944

Source: International Monetary Fund, Bretton Woods Conference Collection Photographs (www.imf.org)

International
Monetary Fund

World Trade
Organization

Organisation for
Economic
Co-operation and
Development

Logos for IMF,
WTO & OECD

Sourced from public domain

of international trade. However, exchange rates became ineffectual because of the rigidity of fixed rates and the infrequent parity changes. In addition, there were often large destabilizing flows of currency, as speculators bet on the value at which the fixed exchange rate would be reset. There were also concerns that a fixed exchange rate system did not allow countries enough freedom to pursue their own monetary and fiscal policies.

Apart from the International Monetary Fund (IMF) that President Roosevelt referred to, Bretton Woods also saw the origins of two other organizations—the World Bank and the World Trade Organization (WTO). The International Trade Organization (ITO) that had been planned in the agreement could not be realized in its initial form as the U.S. Congress would not endorse it. Meanwhile, in 1947, the General Agreement on Tariffs and Trade (GATT), was established and soon signed by the U.S. and 23 other countries. Effectively, it provided an alternative that rendered the ITO obsolete. The GATT was succeeded by the WTO in 1995.

These organizations are among the key players in the international monetary system.

Figure 4.3 — U.S. President Franklin Delano Roosevelt

Source: Getty Images

The World Bank helps provide financial and technical assistance to developing countries around the world, while the WTO encourages trade between member nations, administers global trade agreements, and resolves disputes when they arise. Another key organization in fostering global trade and development is the Organization for Economic Co-operation and Development (OECD). Primarily, it acts as a forum on economic development at governmental level. The main aim of the OECD is the promotion of sustainable economic growth in its member countries which, in turn, contributes to the expansion of world trade.

An integral part of the Bretton Woods system was the establishment of the IMF, which oversees the international monetary system. Member nations subscribe to this system by lending their currencies to the IMF. The IMF then re-lends these funds to help countries that are experiencing balance of payments difficulties. In fact, the core function of the IMF is to make temporary loans to countries to help them tide over difficulties with current account deficits and financial crises. Member countries are entitled to borrow from the IMF up to a certain limit—that country's contribution to the IMF. Beyond that limit, the IMF's lending is conditional upon the borrowing country's acceptance of IMF surveillance over its economic policies.

This is how the IMF explains this conditionality clause: "When a country borrows from the IMF, its government makes commitments on economic and financial policies—a requirement known as conditionality." Conditionality provides assurance to the IMF that its loan will be used to resolve the borrower's economic difficulties and that the country will be able to repay promptly, so that the funds become available to other members in need. In recent years, the IMF has worked to focus and streamline the conditions attached to its financing, in order to promote national ownership of strong and effective policies.

NOTE
SPECIAL DRAWING RIGHTS

In the 1960s, the global economy threatened to slow down because there were inadequate reserves of gold and U.S. dollars to back economic expansion. New supplies of gold could not keep up with global economic growth. The supply of dollars to be kept on reserve by other nations depended on the willingness of the U.S. to spend and invest more money overseas than it received on its own shores. This could not be counted upon in the long run and a shortage of reserves became a real possibility. In response, the IMF was empowered in 1969 to issue an asset called Special Drawing Rights (SDRs), which members could add to their holdings of foreign currencies and gold held in their central banks. SDRs are regarded as an artificial currency, used by the IMF, and is defined in terms of a basket of major currencies, such as the U.S. dollar, euro, pound sterling, and yen.

GLOBAL TRADE AND TRADE AGREEMENTS

Total global merchandise trade in 2005 was estimated at US$10.2 trillion. Since the end of World War II, there has been a steady liberalization of international trade, with the elimination of artificial barriers and other protectionist tools like tariffs, quotas, and subsidies that countries use to protect their domestic markets. Countries have pursued the objective of trade liberalization primarily by seeking agreements among themselves in rounds of multilateral negotiations under the GATT and later the WTO. The latter was created in 1995, by the passage of the provisions of the Uruguay Round of the GATT. Prior to the Uruguay Round negotiations, GATT had focused on promoting world trade by pressuring countries to reduce tariffs. But with the creation of the WTO, this agenda was expanded to also target non-tariff barriers to trade—essentially any national or local protective legislation that might have an impact on trade.

More recently, countries have also begun to negotiate bilateral and regional free-trade agreements (FTAs), which eliminate almost all trade restrictions and subsidies. The FTAs, such as the North American Free Trade Agreement, have been crafted in the hope that they will have a net beneficial effect on the economies of the participating countries. There is some concern though that the pursuit of free-trade agreements could divert the world from multilateral negotiations and lead to the development of rival trading blocs centered on the United States, the European Union, Japan, China, and other major countries.

On this dilemma, WTO director-general Pascal Lamy said, in a speech in Bangalore, India in January 2007, that "… it is clear that the sole work of market forces will not be enough to spread the benefits of globalization to all and that we have to develop instruments to harness globalization, ensuring that both developed and developing countries benefit alike from it and that those in our societies who suffer from the transformations that globalization bring about are adequately taken care of." Still, the procession of preferential trade agreements in recent years contradicts the non-discrimination principle that is one of the cornerstones of the WTO. Indeed, the vast majority of WTO members are party to one or more regional trade agreements, and the growth of such agreements has continued unabated since the early 1990s. By the end of 2005, the number of regional trade agreements notified to the WTO was estimated to have approached 300 (see Figure 4.5 for some of the major ones). Lamy predicted that by 2010, around 400 such agreements could be active.

GLOBAL TRADE GROWTH

World trade has been growing at an accelerating pace. As indicated in Figure 4.4, monthly exports and imports grew from less than US$10 billion per month in 1957 to over US$2.5 trillion per month in 2007.

Figure 4.4 — World Trade—Monthly US$ Billion

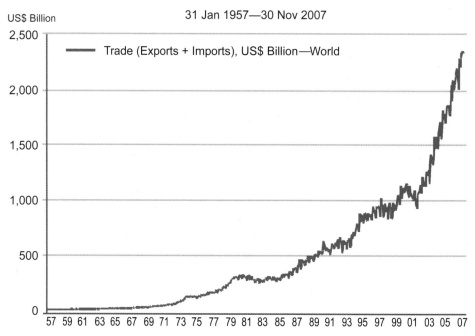

US$ Billion   31 Jan 1957—30 Nov 2007

Source: *International Monetary Fund*

NEWS CLIP
U.S.–SINGAPORE FREE TRADE AGREEMENT

The leading edge U.S.–Singapore Free Trade Agreement is the first U.S. FTA with an Asian nation and the first FTA signed by President George W. Bush. The U.S.–Singapore FTA expands U.S. market access in goods, services, investment, government procurement, intellectual property, and provides for groundbreaking cooperation in promoting labor rights and the environment. This agreement will serve as the foundation for other possible FTAs in Southeast Asia under President Bush's Enterprise for ASEAN Initiative (EAI).

The U.S.–Singapore FTA negotiations were launched on November 16, 2000. The first round of negotiations was held that year, in Washington DC, from December 4 to December 21. The final round was in Singapore, November 11 to 17, 2002, and the agreement was concluded on January 15, 2003. At over 1,400 pages and containing 21 chapters, the agreement fully achieves all of the negotiating objectives Congress called for in the Trade Act of 2002 (TPA). The U.S.–Singapore FTA will further enhance an already strong and thriving commercial relationship with America's 12th largest trading partner. Annual two-way trade of goods and services between the United States and Singapore approached US$40 billion. Singapore guarantees zero tariffs immediately on all U.S. goods, and the FTA ensures that Singapore cannot increase its duties on any U.S. product. For Singapore products entering the U.S. market, duties are phased-out at different stages, with the least sensitive products entering duty-free upon entry into force of the FTA and tariffs on the most sensitive products phased-out over a 10-year period.

In services, the U.S.–Singapore FTA provides the broadest possible trade liberalization Singapore will treat U.S. services suppliers as well as its own suppliers. Market access in services is supplanted by strong disciplines on regulatory au-thority. U.S. foreign direct investment in Singapore was over US$27 billion in 2001. The U.S.–Singapore FTA provides important protection for U.S. investors. U.S. investors will be treated as well as local Singaporean investors or any other foreign investor.

Source: Office of the United States Trade Representative, May 6, 2003

Figure 4.5 — Some Regional Trade Groupings/Agreements

AFTA	ASEAN Free Trade Area	Brunei Darussalam, Cambodia, Indonesia, Laos, Malaysia, Myanmar, Philippines, Singapore, Thailand, Vietnam
ASEAN	Association of South East Asian Nations	Brunei Darussalam, Cambodia, Indonesia, Laos, Malaysia, Myanmar, Philippines, Singapore, Thailand, Vietnam
CAN	Andean Community of Nations	Bolivia, Colombia, Ecuador, Peru
CARICOM	Caribbean Community	Antigua and Barbuda, Bahamas, Barbados, Belize, Dominica, Grenada, Guyana, Haiti, Jamaica, Monserrat, St. Kitts and Nevis, St. Lucia, St. Vincent and the Grenadines, Suriname, Trinidad & Tobago
CACM	Central American Common Market	Costa Rica, El Salvador, Guatemala, Honduras, Nicaragua
CER	Closer Economic Relations	Australia, New Zealand
CIS	Commonwealth of Independent States	Armenia, Azerbaijan, Belarus, Georgia, Kazakhstan, Kyrgyzstan, Moldova, Russian Federation, Tajikistan, Ukraine, Uzbekistan
COMESA	Common Market for Eastern and Southern Africa	Angola, Burundi, Comoros, Democratic Republic of Congo, Djibouti, Egypt, Eritrea, Ethiopia, Kenya, Libya, Madagascar, Malawi, Mauritius, Rwanda, Seychelles, Sudan, Swaziland, Uganda, Zambia, Zimbabwe
EU	European Union	Austria, Belgium, Bulgaria, Cyprus, Czech Republic, Denmark, Estonia, Finland, France, Germany, Greece, Hungary, Ireland, Italy, Latvia, Lithuania, Luxembourg, Malta, Netherlands, Poland, Portugal, Romania, Slovakia, Slovenia, Spain, Sweden, United Kingdom
MERCOSUR	Southern Common Market	Argentina, Brazil, Paraguay, Uruguay
MSG	Melanesian Spearhead Group	Fiji, Papua New Guinea, Solomon Islands, Vanuatu
NAFTA	North American Free Trade Agreement	Canada, Mexico, United States

Source: *World Trade Organization*

Figure 4.6 shows the extent of global merchandise trade in 2005. The three biggest trading blocs that year were Europe, Asia, and North America, accounting for almost 85% of total global merchandise trade. Figure 4.6 also shows that trade within Europe accounted for 31.5% of total merchandise trade while trade within Asia accounted for 14% of the total. With international and inter-regional trade, participants are exposed to foreign exchange. This table demonstrates the extent of that exposure. However, total global merchandise trade remains a fraction of the turnover in foreign exchange markets annually.

Figure 4.6 — Intra- and Inter-Regional Merchandise Trade in 2005—US$ billion

Origin	Destination							
	North America	South and Central America	Europe	CIS	Africa	Middle East	Asia	World
North America	824	87	238	7	18	34	270	1,478
South and Central America	118	86	68	6	10	6	48	355
Europe	398	58	3,201	109	112	122	332	4,372
Commonwealth of Independent States (CIS)	19	7	178	62	5	11	40	340
Africa	60	8	128	1	26	5	49	298
Middle East	66	3	87	3	15	54	281	538
Asia	608	51	498	37	54	89	1,424	2,779
World	2,093	301	4,398	224	240	321	2,443	10,159

Share of Regional Trade Flows in World Merchandise Exports (%)

	North America	South and Central America	Europe	CIS	Africa	Middle East	Asia	World
North America	8.1	0.9	2.3	0.1	0.2	0.3	2.7	14.5
South and Central America	1.2	0.8	0.7	0.1	0.1	0.1	0.5	3.5
Europe	3.9	0.6	31.5	1.1	1.1	1.2	3.3	43.0
Commonwealth of Independent States (CIS)	0.2	0.1	1.8	0.6	0.0	0.1	0.4	3.3
Africa	0.6	0.1	1.3	0.0	0.3	0.1	0.5	2.9
Middle East	0.7	0.0	0.9	0.0	0.2	0.5	2.8	5.3
Asia	6.0	0.5	4.9	0.4	0.5	0.9	14.0	27.4
World	20.6	3.0	43.3	2.2	2.4	3.2	24.0	100.0

Source: *World Trade Organization*

Figure 4.7 — Asian Export Shares to U.S. and China

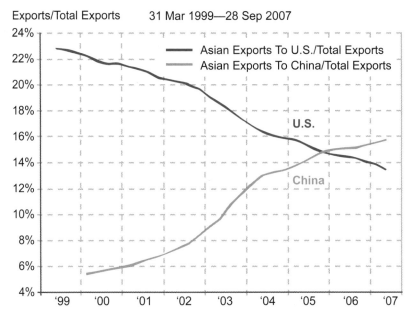

Exports/Total Exports   31 Mar 1999—28 Sep 2007

— Asian Exports To U.S./Total Exports
— Asian Exports To China/Total Exports

U.S.

China

* Data smoothed by 12-mths moving average; includes Hong Kong, Taiwan, South Korea, Singapore, Malaysia, Thailand and the Philippines

Source: *Factset*

One example of the growing integration of regional trade is the expanding percentage of trade between China and the rest of Asia.

As shown in Figure 4.7, Asian exports to China, in 1999, represented about 5% of the region's total exports. However, by 2007 it had reached almost 16% of their total exports. During that time Asian exports to the U.S. declined from about 23% to 13%. Of course, it is important to remember that the total US$ value of exports to the U.S. still grew during this period.

BALANCE OF PAYMENTS

The balance of payments accounts of a country record the payments and receipts of the residents of that country in their transactions with residents of other countries. Strictly defined, the balance of payments of a country is a way of measuring the flow of payments during a specific period of time (usually one year) between that country and all other countries. The calculation includes the country's exports and imports of goods, services, and financial transfers so that all payments and liabilities to foreigners (the debits) and all payments and obligations received from foreigners (the credits) are recorded.

The forces affecting a country's balance of payments give a deeper insight into the demand and supply for its currency. If all transactions are included, the payments and receipts of each country must be equal. Any inequality simply leaves one country acquiring assets in the others. For example, if Singaporeans buy apples from Australia, and have no other transactions with Australia, the Australians end up holding the Singapore currency, which they may keep in the form of bank deposits in Singapore or some other Singapore investment. Or, if they insist on being paid in U.S. dollars, the main international trading currency, they would add that to their foreign reserves. The payments of Singaporeans to Australia for apples are balanced by the payments of Australians to Singapore for assets in the latter. Although the totals of payments and receipts are necessarily equal, there will be inequalities—in the form of deficits or surpluses in merchandise trade, services trade, foreign investment, and private investment.

In the past, many different definitions of the balance of payments deficit or surplus have been used. Until 1973, the focus was on defining a balance of payments that measured a country's foreign exchange capabilities. In essence, would the country be able to exchange its currency for other currencies, or gold, at fixed exchange rates? To meet this obligation, countries maintained a stock of official reserves—known as *foreign reserves*—in the form of gold or foreign currencies, that they could use to support their own currencies. A decline in this stock of official reserves was considered a critical balance of payments deficit because it threatened the country's ability to meet its obligations.

The balance of payments is a summary of transactions between residents of one country with residents of other countries. It includes the (1) current account and (2) financial account.

The *current account* includes the net trade goods and services or balance of trade (exports minus imports), plus net factor income (such items as dividends and interest payments from overseas), and net transfers from overseas such as foreign aid, grants, gifts, etc. Thus: current account = balance of trade + net factor income from abroad + net unilateral transfer from abroad.

The *financial account* encompasses the acquisition or sale of securities or other property, assets which are excluded from the current account. In other words, it includes the net change in foreign ownership of a country's domestic assets. In a country's financial accounts reference must be made to the *capital account* which is the net change in foreign ownership of investment assets. It is calculated by adding foreign direct investment, portfolio investment and other investments.

As the current account and the financial account add up to the total account, there must be a balance. A deficit in the current account must be accompanied by an equal surplus in the financial account and vice versa. Relative to conditions in other countries, a country is more likely to have a deficit in its current account for the following reasons:

- Higher price levels
- Higher GDP
- Higher interest rates
- Lower trade barriers
- Higher exchange rate

The effects of a change in one of these factors on the current account balance cannot be predicted without considering the effect on the other causal factors. For example, if the U.K. government increases tariffs on goods imported from Japan, the British will buy fewer imports, thus reducing its current account deficit.

Typically, the change in official reserves in a given year is very small relative to the current account and the financial account. If a government runs a current account deficit and has no change in official reserves, then the

Figure 4.8 — U.K. Current/Financial Account in 2005 (£ billions)

U.K. Current Account in 2005 (£ billions)

	Credit	Debit	Balance
Goods trade	210.2	-275.8	-65.6
Services trade	105.7	-87.0	18.7
Income flows	184.5	-157.1	27.4
Current transfers	15.9	-28.3	-12.4
Grand total	516.3	-548.2	-31.9

U.K. Financial Account in 2005 (£ billions)

	Credit	Debit	Balance
Capital Account*	4.2	-1.9	2.3
Direct Investment	90.5	-55.6	34.9
Portfolio Investment	131.1	-161.2	-30.1
Other Investment	523.7	-500.5	-23.2
Other Items		-3.2	-3.2
Total	749.5	-722.4	27.1
Errors and omissions			4.8
Grand total			31.9

*The capital account includes such items as land purchases and sales associated with embassies, the transfers of migrants, and EU regional development fund payments.

current account deficit must be balanced by a financial account surplus. The current account table for the U.K. in 2005 (Figure 4.8) shows that goods imports (debit column) exceeded goods exports (credit column) by £65.6 billion, while service exports exceeded service imports by £18.7 billion. These helped contribute to a current account deficit of £31.9 billion. Essentially, this meant that foreign residents added a flow of income to their total asset holdings in the U.K. that exceeded by £31.9 billion the flow of income that U.K. residents added to their total holdings of foreign assets.

FOREIGN DIRECT INVESTMENT (FDI)

The opening up of global economies has seen cross-border currency flows increase in recent years as companies search the world for new investments and sources of profit and income. Recording this growing trend is foreign direct investment (FDI) data from the United Nations Conference on Trade and Development (UNCTAD). According to UNCTAD estimates, global flows of FDI reached US$1.2 trillion in 2006, with the U.S. attracting the largest capital inflows, followed by the U.K. and France. FDI flows to developed countries rose by 48% to US$800 million, with the then 25 countries of the European Union (EU) accounting for about 45% of flows in 2006. Elsewhere, FDI inflows surged to a new record of US$38 billion in Africa, mainly as a result of large investments in oil-rich economies, while FDI flows to Asia and Oceania maintained their upward trend, reaching a new high of US$230 billion—up 15% from 2005. The share of this region in total FDI to developing countries rose from 59% to 63%. China and Hong Kong remain the leading destinations, followed closely by Singapore with some US$32 billion of inflows. India also saw record inflows.

EXCHANGE RATE REGIMES

The global trading and investment activities that we have described so far require an effective international monetary system. In *The International Monetary System, 1945–1981*, author Robert Solomon writes: "Like the traffic lights in a city, the international monetary system is taken for granted until it begins to malfunction and to disrupt people's lives ... a well-functioning monetary system will facilitate international trade and investment and smooth adaptation to change. A monetary system that functions poorly may not only discourage the development of trade and investment among nations but subject their economies to disruptive shocks when necessary adjustments to change are prevented or delayed." The central element of the international monetary system that the IMF administers comprises how foreign exchange rates are determined and how governments can affect exchange rates.

Currency regimes around the world differ in many ways and do not necessarily follow a fixed pattern. These are some typical currency regimes as defined by the IMF:

NOTE
CURRENCY REGIMES

Exchange agreements with no separate legal tender: The currency of another country circulates as the sole legal tender. In such regimes the country may belong to a monetary or currency union in which the same legal tender is shared by the other members of the union. Examples are East Timor, Kiribati, Eurozone countries, Cameroon, and Senegal.

Currency board arrangements: A monetary regime based on a legal commitment to exchange domestic currency for a specified foreign currency at a fixed exchange rate. Examples are Hong Kong and Brunei.

Fixed peg arrangements (different exchange rate margins): The country pegs its currency (formally or de facto) at a fixed rate to a major currency, or a basket of currencies, allowing the exchange rate to fluctuate within different margins around a central rate. Examples are U.A.E., Fiji, Latvia, Denmark and Cyprus.

Crawling pegs: The currency is adjusted periodically in small amounts at a fixed preannounced rate, or in response to changes in selective quantitative indicators. Examples are Bolivia, Tunisia, and Nicaragua.

Managed float with no preannounced path for the exchange rate: The monetary authority influences the movements of the exchange rate through active intervention in the foreign exchange market without specifying, or committing to, a preannounced path for the exchange rate. Examples are India, Indonesia, Thailand, Pakistan, Argentina, and Czech Republic.

Independent floating: The exchange rate is market-determined, with any foreign exchange intervention aimed at moderating the rate of change and preventing undue fluctuations in the exchange rate, rather than at establishing a level for it. Examples are Brazil, Canada, Philippines, U.K., U.S., and Japan.

Source: International Monetary Fund

In addition to the type of exchange rate regime to adopt, a government also decides whether to allow free convertibility of its currency to other currencies. *Current account convertibility* means that foreign exchange can be freely bought and sold provided its use is associated with international trade in goods and services. However, there are still restrictions when the intended use of the foreign exchange is to purchase foreign financial assets, or to make equity investments. Free trade in currencies for the purchase of financial assets, or for equity investments, is called *capital account convertibility*. If convertibility is allowed for transactions in both the current and the capital accounts, we say there is *full convertibility*—this equates to free capital mobility.

THE EUROPEAN UNION (EU)

As far back as 1950, French Foreign Minister Robert Schuman had taken the first step toward economic integration by proposing the common management of the coal and steel industries of Western Europe. Schuman grew up in Luxembourg, witnessing the international tensions that led to World War I and the subsequent shift in the nearby French-German border. He narrowly escaped being sent to a Nazi concentration camp during World War II. In his view, borders created antagonism that contributed to starting wars and he began working for international reconciliation and co-operation. In 1951, his calls for integration were heeded. The European Coal and Steel Community (ECSC) was founded, with six members—Belgium, West Germany, Luxembourg, France, Italy, and the Netherlands. Decisions about the coal and steel industries of these member countries were made by an independent, supranational body called the High Authority.

The success of the ECSC prompted the six countries to integrate other sectors of their economies. The Treaties of Rome were signed in 1957, creating the European Atomic Energy Community (EURATOM) and the European Economic Community (EEC). The countries began to remove trade barriers between them, with the aim of forming a common market. In 1967, the functions of the three European community groups (ECSC, EURATOM and EEC) merged, replaced by a single Commission and a single Council of Ministers, in addition to the existing European Parliament. The members of the European Parliament were originally chosen by the national parliaments but, in 1979, the first direct elections were held, allowing citizens of member states to vote for their candidates. Direct elections are now held every five years.

The number of member countries in the European Union (EU) grew over the years. Denmark, Ireland and the U.K. joined in 1973, Greece in 1981, Spain and Portugal in 1986, and Austria, Finland and Sweden in 1995. Ten more countries joined the European Union in 2004—Cyprus, Czech Republic, Estonia, Hungary, Latvia, Lithuania, Malta, Poland, Slovakia, and Slovenia. Most recently, Bulgaria and Romania joined the European Union in 2007 bringing the total membership of the union to 27. Croatia, Macedonia, and Turkey are expected to join in future years. The economic and monetary union in Europe has been likened to the U.S. economy where different states share the U.S. dollar and have the same key interest rate. For the eurozone, the equivalent of the Federal Reserve is the European Central Bank. The Frankfurt-based bank conducts monetary policy for the eurozone and its board is made up of central bank governors from member countries of the EU.

BIRTH OF A NEW CURRENCY—THE EURO

We rarely see a major new currency born in our lifetimes. The creation of the euro was a significant exception—it represented the largest monetary changeover the world has ever seen. The euro is now regarded as the world's second-most important currency, after the U.S. dollar. The creation of the euro saw disparate and nationalistic European countries come together to form a common economy, fueled by a common currency. The coming of the euro is also an opportunity to show the formation basis for the creation of any currency and the roles that governments, central banks, and other interest groups play. We can see how currency is very much an artificial construct, which takes on a life of its own with unique characteristics and limitations.

On January 1, 1999, the euro became the only legal tender for EU member states participating in the eurozone. It was created by the provisions in the 1992 Maastricht Treaty that established economic and monetary union. To ensure the stability of the new currency system, the participating countries had to adhere to a set of criteria. These are the Maastricht Criteria, named after the city where they were negotiated—Maastricht in the Netherlands.

MAASTRICHT CRITERIA

- **Inflation:** Cannot be higher than 1.5% above the average inflation rate of the three EU countries with the lowest individual inflation rates.

- **Long Term Interest Rates:** Cannot be higher than 2% above the interest rates of the three countries with the lowest individual interest rates.

- **Debt/GDP Ratio:** A country's debt cannot be greater than 6% of gross domestic product (GDP). Also the budgetary deficit must either be lower than 3% of national income, or be falling and almost have reached 3%, or be of a transitory nature. The deficit must also be lower than 60% of national income, or be falling at a sufficient rate towards the 60% mark.

- **Exchange Rates:** The exchange rate of the national currency must have stayed within the normal boundaries of the exchange rate mechanism of the EU countries—also called the European Monetary System (EMS) countries—for two years. The country must have been a member of this mechanism for the same period.

Source: European Central Bank

The "euro" name was selected during the European Summit in Madrid in December 1995. Eleven members of the EU—Austria, Belgium, Finland, France, Germany, Ireland, Italy, Luxembourg, the Netherlands, Spain, and Portugal—discarded their own currencies to create an economic and monetary union. Initially, Greece did not meet the Maastricht Criteria to join the eurozone, but did so on January 1, 2001. The European Union countries' respective currencies (except that of Greece) were irrevocably set at a fixed amount to the euro. These were determined according to their respective market rates on December 31, 1998:

Figure 4.8 — Euro pegs established on December 31, 1998

1 euro =

13.7603 Austrian schillings (ATS)	0.787564 Irish pounds (IEP)
40.3399 Belgian francs (BEF)	1936.27 Italian lire (ITL)
2.20371 Dutch guilders (NLG)	40.3399 Luxembourg francs (LUF)
5.94573 Finnish markka (FIM)	200.482 Portuguese escudos (PTE)
6.55957 French francs (FRF)	166.386 Spanish pesetas (ESP)
1.95583 German marks (DEM)	340.750 Greek drachmas (GRD)

Source: European Central Bank

The notes and coins for the old currencies continued to be used as legal tender until new notes and coins were introduced on January 1, 2002. Three countries—Denmark, Sweden, and the U.K.—decided to keep their own currencies and not adopt the euro. Norway and Switzerland are not part of the European Union. Sweden was scheduled to adopt the euro in 2005, but its people emphatically voted against it, in a referendum of September that year. It should be noted that as soon as the euro was launched, trading in the various currencies to which it was pegged ceased immediately on

Euro coin
Source: Getty Images

foreign exchange markets. In the blink of an eye, hitherto significant global currencies such as the Deutsche mark and the French franc vanished from markets. They are not even referred to now when, for example, analyses on the euro are conducted for time periods that include those prior to its launch. For this purpose, a "synthetic euro" is created, which extrapolates backwards what the euro would have been under the pegs decided upon at the end of 1998.

EURO PERFORMANCE

The euro was created to unite the currencies of the participating European countries with the aim of esytablishing a single market which would rival that of the U.S. A longer-term goal was also to bring these countries a step closer to a more formal confederation of European states. Is it on its way to achieving those goals? In November 2005, *The Economist* magazine expressed a relatively negative view on the progress. It noted: "Economically, the euro's adoption is meant to complete the European single market, bolstering cross-border mergers, improving price transparency and eliminating exchange rate risk. But it engages a variety of free-rider problems, by spreading risk among the countries that use it, while doing little to synchronise broad aspects of the zone's economies. The euro's credibility has also been undermined by the failure of the stability and growth pact, which seeks to limit members' budget deficits."

The European Central Bank (ECB), on the other hand, had a more optimistic outlook. In a speech at the 13th International Monetary Symposium in Tokyo in November 2004 titled "The Euro: Five Years On—Implications For Asia," ECB vice-president Lucas Papademos said the euro is a solid, stable currency in which the markets and the public have confidence. He noted: "Looking back on the period since the introduction of the euro in 1999, I will simply let the facts speak for themselves: during the first five years of the existence of our new currency, the average rate of inflation in the euro area has been precisely 2% which is in line with the ECB's definition of price stability. Even though inflation has occasionally risen above the 2% ceiling—as has been the case in recent months—this was a consequence of a number of shocks of various types, the most recent being the oil price shock. As the ECB's monetary policy strategy has a clear medium-term orientation, our response to supply shocks and euro area-specific shocks has been measured. What should be emphasised, however, is that in these first years of the euro's existence, inflation expectations have remained firmly anchored to a rate close to, or less than, 2%, as can be inferred from the yields of index-linked long-term bonds. Clearly, the markets and the public have confidence in the euro and in the ability and determination of the ECB to maintain price stability."

A graph of the euro vs the U.S. dollar is shown in Figure 4.9. The higher the euro is on the graph, the stronger it is relative to the U.S. dollar. It reflects how the euro fell after its launch on January 1, 1999. This reflected a lack of confidence in the foreign markets on whether the new currency would work. The euro has since rebounded strongly against the dollar, hitting all-time highs in November 2007 of nearly 1.50 U.S. dollars to the euro.

CURRENCY CRISES

The international monetary system is not a foolproof system, and this is regularly manifested by currency crises. Taking the 1990s for example, currency crises occurred in Europe in 1992, in Mexico in 1994, in East Asia in 1997, and in Russia in 1998. Furthermore, during that decade, Argentina went from

Figure 4.9 — Euro: U.S. dollars per euro

US$ per euro   01 Jan 1999–30 Nov 2007

Spot Rates, USD/EUR, Close Daily - United States
[Max: 1 (26 Nov 07), Min: 1 (26 Oct 00), Last: 1 (30 Nov 07)]

being an IMF darling for efforts to liberalize its economy to an economic pariah, exhibiting how a currency crisis can pervade and damage an economy.

A "currency crisis" can be described as a speculative attack on a country's currency that can result in a forced devaluation of that currency and subsequent national debt default. For example, during the East Asian financial crisis, there were grave concerns about how Indonesia's government and companies would service their foreign currency debt after the value of the local currency collapsed. Currency crises are often attributed to a variety of economic conditions, including large deficits, inflation, and low foreign reserves. There's also an element of contagion in currency crises as they sometimes appear to be triggered by similar crises nearby, though not all neighboring economies need be affected. This was clear in the East Asian crisis, which started in Thailand, spread to Indonesia and South Korea, but had less of an impact on Hong Kong (because its local currency is pegged to the U.S. dollar), Singapore, and Taiwan. Figure 4.10 shows the amount of U.S. dollars needed to buy 100 units of the local currency just before Thailand floated its currency on July 1, 1997 and the amount of U.S. dollars needed at the end of that year. The rightmost column shows by how much each of these Asian currencies fell in value against the U.S. dollar over that period in percentage terms.

What happened to the Thai baht, Indonesian rupiah, and Philippine peso, between 1997 and 2007, is demonstrated by Figures 4.11, 4.12, and 4.13 respectively. These charts illustrate how dramatically currencies can fall and recover. Although the Asian crisis resulted in sharp falls in these currencies, after a number of years they had substantial and often unexpected recoveries.

Figure 4.10 — Impact of the Asian financial crisis on its currencies

	US$ per 100 units of local currency 30/6/1997	US$ per 100 units of local currency 31/12/1997	% Change 30/6/1997 to 31/12/1997
Thailand	4.05	2.08	-48.7
Malaysia	39.53	25.70	-35.0
Indonesia	0.04	0.02	-44.4
Philippines	3.79	2.51	-33.9
Hong Kong	12.90	12.90	0.0
South Korea	0.11	0.06	-47.7
Taiwan	3.60	3.06	-14.8
Singapore	69.93	59.44	-15.0

Source: *Institute for International Economics*

Note that while Figure 4.10 gives the amount of US$ that could be purchased with 100 units of the various Asian currencies, Figures 4.11, 4.12, and 4.13 show the amount of local currency that could be purchased with one U.S. dollar. The chart axes are reversed so that a falling line indicates a weakening of the currency—when one U.S. dollar can purchase more of the local currency, while a rising line indicates a strengthening of the local currency—when one U.S. dollar purchases less of the local currency.

Figure 4.11 — Thailand: Exchange Rate Vs U.S. dollar

Thai baht per U.S. dollar   01 Jan 1997–07 Dec 2007

Spot Rates, THB/USD, Close Daily - Thailand
[Max: 56 (12 Jan 98), Min: 22 (17 Jun 97), Last: 30 (07 Dec 07)]

01/01/97 01/01/98 01/01/99 03/01/00 01/01/01 01/01/02 01/01/03 01/01/04 03/01/05 02/01/06 01/01/07

Figure 4.12 — Indonesia: Exchange Rate Vs U.S. dollar

Indonesian rupiah per U.S. dollar   01 Jan 1997–07 Dec 2007

Spot Rates, IDR/USD, Close Daily - Indonesia
[Max: 16595 (17 Jun 98), Min: 2360 (03 Jan 97),
Last: 9267 (07 Dec 07)]

Source: *Institute for International Economics*

Figure 4.13 — Philippines: Exchange Rate Vs U.S. dollar

Philippine pesos per U.S. dollar   01 Jan 1997–07 Dec 2007

Spot Rates, PHP/USD, Close Daily - Philippines
[Max: 56 (22 Mar 04), Min: 26 (02 Jan 97),
Last: 42 (07 Dec 07)]

Source: *Institute for International Economics*

Since the 1970s, when currency crises first appeared in Latin American countries, economists have regularly put forward theories on why they happen. The early models of currency crises, developed by economists such as Paul Krugman in the late 1970s, identify one of the key causes as the perceived inability of governments to control their budgets. According to these models, speculative attacks on currencies can result from an increasing current account deficit or from the anticipation that a government is going to effect monetary measures, such as increasing money supply or increasing borrowing to reduce its fiscal deficit. The speculative attack can result in a sudden devaluation when the central bank's store of foreign reserves is depleted and it can no longer defend the domestic currency. Investors perceive that the government's desire to finance its debt has become its most important concern, with the fear is that this will lead to a monetising of its fiscal deficit. Such a growing perception in the market is likely to contribute to devaluation in the local currency, and a crisis is triggered when investors sense that a government may abandon a fixed exchange rate.

While these early models are useful in that they show the links between governments' concerns over servicing their debt and the country's exchange rate, they don't really explain why contagion takes place in currency crises. More recent models were developed in the currency crisis-filled 1990s. For example, one issue is that devaluation in a national currency affects its current account due to falls in exports to a neighboring country. In such a situation, devaluation in the neighboring country also becomes increasingly likely. Furthermore, an economic shock that is common to a region or a group of trading partners, such as steeply rising oil prices, can affect those economies simultaneously. Expectations that currency problems are on the horizon can heighten either because countries are trade partners or because they have similar macroeconomic policies or conditions, such as high government debt.

CASE STUDY: PORTRAIT OF A CURRENCY CRISIS—ARGENTINA

The theories about currency crises are clearly manifested in the problems that Argentina has faced during its numerous financial crises. In 1989, all tiers of government in Argentina were undertaking heavy spending programmes but were reluctant to raise taxes to help finance this spending. Instead, they borrowed money to make up the shortfall. A lot of extra money went into circulation, causing prices to soar into hyperinflation. Wages didn't keep up and devastated Argentinians saw their savings fall steeply in value. President Raúl Alfonsín had to resign five months before the end of his term amid civil riots and President Carlos Menem took over the presidency. Menem managed to reduce inflation in 1990, but it was in 1991 that greater inroads were made in addressing the problem. Dramatic progress came in the shape of Harvard-educated economist Domingo Cavallo, whom Menem named as Economy Minister. Under the guidance of the IMF, Cavallo implemented a law that required the Argentine central bank to hold U.S. dollars or U.S. dollar-denominated assets in its reserves for every Argentine peso in circulation in the country. The Argentine peso and the U.S. dollar were set at one-to-one parity in an Argentine Currency Board arrangement called the Convertibility Plan. Initially, the impact was startling. Within four months inflation was down to 1.5% and foreign capital inflows surged—US$9.2 billion in 1992, and US$13.5 billion in 1993. Local companies invested too, contributing to growth in output. Until 1995, foreign inflows and domestic investment contributed to fostering a bright outlook for Argentina's economy.

However, the devaluation of the Mexican peso in late 1994 started a chain of events which would ultimately lead to the collapse of the Argentine economy in 2001–2. The Mexican devaluation prompted many foreign investors in Argentina to sell their assets there on fears that Argentina would do the same. They converted their Argentine pesos to U.S. dollars and took their money out of the country. Bank deposits fell sharply, and the government had to intervene to prevent a banking crisis. Not long after that, in 1997, the Argentine economy received a further blow from the Asian financial crisis, which began in Thailand. This crisis caused many economies around the world to devalue their currencies against the U.S. dollar, rendering Argentina's economy uncompetitive because of its link to the U.S. dollar. Indeed, Argentina's export growth came to a halt in 1998, increasing the current account deficit. Then, in 1999, Argentina's biggest trading partner, Brazil, devalued its own currency against the U.S. dollar which also resulted in the U.S. dollar, and the Argentine peso, rising in value. Argentina's current account deficit soared further and when capital inflows failed to rise to compensate, despite loans from the IMF, the outflow of U.S. dollars to pay for imports caused the amount of money in circulation to shrink. This cut people's spending power, forcing domestic producers to slash prices and lay off staff. Unemployment rose to around 20% in 2000.

In early 2001, the next president, Fernando de la Ruà, brought back Domingo Cavallo who had been sacked by Menem in 1996 after the harshness of his policies caused riots. Not long after being reinstalled, Cavallo announced that he wanted to change the law so that the Argentine peso could be backed by both the U.S. dollar and the euro. This was his attempt to make Argentina's exports more competitive, but in doing so he destroyed the confidence that foreign investors and the Argentinean public held in the legislated link between the peso and the U.S. dollar. Sensing a devaluation of the peso on the horizon, people rushed to convert their pesos to U.S. dollars. The rush turned into a panic by June of that year when Cavallo said that parity would not be maintained for ever. Wealthy Argentinians exchanged their pesos for U.S. dollars at the one-to-one rate, and parked their proceeds in assets overseas, especially in Uruguay. By December 2001, almost US$20 billion had left the country. Tax collections were sharply lower by December, making it harder for the country's government to deal with its ever-deteriorating finances. Provincial governments' revenues dropped too. Buenos Aires Province, where more than a third of Argentina's citizens live, was forced to cancel a bond issue, in

July 2001 as the nation's economic problems mounted. It couldn't pay its employees or keep schools and hospitals running. With debts of about US$6 billion, the provincial government printed its own currency, called the Patacón, from late August 2001, and began to finance its obligations by paying with that. Indeed, a number of provinces introduced their own currencies, which were circulated alongside the beleaguered peso to stave off economic paralysis. Finally, in January 2002, the one-to-one Argentine peso–U.S. dollar parity was abandoned. The peso promptly lost a large part of its value. After a few months, the exchange rate was left to float more or less freely.

In the next five years, the Argentina economy shared a dramatic turnaround under President Nestor Kirchner. It was the fastest growing in the Western Hemisphere during that period. The key factor was that the government got its basic macroeconomics polices right, economists say. After living with an overvalued currency for a long time, Argentina targeted a stable and competitive exchange rate. The authorities also kept interest rates low and made growth its top priority.

SUMMARY

The key organizations that support the international monetary system include the IMF and WTO. The Federal Reserve Bank of New York describes the international monetary system as "the legal and institutional framework —the laws, rules, customs, instruments, and organizations—within which the foreign exchange market operates." Global trade developed in the years that followed the Bretton Woods agreement and, more recently, bilateral free trade agreements (FTAs) have become popular as barriers to trade across borders are continuously torn down. The FTAs, such as the North American Free Trade Agreement, have been crafted in the hope that they will have a net beneficial effect on the economies of countries participating in the agreements. Against these developments, balance of payment and inflation data give us an idea about which direction currencies flow within the international monetary system. The current account and trade deficits or surpluses within countries, and the differences in inflation rates between countries allow us to ascertain the demand and supply for their currencies, which ultimately have an impact on exchange rates. Meanwhile, there are several different kinds of currency regimes including fixed rate systems and floating rate systems, and governments choose currency regimes that best suit their prevailing political and economic needs. Finally, the euro offered a rare chance to see a new major currency born. On January 1, 1999, the euro became the only legal tender for participating countries in the European Union. It was established by the provisions in the 1992 Maastricht Treaty on European Union that was used to establish an economic and monetary union. The euro is now regarded as the world's second most important currency, after the U.S. dollar. It should be noted that the international monetary system is not fool-proof and has been pressured numerous times in recent years, with a classic example being the Argentine peso crisis in the 1990s and early 2000s.

 QUICK QUIZ

1. Which current global organizations have their origins in the Bretton Woods meeting?

2. Why did Special Drawing Rights have to be devised?

3. Name five regional trade groupings or trade agreements.

4. Name three factors that can cause a country to show a current account deficit.

5. What does "full convertibility" mean?

6. What are the Maastricht Criteria for joining the euro?

7. Which was the 12th country to join the euro?

8. What was the currency board arrangement between the Argentine peso and the U.S. dollar, set in the early 1990s?

9. What exchange rate regime does your own country follow?

THE GLOBAL FOREIGN EXCHANGE MARKET

5

FOREIGN EXCHANGE TURNOVER

It is easy to say that the foreign exchange market is the world's most important financial market. The rapid increase in world trade and investment that we have witnessed in recent years means that the exchange of different currencies has accelerated. According to the Bank for International Settlements' (BIS) April 2004 "Triennial Central Bank Survey of Foreign Exchange and Derivatives Market Activity," average daily international foreign exchange trading volume was almost US$1.9 trillion (see Figure 5.1). That foreign exchange trading survey collected national foreign exchange and derivatives market data from 52 central banks and monetary authorities around the world. BIS said in its report that the growth in turnover was driven by all types of counterparties, with trading between banks and financial customers rising most strongly. The report noted that foreign exchange turnover among banks and their financial customers rose because of the increase in activity of hedge funds and commodity traders, as well as robust growth in trading by asset managers. This contrasts with the period between 1998 and 2001, when activity in this market segment had been driven mainly by asset managers, while the role of hedge funds had reportedly declined. Foreign exchange turnover grew strongly between 1989 and 2001, then took a dip in 2001, before surging again in 2004. The decline in 2001 was partly attributed to the advent of the euro in 1999, which saw the end of trading in important currencies like the Deutsche mark and the French franc. Another reason cited was rationalization in the global banking sector in the wake of the Asian financial crisis in 1997 and the bursting of the dot.com bubble in early 2000.

In 2006, the average daily turnover on the New York Stock Exchange was estimated at about US$90 billion, while the trading volume in foreign exchange, at US$1.9 trillion *per day*, was more than 10 times the average daily turnover of all the world's other stock markets. Considering that the free-floating currency system, which is at the center of foreign exchange trading, only began in the 1970s, the daily trading figure is staggering. And trading volumes are growing robustly. It is estimated that the average daily volume in global foreign exchange could soon reach as high as US$3 trillion.

Figure 5.1 — Global Foreign Exchange Market Turnover Daily Average in April (US$ billions)

	1989	1992	1995	1998	2001	2004
Spot Transactions[1]	317	394	494	568	387	621
Outright forwards[2]	27	58	97	128	131	208
Foreign exchange swaps[3]	190	324	546	734	656	944
Estimated gaps in reporting	56	44	53	60	26	107
Total Turnover	590	820	1,190	1,490	1,200	1,880

Source: *World Trade Organization*

[1]**Spot transactions:** Single outright transactions involving the exchange of two currencies. Transactions are done at a rate agreed on the date of the contract for value or delivery (cash settlement), typically within two business days.

[2]**Forward contracts:** Over-the-counter agreements by counterparties to exchange a specified amount of different currencies at some future date, with the exchange rate being set at the time the contract is entered into. With a forward contract, a price is established on the trade date, but cash changes hands only on the settlement date.

[3]**Foreign exchange swap:** An over-the-counter, short-term derivative instrument. Two parties exchange agreed-upon amounts of two currencies as a spot transaction, simultaneously agreeing to unwind the exchange at a future date, based on a rule that reflects both interest and principal payments. In practice, a foreign exchange swap is the combination of a spot and forward transaction.

OPINION
SMART MONEY MOVES TO FX TRADE

Daily currency trading volumes could climb to more than US$3,000 billion a day by 2010—half as much again as current levels—according to a study to be released today.

"Based on the past five years, the market has shown growth of around 15% a year and this shows no signs of abating," said Justyn Trenner,

principal of ClientKnowledge. His US$3,000 billion estimate is based on trading volumes now over US$2,000 billion a day and growth of 10% between now and then, meaning at the current pace it could be more like US$3,400 billion.

Source: Jennifer Hughes, *Financial Times*, June 5, 2006

CASE STUDY: AUSTRALIAN SPOT MARKET TURNOVER IN 2006

Figure 5.2 shows the large increase in the size of the Australian foreign exchange market over the past two decades. Trading in spot contracts, in all currencies, has grown from A$4 billion a day in 1985 to over A$70 billion a day in April 2006. By way of comparison, this 15% annual increase compares to an increase in Australia's nominal GDP of 7% over the same period. Figure 5.2 shows particularly strong growth during 2006. This surge also occurred in the other markets, such as London and New York, where the growth has been almost identical to that in Australia. This large growth in turnover could be related to the increased treatment of foreign exchange as an asset class in its own right and the rapid growth in funds under management by hedge funds, a number of whom have currency-related strategies.

Figure 5.2 — Australian Spot Market Turnover

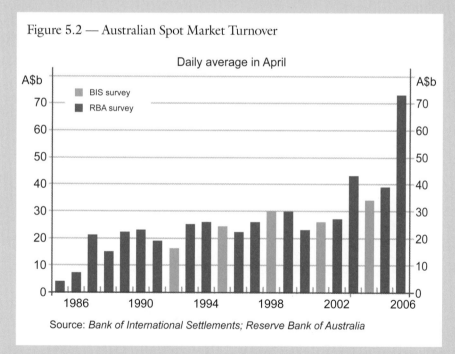

Source: *Bank of International Settlements; Reserve Bank of Australia*

Source: *For both text & graph, Reserve Bank of Australia*

SPECULATION IS THE KEY DRIVER

The most important component of daily trading volume is speculative activity—this usually relates to global capital seeking the most profitable return in the shortest period of time. It is estimated that 95% of foreign exchange transactions are speculative. More than 40% of trades last less than two days, while about 80% of trades last less than one week. In December 2004, the BIS published a follow-up report to its triennial survey of April, titled "Why has FX trading surged? Explaining the 2004 Triennial Survey." The report confirmed that the surge of activity between banks and financial customers could reflect the broad search for yield that has characterized financial markets in recent years. It noted that, in this search, currency market players worldwide have followed two key strategies—one is based on interest rate differentials and the other on trends in exchange rates. The report said: "The first strategy exploited the forward bias by investing in high-yielding currencies. A popular form of this investment strategy among leveraged players and real money managers was the so-called carry trade." In a "carry trade," an investor borrows in a low interest-rate currency and, with these funds, takes a long position (buys) in a higher interest-rate currency, betting that the exchange rate will not change so as to offset the interest rate differential between the two currencies. "While the U.S. dollar depreciated and the interest rate differential persisted, such investment strategies were profitable and a likely factor contributing to turnover growth," it said. The second strategy involved "momentum trading," where investors took large

"On the foreign-exchange markets today, the dollar fell against all major currencies and the doughnut."

© The New Yorker Collection 1987 Robert Mankoff from cartoonbank.com. All Rights Reserved.

positions in currencies aimed at exploiting long swings or "runs" in exchange rates. Such trades added weight to the underlying trends in exchange rates between countries. "Following the April 2001 survey, there was a strong pattern of U.S. dollar depreciation as the price of a dollar in different major currencies fell steadily until early spring 2004. U.S. dollar depreciation ranged from about 15% against the Canadian dollar and Japanese yen, to more than 30% against the Australian dollar." Beyond the position-taking related to profit opportunities associated with exchange rate trends, the report said such runs may also be associated with growth in hedging-related turnover. "Multinational firms face greater incentives to hedge in the face of long swings in currencies in order to minimise losses associated with currency positions. For instance, the European exporter invoicing in dollars in the midst of a long run of dollar depreciation has an incentive to hedge against further depreciation," it added.

FOREIGN EXCHANGE MARKET CHARACTERISTICS

In recent years, the three major foreign exchange markets have been London, New York, and Tokyo. According to the 2004 BIS survey the U.K. and U.S. accounted for more than 50% of daily turnover, while Japan accounted for slightly more than 8%. Singapore was also an important player with about 5% of the average daily turnover (see Figure 5.3).

Although we identify the countries where foreign exchange trading takes place, this trading is distinct from equities markets or commodities markets insofar as foreign exchange markets have no fixed location. Foreign exchange markets are actually decentralized over-the-counter markets

Figure 5.3 — Average Daily Turnover by Country

Country	Share
United Kingdom	31.3%
United States	19.2%
Japan	8.3%
Singapore	5.2%
Germany	4.9%
Hong Kong	4.2%
Australia	3.4%
Switzerland	3.3%
France	2.7%
Canada	2.2%
Others	15.3%
Total	100%

Source: *Bank of International Settlements Triennial Survey 2004*

© The New Yorker Collection 1998 Leo Cullum from cartoonbank.com. All Rights Reserved.

that cut across borders. They are also the least regulated of all financial markets. Here are some of the commonly cited characteristics of the foreign exchange markets:

- **24-Hour Market:** The currency market doesn't sleep during the working week and players can enter or exit trading positions at any time. There is no opening bell as the global trading day starts in Wellington, New Zealand, moves westward via Sydney, Tokyo, and Singapore, then Moscow, Frankfurt, London, and finally New York and San Francisco, before starting a new global day in Wellington again. Traders can, therefore, effectively choose when they want to trade morning, noon, or night.

- **Liquidity:** The foreign exchange market has better depth and breadth than any other capital market. Financial instruments like stocks and commodities are all subject to what is available in an order book and investors may not get all they want in one go. A foreign exchange order has the potential to be filled instantaneously at one rate and in a good size.

- **Easy Entry:** Anyone who wishes to trade in currencies can do so by using any of a number of companies to set up online trading accounts that operate around the clock.

- **Simple Trading Decisions:** Only a few of the world's currencies represent the bulk of the average daily turnover. This is in contrast to thousands of stocks to choose from in the world's stock markets. As such, the decision to buy or sell can be reached more quickly.

- **Neutral Conditions:** Currencies trade in pairs and typically one side of every currency pair constantly moves relative to the other side. When you buy a currency, you are simultaneously selling the other currency in the pair. So, if some currencies go up, others have to go down. There's no structural bias and profits can be made as currencies go up or down.

- **High Leverage Possible:** Participants can typically leverage their positions to as much as 100 times the cash they put up. This means that the foreign exchange market trader need only deposit US$1,000 for each US$100,000 position traded. This makes currency trading accessible to a wider range of traders because the initial funds requirement is very low relative to the size of the trading positions they hold. But the risks are commensurate—if a bet goes wrong, they can lose by a correspondingly high amount.

- **Low Transaction Costs:** Transaction costs are normally lower in the foreign exchange market and currencies are cheaper to trade than stocks. Foreign exchange trading is typically commission-free and there are no exchange or clearing fees. Thus, bottom line visibility is clearer for traders, making decisions about taking new trading positions, or what to do with existing ones, quicker and more efficient.

- **Tight Bid-Ask Spreads:** Because of the high liquidity within the currency market, bid-ask spreads are generally tighter when compared with bonds, equities or futures. The spread reflects transaction costs in the foreign exchange market.

- **Real-Time Quotes, Instant Execution:** Players in the foreign exchange market can execute their trades directly off real-time bid-ask quotes. This means that trades can be executed with much more certainty than, for example, transactions that have to be executed on an exchange floor.

Against this backdrop, the dynamic nature of the foreign exchange market is an attractive proposition to many investors. As is the case with any type of investment vehicle, there are risks and rewards in currency trading. These risks and rewards are amplified in the foreign exchange market because it is relatively unregulated. For instance, a stock exchange is a highly regulated environment, with tight rules placed on buying and selling. This helps to keep the playing field fair for everyone and takes away, for example, the opportunity for companies to manipulate stocks for their own ends. While the potential for a skilled investor to realize significant profits in the foreign exchange market is large, good investors will also familiarize themselves with potential downside risks, which can be magnified by margin trading.

REGULATION

Each foreign exchange transaction comes with its own associated risks, including volatility, exchange rate risk, credit risk, monetary risk, and interest rate risk, as well as the possibility of central bank intervention. Because the foreign exchange market is largely unregulated on an international scale, trading activity is generally subject to the laws and customs of each participant's home nation. Regulatory organizations in various countries include:

- **Australia:** Australian Securities and Investments Commission

- **Canada:** British Columbia Securities Commission, Ontario Securities Commission

- **Denmark:** Finanstilsynet (Danish Financial Supervisory Authority)

- **Germany:** Bundesanstalt für Finanzdienstleistungsaufsicht (Federal Financial Supervisory Authority)

- **Hong Kong:** Securities and Futures Commission

- **Japan:** Financial Services Agency

- **Spain:** Comisión Nacional del Mercado de Valores (Spanish Securities Market Commission)

- **Sweden:** Finansinspektionen (Swedish Financial Supervisory Authority)

- **Switzerland:** Groupement Suisse des Conseils en Gestion Indépendants; Federal Department of Finance; Commission fédérale des banques (Swiss Federal Banking Commission)

- **United Kingdom:** Financial Services Authority

- **United States:** U.S. Securities and Exchange Commission; Commodity Futures Trading Commission; National Futures Association

LEADING CURRENCIES

Typically, a country's currency comprises paper notes and coins circulating within its economy. Today, currencies get their value purely on the basis of their acceptability to people. Their value is not guaranteed, as opposed to the past when each unit represented a specific amount of a commodity like gold or silver. As we have mentioned, this is known as fiat money—that is, money issued on the authority, or fiat, of a government, but not tied in value to the precious commodity. Each country has control over the supply and production of its own currency. Exceptions are the member countries of the Economic and Monetary Union, which have ceded control of monetary policy to the European Central Bank (ECB).

The four most important currencies in foreign exchange markets in terms of trading volume, are the U.S. dollar, the euro, the Japanese yen, and the U.K. pound sterling (see Figure 5.4).

Figure 5.4 — Proportion of international foreign reserves

Currency	2000	2001	2002	2003	2004	2005	2006
U.S. dollar	70.5%	70.7%	66.5%	65.8%	65.9%	66.4%	65.7%
Euro	18.8%	19.8%	24.2%	25.3%	24.9%	24.3%	25.2%
U.K. pound	2.8%	2.7%	2.9%	2.6%	3.3%	3.6%	4.2%
Japanese yen	6.3%	5.2%	4.5%	4.1%	3.9%	3.7%	3.2%
Swiss franc	0.3%	0.3%	0.4%	0.2%	0.2%	0.1%	0.2%
Others	1.4%	1.2%	1.4%	1.9%	1.8%	1.9%	1.5%

Source: *International Monetary Fund, European Central Bank*

The International Organization for Standardization (ISO) has assigned the following codes to the four main currencies: USD, EUR, JPY, and GBP respectively. Generally, the currency code is composed of the country's two-character country code plus an extra character to denote the currency unit. After the USD, EUR, JPY, and GBP, the next most heavily traded currencies in the world are the Swiss franc (CHF), the Canadian dollar (CAD), the Australian dollar (AUD), and the New Zealand dollar (NZD).

As we have noted, currencies trade in pairs in the foreign exchange market. This involves simultaneously buying one currency and selling another currency. The most important currency pairs are EUR/USD, USD/JPY, GBP/USD, and USD/CHF. USD/CAD, AUD/USD, and NZD/USD are known as the "dollar Bloc" currencies. These currency pairs are referred to as "majors," which distinguish them as the most liquid and widely traded currency pairs in the world. Trades involving majors are estimated to make up about 90% of all trading in foreign exchange markets. EUR/USD is the

NOTE
CURRENCY NICKNAMES

Traders often use nicknames for some of the major currencies. The origins of the "aussie," "kiwi," and "swissy" are self-evident and correspond to the currencies of Australia, New Zealand, and Switzerland respectively. The origins of some other nicknames are more intriguing. The U.S. dollar is often referred to as the "greenback," a moniker that dates back to the days of U.S. President Abraham Lincoln. Between 1862 and 1863, Lincoln introduced a paper currency, colored green on the reverse side, to help finance the Civil War and bring it to a conclusion. It was issued against the credit of the country and not against gold or silver. In other words it was fiat currency. The move came in response to the high interest rates that were hitherto charged by international bankers on their loans to his government. Lincoln received Congressional approval to borrow US$450 million from the people by selling them bonds, or greenbacks. They were not redeemable until 1865 when three could be exchanged for one in silver. They were made full legal tender in 1879. Lincoln said: "The privilege of creating and issuing money is not only the supreme prerogative of Government, but is the Government's greatest creative opportunity. By the adoption of these principles, the taxpayers will be saved immense sums of interest." Lincoln's move may have ultimately led to his assassination in 1865. Indeed, Otto von Bismarck, the German Chancellor (1871–90), was in no doubt that the introduction of the greenback had led to Lincoln's demise. Bismarck said: "He obtained from Congress the right to borrow from the people by selling to it the "bonds" of States ... and the Government and the nation escaped the plots of the foreign financiers. They understood at once, that the United States would escape their grip. The death of Lincoln was resolved upon."

The Canadian dollar is nicknamed the "loonie," which is the name Canadians gave to a gold-colored, bronze-plated, one-dollar coin introduced in 1987. It bears images of the common loon, or great northern diver, which is a well-known Canadian bird.

The U.K. pound versus the U.S. dollar is also known as "cable." The origins of this term come from the fact that, in the late 1800s, the exchange rate for the U.S. dollar against the U.K. pound sterling was transmitted overseas via transatlantic telegraph cable.

Source: www.xat.org/xat

most actively traded pair, accounting for almost 30% of global average daily turnover. The next two most important pairs in terms of daily turnover are USD/JPY and GBP/USD.

Note that there is a system to the way that currency pairs are quoted. The first currency in the pair is considered the *base currency* and the second currency is the *quote currency* or *counter currency*. For example, the euro is the base currency and the U.S. dollar is the quote currency in the EUR/USD pair. Or for USD/JPY, the U.S. dollar is the base currency while the Japanese yen is the quote currency. Most of the time, the U.S. dollar acts as the base currency. Quotes are expressed in units of US$1 per quote currency.

CURRENCY TRADING TRENDS

The BIS triennial survey of 2004 revealed some interesting global trends, in terms of currency and geographical share of turnover, compared to the previous survey in 2001. As mentioned, the EUR/USD was the most widely traded currency pair, averaging US$501 billion per day or 28% of total turnover (see Figure 5.5). However, the share of the EUR/USD was slightly down from 30% in 2001. This was attributed to factors including an investors' drive for diversification into a wider range of currencies, to seek better returns on their investments, and greater demand for hedging in a wider range of currencies by companies exposed to different foreign currencies. The second most actively traded currency pair was the USD/JPY, with 17% of turnover or US$296 billion per day. The pair's share of total trade was also down from 20% in 2001. Meanwhile, the share of GBP/USD increased from 11% in 2001 to 14% in 2004. In this instance, traders were seeking greater volatility amid

Figure 5.5 — Average Daily Turnover by Currency Pair, 2004

Country	Share
EUR/USD	28%
USD/JPY	17%
GBP/USD	14%
AUD/USD	5%
USD/CHF	4%
USD/CAD	4%
EUR/JPY	3%
EUR/GBP	2%
EUR/CHF	1%
Others	22%
Total	100%

Source: *Bank of International Settlements Triennial Survey 2004*

NOTE
HOW THE $ SIGN CAME ABOUT

Ever wondered how the dollar, or $, came about? The answer is not as obvious as it seems, even though $ is probably the most widely recognized symbol in the world. You will see it in news stories, books, your handphone memory, the keyboards of computers, programming languages, and even as a design element in clothes and accessories. In fact, it's so dominant that you tend to forget the other important symbols of the foreign exchange market such as the euro (€), the pound sterling (£), and the Japanese yen (¥).

The $ is believed to have its origins in Spanish currencies used in the early days of U.S colonization. Spanish pesos were also called piastres, Spanish dollars, and pieces of eight, and were circulated in many parts of the world. Since three of the four names—pesos, piastres, and pieces—given for the Spanish dollar start with p and are pluralized with s, it was natural for abbreviations like p and ps to be used. Sometimes ps was written as Ps. The theory goes that when P with a superscript s is written quickly, there is a tendency to join the letters. If you look at the top part of the resulting symbol, that's the $ sign. Although the $ sign originally referred to a Spanish coin, it was the British colonists of America who made the transition from ps to the new sign. This is also why $1 is the norm rather, than 1$, as it follows the British convention of placing the pound sign in front.

Source: Mark Brader, "Origin of the Dollar Sign"

the lack of such opportunities in the USD/JPY. Turnover in AUD/USD exceeded that in USD/CHF for the first time since BIS started conducting these surveys in the 1980s (the BIS first conducted a survey of the U.S., U.K., Japan, and Canada in 1986), making it the fourth most traded currency pair in the world with US$90 billion in daily turnover. This was almost double the US$47 billion measured in 2001. Average daily turnover in USD/CHF and USD/CAD also rose to US$78 billion (from US$57 billion in 2001) and US$71 billion (from US$50 billion) respectively.

In terms of individual currencies, the U.S. dollar was the most heavily traded with 88.7% of average daily turnover followed by the euro at 37.2% (see Figure 5.6). Both were a tad below their shares from the 2001 survey, which were 90.3% and 37.6% respectively. The share of the yen was also

Figure 5.6 — Average Daily Turnover by Currency, 2004

Country	Share
USD	88.7%
EUR	37.2%
JPY	20.3%
GBP	16.9%
AUD	6.1%
CHF	5.5%

Source: *Bank of International Settlements Triennial Survey 2004*

down, from 22.7% to 20.3%, with the pound taking up some of the slack with a 16.9% share of turnover, up from 13% in 2001. The Swiss franc maintained its position from 2001 at 6.1%, while the Australian dollar's share rose to 5.5% from 4.2% in 2001. (Note, the total share exceeds 100% due to double counting or more on currency pairs.)

CURRENCY AS AN ASSET CLASS

The surge in foreign exchange trading signifies a growing recognition that currencies are an asset class in their own right. In *Why has FX Trading Surged? Explaining the 2004 triennial survey,* authors Gabriele Galati and Michael Melvin noted the attractiveness of currencies, compared to bonds and stocks, in investors' search for yield. They said that interest in currencies as an asset class was reinforced by disappointing yields in stock and bond markets at different times. As returns on stocks and bonds waned, investors found currency strategies to be quite profitable over the 2001 to 2004 period. Following the 2001 survey, there was a long run of dollar depreciation that was actively exploited by investors. It can be seen that, in general, at that time equity markets were falling well into 2003 before beginning an upward run that lasted less than a year. Bond yields were low and fairly flat over the period. So, the strong trend in the foreign exchange market offered an attractive alternative to stocks and bonds.

Thus, the major attraction of currencies as an asset class is for portfolio diversification since their movements are often uncorrelated to other asset classes. The following article from *Charity Times*, a leading business and management magazine for non-profit professionals, shows how practitioners in foreign exchange markets manage currencies as an asset class:

NOTE
CURRENCY AS AN ASSET CLASS

Promising returns with a low correlation to other asset classes, currency has come into its own right. It is being used by a growing number of larger pension funds and charities to generate absolute returns and to diversify existing portfolios. But active currency management is not widely understood. Part of the reason for this is its complexity. Currency traders do not measure their returns in relative, but in absolute terms. Risk and return tolerances are agreed in advance with the investor. Active currency management also polarises around two core approaches, fundamental or technical, although in truth most managers use a combination of both to varying degrees. "Technical trading is driven by past exchange rate data, and fundamental trading by economic market data," observes Bill Muyskin, senior consultant and currency expert at Mercer Investment Consulting. Each approach can be further characterised as predominantly quant or judgemental. Quant uses pre-programmed trading; judgemental, as its name implies, allows for decisive human intervention. Of the 117 managers measured by Mercer in their currency universe, most use some blend of technical and fundamental. By the same token, even the most rigorous quant must allow for intervention when unique, market-moving events take place, and the most opinionated judgemental manager will still consult a model against which to test themselves.

This highlights a fundamental point about the active management of currency. "There is no single process or style that you can say is dominant and best," argues Mike Victoros, head of global FX products at ABN AMRO. "We have been lucky that our relatively judgemental approach works well in the current environment." Some examples bear this out. At Oppenheim Asset Management, one of Germany's leading active currency managers, only 15 currencies are traded, mostly developed ones. "Our model throws out a plus, minus or neutral," says their currency chief Christian Walde, "We can go against it within pre-determined limits."

Meanwhile, Credit Suisse Asset Management has a somewhat different decision taking process. This attributes 60% of each decision to fundamentals and 40% to behavioural or short-term factors. Within the 60%, more than half (35%) is attributed to macro-economic variables, 10% to aggregate flows of money, and 15% to fundamental quantitative analysis and forecasting. Of the remaining 40%, just over half (more than 25% of total) is technical analysis using charts, and the remaining 15% to market sentiment. By contrast to Oppenheim, CSAM trades more than 20 currencies, particularly emerging ones, and they expect to increase this number in future. These two examples illustrate the difference in sophistication between the models used by different managers. For instance, managers no longer only form their views on currency pairs, but some instead take an absolute approach, valuing currencies individually then blending these valuations into pairs. Research from Hymans Robertson finds that managers are split almost equally between pairwise, absolute and some blend of the two. Needless to say, the size of the set of currency pairs traded by any manager is an important clue as to their resources and aspirations. As a rule of thumb, this market breaks down into two groups; those that trade only developed currencies and those that trade a wider range including the main emerging currencies.

Source: *Charity Times Investment Quarterly*, Q3, 2006

SUMMARY

Foreign exchange trading volumes are collated once every three years by the Bank for International Settlements. Its triennial survey for 2004 showed the staggering extent of the foreign exchange trading—then at $1.9 trillion a day—and by most accounts trading volumes have grown since then. Growth has been driven by hedge funds, central banks and other investors, adding to the liquidity already provided by commercial and investment banks. It should be stressed that the most important component of daily trading volume is speculative activity—this usually relates to global capital seeking the most profitable return in the shortest period of time. It is estimated that 95% of foreign exchange transactions are speculative. In recent years, the three major foreign exchange markets have been London, New York and Tokyo. According to the Bank for International Settlements' triennial survey for 2004, the U.K. and U.S. accounted for more than 50% of the daily turnover, while Japan accounted for slightly more than 8%. Singapore was also an important player with about 5% of the average daily turnover. The major attractions of foreign exchange markets include: (1) high liquidity levels; (2) high accessibility for many different types of participants; and (3) efficiency. The U.S. dollar, the euro, the U.K. pound and the Japanese yen continue to be the four most important currencies in the world and account for the dominant share of foreign exchange trading. There is also a notion that currencies have become an asset class in themselves as investors search for yield around the globe.

QUICK QUIZ

1. How often does the Bank for International Settlements carry out its survey of central banks to determine world trends in foreign exchange trading?

2. What percentage of today's world-wide foreign exchange trading is believed to be speculative?

3. What is a carry trade? Why are interest-rate differentials important for carry trades?

4. Name five commonly cited characteristics of foreign exchange markets.

5. What are the advantages of leverage in foreign exchange trading? What are the negatives?

6. What is fiat money and how does it work?

7. What are the four most important currencies in the world, in order of their importance?

8. Why are currencies gaining in importance as an asset class even though they have no intrinsic value?

EXCHANGE RATES
AND THEIR MOVEMENTS

CURRENCY MOVEMENT FACTORS

To date, there is no exchange rate model that can predict future currency prices with 100% accuracy. In rapidly growing global foreign exchange markets, currency movements become harder to predict as more participants enter the market on a daily basis, bringing with them all their research, opinions, emotions, and expectations about where currencies should be headed. Currency movements in the short term can be influenced by publicly available information like the release of a country's gross domestic product (GDP) data, the consumer price index, or employment data. The following publicly available information can have an immediate impact on currency movements:

- Local economic data releases and the anticipation of those releases.

- Economic data releases in foreign countries, especially of major trading partners, and the anticipation of those releases.

- Central banks, such as the U.S. Federal Reserve or the European Central Bank, raising or lowering interest rates.

- Central banks making public their thoughts on monetary policy.

- Expectation of central banks making public their views on local interest rates or monetary policy.

- Political developments, both globally and in individual countries.

- Natural disasters and perceptions about how they will impact economies.

- Changes in commodity prices, particularly oil and gold.

This list is not exhaustive, but these factors would be among the more important catalysts for currency movements.

But there is also information that is not immediately publicly available, such as individual traders' in-house strategic analyses on currencies, or buy and sell orders that come from customers, which can affect the decision processes of market participants. The activities of market participants such as central banks, commercial banks, hedge funds, individual investors, and multinational corporations will be influenced by a mixture of all these factors.

In *The Psychology of the Foreign Exchange Market*, author Thomas Oberlechner says "… to many, the foreign exchange market is a mystery, and the exchange rates it produces are ultimately incomprehensible. Changes in exchange rates seem random, or at best, governed by complex mathematical principles understood by a select few." Oberlechner took a micro view of currency trading by interviewing countless traders who provided valuable insights about how they conduct their trades. However, macroeconomic views on exchange rates are often put forward when currency movements are reported in the press or in reports generated by market participants such as central banks and investment funds. For example, the Federal Reserve Bank of New York's description of the performance of the U.S. dollar and the euro for the period from July to September 2005 provides an insight into the factors that can influence appreciation and depreciation related to currency pairs.

" OPINION
FEDERAL RESERVE OPINION
THE DOLLAR APPRECIATES

"*The euro-dollar currency pair (EUR/USD) traded within a range of about 1.1900 to 1.2550 during the period. This fairly narrow trading range contributed to low levels in both actual and implied volatility of the currency pair over the period. The dollar ended the quarter moderately stronger against the euro, at $1.202 per euro. The dollar's depreciation against the euro in late August partly reflected increased uncertainty about the U.S. economic outlook in the aftermath of Hurricanes Katrina and Rita and the potential impact of rising energy prices. Investors also questioned whether or not the Federal Open Market Committee (FOMC) would continue to raise the target federal funds rate after 25-basis point (0.25%) increases at both the June 30 and August 9 meetings. These concerns prompted U.S. interest rates to decline and* *interest rate differentials between the United States and the euro area to narrow markedly following Hurricane Katrina's landfall on August 29. Narrower interest rate differentials, in turn, put downward pressure on the dollar in early September. Uncertainties about monetary policy and growth proved to be short-lived. Many economists' estimates indicated that any negative impact that Hurricane Katrina might have on growth would likely be confined to the third and fourth quarters of 2005, with the potential for a subsequent increase in growth in 2006 as the rebuilding effort in the U.S. Gulf Coast got under way. Analysts also reported that commentary from Federal Reserve officials was consistent with expectations for further increases in the federal funds target rate by the FOMC. Despite some lingering uncertainties about the likely impact of elevated energy prices and the extent of economic disruption in the U.S. Gulf Coast region, concern about the*

hurricane's effect on the broader economy appeared to ease over the month of September. As expectations for further policy rate increases by the FOMC rose, interest rate differentials between the United States and the euro area widened again in September. The dollar recovered from its recent lows and finished the quarter 0.7% stronger against the euro. Expectations for further policy rate moves were confirmed near quarter-end when the FOMC raised the target federal funds rate by another 25 basis points to 3.75% at the September 20 meeting. Some market participants reported that the close results of the German parliamentary elections on September 18 also pressured the euro lower as investors speculated that the absence of a majority governing party in Germany could stall structural reform in Europe's largest economy."

Source: *"Treasury and Federal Reserve Foreign Exchange Operations,"* Federal Reserve Bank of New York, July–September 2005

Central banks around the world, such as the U.S. Federal Reserve, carry out actions called "monetary policy" to influence the availability and cost of money and credit. They do this to achieve certain national economic goals such as lowering inflation or promoting growth. In 1913 the passage of the U.S. Federal Reserve Act gave monetary policy power to the Federal Reserve. There are three tools of monetary policy that the Federal Reserve or "Fed" uses: (1) open market operations, (2) the discount rate and (3) reserve requirements. While the Fed's Board of Governors makes decisions regarding the discount rate and reserve requirements, the Federal Open Market Committee (FOMC) is responsible for so-called "open market operations." By using those tools the Fed is able to influence the balances that banks and other depository institutions hold at Federal Reserve banks and are thus able to alter the federal funds rate which is the interest rate which banks lend to each other overnight. A change in the federal funds rate influences a whole host of financial and economic events such as: Other short-term interest rates, foreign exchange rates, long-term interest rates, the amount of money and credit, and such economic variables such as employment, production output, and prices of various goods and services. The 12 members on the FOMC, including various officials of the Federal Reserve System, hold eight annual meetings where they determine monetary policy after they have reviewed economic and financial conditions and any risks to price stability. The Federal Reserve's commentary shown above illustrates how such variables as natural disasters, energy prices, political uncertainties and interest rate changes can influence currencies.

Currency strategists will look at such factors to forecast price targets for currencies. For example, if a strategist was tasked to predict the expected performance of the Canadian dollar against the U.S. dollar through 2007, he would probably factor in the expected performance of the U.S. dollar over the previous period, as well as expectations of commodity prices that Canada exports such as oil, the direction of interest rates in Canada, and the corresponding rate environment in the U.S. The strategist is also likely to look at expectations of capital and trade flows associated with the Canadian economy, and how Canada's political landscape is likely to evolve over the period. Thus, in forecasting the expected performance of the "loonie," the strategist essentially conducts a fundamental analysis of a country's underlying economic conditions. To get a feel for these fundamental analyses, here are some common scenarios that can have an impact on currencies:

- **If a country's stock market rallies, its currency could strengthen.** A stock market rally provides an ideal investment opportunity for individuals regardless of geographic location. As a result, there is a positive correlation between a country's equity market and its currency. If the stock market is rising, funds will rush in to seize the opportunity. Alternatively, falling stock markets will see investors selling their shares to seek opportunities elsewhere. The correlation between stocks and currencies is strong enough to make currency traders watch stock markets for cues on the performance of currencies.

- **If oil prices surge to record highs, it can have a negative impact on some currencies.** A country's dependence on oil is very important in determining how its currency will be hit by a spike in oil prices. There will be a greater negative impact on countries that are net oil importers. For example, the U.S. is among the world's largest net oil importers and thus its economy will be more sensitive to changes in oil prices than many other countries. Countries with alternative fuel sources, and other resources, have the ability to switch from strict oil dependence to other energy sources, which helps to reduce their exposure and sensitivity.

- **An increase in a country's unemployment numbers can have a negative impact on its currency.** Currency prices reflect the balance of supply and demand for those currencies. A primary factor affecting supply and demand is the overall strength of the economy. The unemployment rate is a strong indicator of a country's economic strength and therefore a contributor to the underlying shifts in supply and demand for that currency. When unemployment is high, the economy may be weak—and its currency may fall in value.

- **If a country's central bank makes a surprise decision to raise rates by more than expected, its currency could rally.** Currency traders look at data related to interest rates very closely as interest rate differentials are strong indicators of relative currency movements. If a country raises its interest rates, its currency can strengthen in relation to those of other countries because high interest rates help nations attract foreign investment. Economic indicators that have the biggest impact on interest rates are the producer price index, consumer price index, and GDP. Generally, the timing of an interest rate decision is known in advance. They take place after regularly scheduled meetings by the Federal Reserve, ECB, BOJ, and other central banks.

THE IMPACT OF REAL INTEREST RATES

Traditional macroeconomic exchange rate models are based on fundamental analyses. In these models, the basic force that drives exchange rates comes from the balance between supply and demand. For example, if the demand for the U.S. dollar exceeds its supply at the current exchange rate against the euro, the price of U.S. dollars in terms of the euro will rise. Conversely, if supply exceeds demand, the price will fall. Demand and supply factors that govern exchange rates become much more complex than that because people don't use currencies just to purchase foreign goods and services, but also for activities like cross-border investment and speculation. This opens up many other variables that must be considered when addressing exchange rate movements, as underscored in the Federal Reserve Bank of New York's commentary cited previously. One of the most important factors, for example, is how investors ride interest rate differentials between countries.

We know that interest is the price paid to entice people with funds to save rather than spend, or to invest in long-term assets rather than hold cash. Therefore, interest rates reflect the interaction between the supply of savings and the demand for capital, or between the demand for money and its supply. A key determinant of these interest rates is inflationary expectations. Global investors broadly desire a real return from their investments, and changes in forecasts over future inflation are consequently reflected in current exchange rates. "Real return" here refers to the interest rate minus the inflation rate.

CASE STUDY: FISHER EFFECT

The so-called Fisher Effect was developed by the economist Irving Fisher which says that, all things being equal, a rise in a country's expected inflation rate will eventually cause an equal rise in the interest rate (and vice versa). Fisher believed that in order to understand the relationship between money, inflation and interest rates it was necessary to understand the difference between the "nominal" interest rate and "real" interest rate. The nominal interest rate is the stated rate given by banks, for example, interest on a savings account while the real interest rate corrects the nominal rate for the impact of inflation in order to tell how fast the purchasing power of a savings account will change over time. Simply put, the real interest rate is the nominal interest rate minus the expected inflation rate:

Real interest rate = Nominal Interest Rate - Expected Inflation Rate

Nominal Interest Rate = Real interest Rate + Expected Inflation Rate

If the bank interest rate is 5% and inflation is 6% then the real interest rate is –1% which means that the bank deposit is losing its

Irving Fisher
Photography sourced from public domain

purchasing power. On the other hand if the inflation rate is 3% then the real interest rate is 2% and the bank deposit is gaining in purchasing power.

Fisher received the first Ph.D. in economics from Yale University in 1891 and produced a thesis based on mathematical and monetary economics which was considered innovative in the U.S. at that time. He was also a health campaigner after he recovered from a bout of tuberculosis. As a result he advocated vegetarianism, avoiding red meat, avoiding alcoholic drinks, and exercise. He also believed in a theory that mental illness was caused by infectious materials in the teeth roots, bowels and other places of the body so that surgical removal would cure metal disorders. When his daughter was diagnosed with schizophrenia, he had sections of her bowel and colon removed which resulted in her death.

He was a prolific writer on the problems of World War I, the prosperous 1920's and the 1930's depression. The 1929 stock market crash and the following Great Depression was a blow to Fisher since he lost a great deal of his personal wealth. His academic reputation was also damaged when a few days before the Stock Market Crash of 1929 he said: "Stock prices have reached what looks like a permanently high plateau." He said that the market was "only shaking out the lunatic fringe" and explained that he felt stock prices had not caught up with their real value and might go higher. After the Crash, he continued to state that a recovery was imminent.

Nevertheless his contribution to economics is clear. Not only was he the first economist to distinguish clearly between real and nominal interest rates but he also was a pioneer in the statistical analysis of money stock, interest rates and price levels. He believed that people generally had "money illusion" insofar as they could not differentiate between the money and the products money could actually buy.

Here is an example of how this works: If Australia's interest rates are higher than Japan's, then Japanese investors will, for example, want to buy Australian bonds to take advantage of the higher rates and corresponding returns. But to do so, they must first sell Japanese yen and buy Australian dollars at the current exchange rate between the two currencies. Next, Japanese investors are not likely to park their money in Australian bonds indefinitely and, at some point in the future, will want to bring their proceeds home and convert them back to yen. So they will also be interested in having an idea of what the exchange rate between the yen and the Australian dollar will be in the future. The expected return for these investors will have to factor in both the interest rate and the expected movement in exchange rates between the two currencies. That is, the demand for yen will depend not only on the current exchange rate, but also on anticipation of future exchange rate movements against the Australian dollar. The Japanese investors' exchange rate predictions will, in turn, be influenced by their estimate of what the inflation rates will be in each country. If inflation in Australia rises above the prevailing interest rates, the Japanese investors will then expect a weakening of the Australian dollar. If Japanese inflation is lower than the prevailing interest rates then the Japanese yen will become more attractive.

SPECULATION AND OTHER FACTORS

The demand for foreign exchange to support international trade is not as complex as interest rate differential considerations since short-term trade patterns are reasonably predictable—for example, the market will know roughly at which levels domestic importers will buy foreign currencies with their local currency to pay for the goods they buy overseas, and they will also know where exporters will sell foreign currencies which they receive for goods sold in their export markets. Speculative demand, on the other hand, causes most of the short-term fluctuations in currency markets. Speculators have to guess constantly where currencies are headed, and their guesses are often revised when their short-term targets are reached or if currency movements run contrary to their initial guesses. As foreign exchange speculators change their views about the future, their demand for currency changes, resulting in exchange rate fluctuations.

In addition to all these drivers, central banks also intervene in foreign exchange markets for reasons that can be quite different from those of the other participants. For instance, the Bank of Korea could easily decide to sell won in foreign exchange markets. The bank's intention could be to keep the value of the won low so that the country's exports are more competitive. The greater demand for South Korea's exports will feed back positively into its economy.

The scenarios just described generate supply and demand drivers for currencies across the globe. The accompanying foreign exchange transactions come on the back of thousands upon thousands of decisions, made each day, to buy or sell currencies. To determine exchange rates, we would have to consider the influence of these decisions on currencies, which is by no means an easy task. Different empirical exchange rate models incorporate one or more of these variables—all of which can have an impact on exchange rates.

FOREIGN EXCHANGE MODELS

Three of the most regularly cited exchange rate models are outlined below:

- **Monetarist Model:** In this model, currency prices are viewed as simply any other commodity price and are assumed to be flexible just like any other item. Formal devaluations and revaluations of currencies are viewed as unnecessary as a country's foreign exchange rate responds to the forces of supply and demand.

- **Portfolio Balance Model:** This model takes a short-term view of exchange rates and broadens the focus from currency demand and supply conditions to take into account other financial asset demand and supply conditions. According to the portfolio balance theory in its simplest form, foreign exchange market participants balance their portfolios between domestic money, domestic bonds, and foreign currency bonds, modifying their portfolios as conditions change. The process of bringing the total demand for and supply of

CASE STUDY: PPP BETWEEN U.S. DOLLAR AND CHINESE RENMINBI

In determining the exchange rate of the U.S. dollar against the Chinese renminbi, the analyst would create the Purchasing Power Parity (PPP) line by dividing the U.S. inflation rate by the Chinese inflation rate and track it on a monthly basis. The exchange rate of the U.S. dollar against the renminbi should follow the PPP line. An example is shown in Figure 6.1:

Figure 6.1 — China Currency

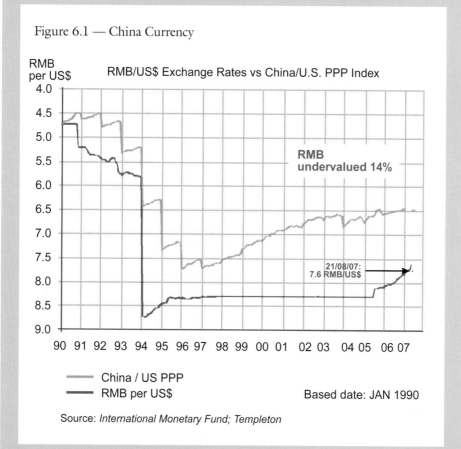

The lighter PPP line shows that between 1990 and 1997, inflation in the U.S. was lower than inflation in China and therefore the Chinese currency should have been weaker against the U.S. dollar. This is confirmed by the darker falling exchange rate line. But then, in 1994, the Chinese government decided to lower the exchange rate and fix it against the U.S. dollar so that until 2005 the rate was not allowed to change. Meanwhile, in 1997 inflation in the U.S. started rising against inflation in China, which meant that the Renminbi should have strengthened against the U.S. dollar. However, the Chinese government would not allow an exchange rate revision causing pressure for change to build up. This created a difference between the PPP line and the actual exchange rate of 14%, this figure indicating how much the renminbi was undervalued against the U.S. dollar. PPP is useful in assessing long-term exchange rate trends and can provide valuable information about long-run equilibrium. But as Figure 6.1 shows, it has not met with much success in predicting exchange rate movements over short- and medium-term horizons for widely traded currencies.

financial assets in each country to an equilibrium state is what determines the exchange rate.

- **Purchasing Power Parity (PPP) Model:** The theory holds that in the long run, exchange rates will adjust to equalize the relative purchasing power of currencies. This concept follows from the law of one price—that is, in competitive markets, identical goods will sell for identical prices when valued in the same currency. The PPP can be tracked by dividing the inflation rate in one country by the inflation rate in another country.

By taking a standard product such as a McDonald's Big Mac, currency researchers have an informal way of measuring the PPP between two currencies. It provides an intuitive test of the extent to which market exchange rates result in goods costing the same in different countries. *The Economist* magazine introduced such an index in 1987 (see Figure 6.2).

While macroeconomic exchange rate models provide some insight into exchange rate movements, they took a credibility hit after Richard Meese and Kenneth Rogoff concluded, in a study titled *"Empirical Exchange Rate Models of the Seventies: Do They Fit Out of Sample?"* that such models do a poor job of tracking movements over short time horizons. Their study, released in 1983, compared time series and rate models on the basis of their out-of-sample forecast accuracy. Meese and Rogoff found that a random walk model would have predicted major exchange rates as well as any of the exchange rate models they chose to study. "Significantly,

Figure 6.2 — *The Economist's* Big Mac Index (2007)

	Big Mac prices in dollars*	Implied ppp of the dollar[1]	Under (-)/ over (+) valuation against the dollar, %
United States[‡]	3.41	-	-
Argentina	2.67	2.42	-22
Australia	2.95	1.01	-14
Brazil	3.61	2.02	+6
Canada	3.68	1.14	+8
Chile	2.97	459	-13
China	1.45	3.23	-58
Czech Republic	2.51	15.5	-27
Denmark	5.08	8.14	+49
Egypt	1.68	2.80	-51
Eurozone**	4.17	1.12[††]	+22
Hong Kong	1.54	3.52	-55
Hungary	3.33	176	-2
Indonesia	1.76	4,663	-48
Japan	2.29	82.1	-33
Malaysia	1.60	1.61	-53
Mexico	2.69	8.50	-21
New Zealand	5.89	1.35	+73
Peru	3.00	2.79	-12
Philippines	1.85	24.9	-46
Poland	2.51	2.02	-26
Russia	2.03	15.2	-41
Singapore	2.59	1.16	-24
South Africa	2.22	4.55	-35
South Korea	3.14	850	-8
Sweden	4.86	9.68	+42
Switzerland	5.20	1.85	+53
Taiwan	2.29	22.0	-33
Thailand	1.80	18.2	-47
Turkey	3.66	1.39	+7
United Kingdom	4.01	1.71[§]	+18
Venezuela	3.45	2,170	+1

*At contemporary exchange rates   [1]Implied purchasing power parity: local price divided by price in U.S.
[‡]Average of New York, Chicago, Atlanta, and San Francisco
**Weighted average of prices in eurozone   [††]Dollars per euro   [§]Dollars per pound

Sources: McDonald's; *The Economist*

NEWS CLIP
IPOD SWALLOWS BIG MAC INDEX

In a sign of the times, a new indicator for foreign exchange movements, based on Apple's iPod music player, has been developed as an alternative to the Big Mac Index. Launched yesterday, the CommSec iPod Index predicts a 15% drop in the Australian dollar against the U.S. dollar—music to exporters' ears.

In 1986, *The Economist* launched a tongue-in-cheek index based on the McDonald's hamburger as a way of assessing whether a particular currency was undervalued or overvalued against other currencies. Currency analysts have a range of ways to explain exchange rate levels and forecast future movements, but a long-term measure is purchasing power parity, or PPP. The Big Mac and iPod index theories are that if an object in Australia is dearer than in America when expressed in U.S. dollars, the Australian dollar may be perceived as overvalued. One way that this imbalance in Big Mac prices may be corrected would be for the Australian dollar to fall against the U.S. currency. *The Economist* used the burger because it is made the same way the world over. However, Commonwealth Securities chief economist Craig James said the Big Mac Index could be distorted by taxes, transport costs, labour laws and trade barriers in each country. "No PPP approach is perfect, just

as no currency model is completely accurate."

Twenty years on, and with the same light-hearted approach, Commonwealth Securities devised the CommSec iPod Index. "A key difference between the iPod and Big Mac approaches is that Big Macs are made in a host of countries across the globe whereas iPods are predominantly made in China," Mr James said. "Simply, an iPod nano should broadly cost the same across the globe. If there were substantial price differences customers would switch their purchases to other countries, especially given the power of the internet."

The first reading of the iPod Index of 26 countries—based on a 2-gigabyte iPod nano in U.S. dollars—suggests that the greenback has potential to rally. Brazil is the dearest place to buy an iPod, at US$327.71. The lowest is in Canada at US$144.20. Australia is in 19th place at US$172.36 (A$219), four places above the U.S. at US$149. Mr James said: "The index suggests that the U.S. dollar has potential to appreciate against a range of major currencies, with the Aussie dollar around 15% overvalued against the greenback."

Source: "iPod swallows Big Mac Index," *The Australian*, January 19, 2007 the structural models fail to improve on the random walk model in spite of the fact that we base their forecasts on actual realised values of future explanatory variables," they said. Their research underscores the view that changes in exchange rates seem random and that the foreign exchange market is a mystery.

Thus, while the variables in macroeconomic models—such as interest rates, prices, and GDP—can reasonably explain exchange rate changes over medium-term to long-term horizons, they are not necessarily useful for tracking rate changes on a daily, weekly, or monthly basis. As such, currency traders and other market participants who focus on the short-term horizon look beyond macroeconomic models for a deeper understanding of the market. More recently, researchers have investigated the impact of order flows on exchange rates and found that they can be used to explain and forecast rates in the short term. This is viewed as a micro-approach to foreign exchange. Order flows are defined as the differences between seller- and buyer-initiated volumes. In practice, models based on order flow analysis are often used in combination with fundamental and technical analyses. A number of empirical studies show that order flow analyses have good explanatory power in the short and medium term, in contrast to fundamental analyses. In 2005, Martin Evans and Richard Lyons showed in a paper entitled "Understanding Order Flow" that micro-based models also have better forecasting power than both standard macro-models and random walk models with a horizon of from one day to one month.

SPOT AND FORWARD RATES

Spot (transactions for immediate settlement) and forward (transactions for future settlement) contracts of currency pairs are two of the main instruments of foreign exchange trading in which the BIS collates information on global trading volumes in its triennial surveys. The pricing of forwards helps us better understand the relationship between currencies and interest rates. The forward contract is similar to the spot exchange except that the time period of the contract is longer. So, forward contracts have an exchange rate that differs from the spot rate and this difference reflects the difference in interest rates between the two currencies. Forward rates, spot rates, and interest rates are related by *interest rate parity*. The principle behind interest rate parity is that there shouldn't be any arbitrage opportunities between the spot market, the forward market, and the term structure of interest

 TERMINOLOGY

RANDOM WALK MODEL—Based on an investment theory that says market prices follow a random path up and down, without any influence by past price movements, making it impossible to predict with any accuracy in which direction the market will move at any point.

NOTE
ORDER FLOWS AND THE TRADITIONAL CONCEPT OF DEMAND

Order flow—the variable that conveys information in the micro approach—is not the same thing as the traditional concept of excess demand. Excess demand equals zero in equilibrium, but order flow generally does not equal zero. Order flow is defined as the cumulative flow of signed transactions, where each transaction is signed positively or negatively depending on whether the initiator of the transaction (the non-quoting counterparty) is buying or selling, respectively. At an even more basic level, then, order flow is not even the same as demand: order flow measures actual transactions, whereas demand changes need not involve any transactions whatsoever. Consider, for example, textbook models of exchange rates. In those models, shifts in macro fundamentals cause shifts in demand and price, but without any transactions taking place, or needing to take place, for the price change to occur; that is, demand is shifting but no order flow is occurring because at the new price people are indifferent again between buying and selling. These textbook models are unable to account for the strong positive correlations between signed order flow and the direction of price changes found in the data because they assume that all demand shifts are driven by changes in public information.

Source: Martin Evans and Richard Lyons, *Frequently Asked Questions About the Micro Approach to FX*, July 2004

rates in the two countries. If interest rate parity is violated, an arbitrage opportunity exists. In other words, the forward rate of the currency should be the spot rate plus the interest to be earned in the time period of the forward contract.

The relationship between the spot and the forward rate is determined by the difference in the rates of interest earned on the respective currencies in the currency pair. Forward rates can be quoted in two ways—as an outright quote or as forward points (also called a swap rate). The outright quote is simply a bid-ask price similar to spot market quotes. The "forward points" are the amounts that need to be added to or subtracted from the spot rates. The "forward premium" or "discount" is typically the difference in short-term interest rates between the two countries.

It is important to note that forward rates are not expectations of what the spot rate will be in the future. It is simply a rate that factors in the interest rate differential between two currencies over the period for which a forward contract is entered into. For example, if you want to calculate the

NOTE
INTEREST RATE PARITY AND ARBITRAGE

According to interest rate parity, the difference between the (risk-free) interest rates paid on two currencies should be equal to the differences between the spot and forward rates. If interest rate parity is violated, then an arbitrage opportunity exists. The simplest example of this is what would happen if the forward rate was the same as the spot rate but the interest rates were different, then investors would:

1. borrow in the currency with the lower rate

2. convert the cash at spot rates

3. enter into a forward contract to convert the cash plus the expected interest at the same rate

4. invest the money at the higher rate

5. convert back through the forward contract

6. repay the principal and the interest, knowing the latter will be less than the interest received.

Therefore, we can expect interest rate parity to apply. However, there is evidence of forward rate bias. This is the tendency of currency markets to over-estimate changes in exchange rates: The actual movements tend to be smaller than the expectations as measured by forward rates.

Source: http://moneyterms.co.uk/

90-day forward rate for the USD/CAD, you will have to factor the Canadian 90-day LIBOR and U.S. 90-day LIBOR into the calculation.

Spot, forward, and interest rates are important drivers in the determination of exchange rates. They also help us understand the key concept of uncovered interest parity, which is discussed by Federal Reserve Bank of San Francisco economist Michele Cavallo below.

CENTRAL BANKS' INFLUENCE ON EXCHANGE RATES

Finally, we need to know the influence that central banks have on exchange rates. In a pure floating exchange rate system, the central bank plays no part in determining exchange rates by intervening in foreign exchange markets. But such pure systems don't really exist and even the likes of the Federal Reserve, ECB, and BOJ do on occasion intervene in the foreign exchange

EXAMPLE
CALCULATION OF FORWARD RATES

Assume:

USD/GBP rate – 1.6000
USD 6-month interest rate – 1.20%
GBP 6-month interest rate – 3.75%

A company with GBP needs to buy US$1 million in six months' time:

- Stage 1 – the bank borrows the GBP equivalent of US$1 million (£625,000) at 3.75%   Interest cost = £625,000 × 3.75% × 182/365 = £11,686

- Stage 2 – the bank converts £625,000 into USD at the current spot rate (1.6000) = US$1 million

- Stage 3 – US$1 million is not required by the customer for 6 months—the bank places this amount on deposit for 6 months. Interest received = US$1,000,000 × 1.20% × 180/360 = US$6,000

- Forward rate calculation = (US$1,000,000 + US$6,000)/ (£625,000 + £11,686) = 1.5800.

Thus, the forward rate is at a discount (minus 0.02 forward points) to the spot rate.

Source: Lloyds TSB Financial Markets

markets. When central banks intervene, their currency systems are known as "dirty floats." There are several reasons that interventions occur. One of the most important reasons is to stabilize fluctuations in the exchange rate. Another is to help reverse a widening trade deficit.

What are the tools that central banks use to conduct their interventions, ultimately aimed at either raising or lowering the value of their local currencies? One way is through changes to the domestic money supply. Intervention often starts with open market operations—for example, buying or selling government bonds—to change the domestic money supply. This will feed into domestic interest rates, and then to exchange rates. This type of intervention can take time, perhaps several weeks, to have the desired impact on exchange rates.

OPINION
THE "CARRY" TRADE

"According to economic theory, an investment strategy based on exploiting differences in interest rates across countries should yield no predictable profits. Consider two countries, one with a high interest rate, and the other with a low interest rate. According to another equilibrium condition of international financial markets called the "uncovered interest parity," the difference in interest rates between the two countries simply reflects the rate at which investors expect the high-interest-rate currency to depreciate against the low-interest-rate currency. When this depreciation occurs, investors who borrowed a given amount in the low-interest-rate currency and then lent it in the high-interest-rate currency will find that their return is worth less. The uncovered interest parity condition implies, indeed, that investors should expect to receive no profits, as they should expect the return from lending in the high-interest-rate currency to be worth ultimately as much as the cost of borrowing in the low-interest-rate currency.

In practice, however, investors in international financial markets do seem able to make profits through such strategies. In fact, market participants and commentators have often cited the carry trade as the source of several recent exchange rate swings.

Why can carry trades be profitable? If the exchange rate between the funding and the target currencies does not move, then the profit from the carry trade is proportional to both the interest rate differential and the forward premium between the two currencies. But, of course exchange rates do move, and, therefore, a carry trade involves exchange rate risk, in particular, the possibility that the target currency will depreciate against the funding currency. In that case, the value of the amount initially borrowed in the funding currency will increase in terms of the target currency, effectively increasing the borrowing cost of the strategy. By the same token, the higher interest rate obtained by lending in the target currency will be worth less in terms of the funding currency, ultimately trimming its profitability.

If the carry trade is a risky strategy, why are investors reported to use it extensively? The answer lies in the "forward premium puzzle." This is a well-known empirical anomaly of foreign exchange markets, and it concerns the implications of the forward premium for the realized rate of change in the value of one currency relative to another. Empirical evidence shows that currencies that are at a forward premium and that, correspondingly, have a low interest rate, actually tend, on average, to depreciate, not appreciate, as the theory of interest parity conditions predicts. Similarly, currencies that are at a forward discount and that, correspondingly, have a high interest rate, tend, on average, to appreciate, not depreciate. This anomaly, then, implies that an investor who enters a carry trade is quite likely to make predictable profits from two sources: the interest rate differential between two currencies and the appreciation of the high-interest-rate currency that was originally bought at a forward discount."

Source: Michele Cavallo, *"Interest Rates, Carry Trades, and Exchange Rate Movements,"* Federal Reserve Bank of San Francisco, November 17, 2006

A more direct method of intervention that central banks adopt is to enter the foreign exchange market to buy and sell their domestic currencies. A central bank could sell its local currency, thereby reducing its value, or it could raise its value by buying the currency. But the ability of a central bank to raise the value of its currency through this type of intervention is related to the amount of foreign exchange reserves it has accumulated. These reserves may run out, as we saw in Argentina's financial crisis.

Therefore, to understand how a central bank's intervention activities can have an impact on its local exchange rate, we simply need to know how its actions affect the country's money supply. A change in the money supply will affect the average interest rate in the short run, and the price level and hence inflation rate in the long run. Because central banks are generally entrusted to maintain domestic price stability, or to assist in maintaining appropriate interest rates, foreign exchange intervention will often interfere with one or more of these other goals. For example, if a central bank believes that current interest rates should be raised gradually in coming months in order to curb inflationary pressures, then an intervention to lower the value of the domestic currency would result in increases in the money supply and a decrease in interest rates, which is the opposite of what the bank wants. These sorts of conflicts usually result in a central bank "sterilizing" its intervention by requiring banks to keep more reserves with the central bank by requiring them to purchase central bank bonds and stopping that money from flowing into the market. Such sterilization counteracts the impact of domestic money supply interventions by offsetting them with purchases or sales of domestic assets.

For example in 2003, the BOJ intervened on behalf of the Ministry of Finance in foreign exchange markets in efforts to reduce the value of the yen. This action was driven by the perception that an excessively rapid rise in the value of the yen would hinder the fledgling economic recovery by reducing the competitiveness of Japan's exports. "Total foreign exchange intervention over the first ten months of 2003 amounted to over 17 trillion yen in assets, almost double the previous record for that length of time," noted senior research advisor Mark M. Spiegel in an essay entitled "Japanese Foreign Exchange Intervention," published in the Federal Reserve Board of San Francisco's *Economic Letter* in December 2003. He also observed that "sterilized intervention requires the central bank to follow the intervention, such as buying dollar assets with yen-denominated currency, with a countervailing sale of yen assets to mop up the extra yen that would otherwise be injected into the economy. Thus, the intervention would have no impact on the domestic money supply and would only alter the public's relative supplies of available yen and dollar assets." But as Spiegel pointed out, the "media characterized the interventions as 'unsterilized' because Japanese money supply had steadily increased along with the intensive intervention activity. The Nikkei Financial Daily noted at the time that the total value of interventions from the beginning of 2003 until the end of August matched almost exactly the increase in the BOJ's current account balance over that period, suggesting that the BOJ left the funds associated with its intervention activity in the market."

 SUMMARY

There are some of the types of publicly available information that can have an impact on short-run currency movements. These include:

- Local economic data releases and the anticipation of those releases

- Economic data releases in foreign countries, especially of major trading partners, and the anticipation of those releases

- Central banks hiking or lowering interest rates

- Central banks making public their thoughts on monetary policy

- The expectation of central banks making public their views on local interest rates or monetary policy

- Political developments globally and in individual countries

- Pronouncements from central banks, especially those of the Federal Reserve and the European Central Bank

- Natural disasters and perceptions about how they will impact economies

- Change in commodity prices, particularly oil and gold

With these factors in mind, efforts have been made to theoretically determine exchange rates through the use of exchange rate models. Some of the more popular exchange rate models include the monetarist model and the portfolio balance model, but none can still accurately predict currency movements. Adding to the mix, and uncertainty, is the concept of uncovered interest parity, which is also used to help explain currency movements. According to uncovered interest parity, the difference in interest rates between the two countries simply reflects the rate at which investors expect the high interest-rate currency to depreciate against the low interest-rate currency. When this depreciation occurs, investors who borrowed a given amount in the low interest-rate currency and then lent it in the high interest-rate currency will find that their return is worth less. The uncovered interest parity condition implies that investors should expect to receive no profits, as they should expect the return from lending in the high interest-rate currency to be worth ultimately as much as the cost of borrowing in the low interest-rate currency. In practice, however, investors in international financial markets do seem able to make profits through such strategies.

 QUICK QUIZ

1. Name four types of publicly available information that can have an impact on currency movements.

2. Why did hurricanes Katrina and Rita have a negative impact on the U.S. dollar?

3. How do rallies in a stock market typically affect its local currency?

4. What is the basis of the purchasing power parity model for exchange rates?

5. Would it be remiss to explain currency movements in terms of random walk models? Why?

6. Explain the difference between a forward premium and a forward discount?

7. What is the main theoretical conundrum associated with uncovered interest parity?

8. Why would central banks have to sterilize their interventions in foreign exchange markets?

7

FOREIGN EXCHANGE PRODUCTS

There are three main types of foreign exchange transactions:

- **Spot transactions:** A currency exchange in which delivery or settlement usually occurs within two business days of the trade date.

- **Forward transactions:** Agreements to buy or sell a currency at a specific date in the future, and at a specific rate agreed in advance.

- **Swaps:** agreements to change one currency for another now, and to convert the currencies back again at a later date, both at agreed prices.

In this chapter, we'll look more closely at these key transactions, why they are used and how they work.

SPOT TRANSACTIONS

As we have mentioned, spot transactions are single outright transactions involving the exchange of two currencies in currency pairs, such as USD/JPY or EUR/USD. This is done at a rate agreed on the date of the contract with cash settlement typically within two business days. There are several key functions of spot transactions:

- **Clearing Transactions**: When an investor in the U.S. buys a rupee bond issued in India, he must exchange U.S. dollars for the Indian rupee to pay for it. Alternatively, if an Australian company imports cars from Japan, it may have to pay for the cars in Japanese yen and thus it will have to exchange the Australian dollar for yen. These currency exchanges are usually done through the investor's or company's bank. For such transactions, banks receive orders from their clients on the spot market. These are usually regarded as "real" transactions, that is, transactions that facilitate the conduct of business in the real economy.

- **Arbitrage:** This action takes advantage of a price differential between the exchange rates of two or more currencies. Trades are executed to profit from the imbalance, or the difference, between the market prices. For example, if the USD/JPY trades at 116.49 in Tokyo and 116.48 in Singapore, traders can make a profit by buying the yen in Tokyo and selling it in Singapore, because the yen is stronger against the U.S. dollar in Singapore. Such arbitrage opportunities are fleeting as equilibrium levels are normally reached quickly between markets in different countries. But they can be very profitable for bigger players, such as banks, as they can trade huge amounts of money to ride on such discrepancies until they are gone. Even if the discrepancies are small the banks can make money because of the large trading volumes. Theoretically, arbitrage helps to promote the efficiency of markets by identifying and taking advantage of differences in pricing. In any market, differences in prices for the same goods and services will be exploited until some sort of convergence price is reached. In currency markets in particular, discrepancies in pricing are traded away instantly, usually via computerised trading platforms that are designed to watch for them.

- **Hedging:** Hedging is a way to reduce or cancel the risk of one investment by taking a risk in another investment. The process can avoid an unwanted business risk, while still enabling a profit from an investment activity. Firms that operate in international markets are exposed to currency risk or exchange rate risk. We know this as the risk that a company's business overseas, or the value of an asset, will be affected by changes in exchange rates. For example, if a U.S. firm orders outdoor garden ornaments from Bali and payment is due in 30 days, the firm incurs a risk that the Indonesian rupiah will strengthen against the U.S. dollar over the period, and it will have to pay more in U.S. dollar terms. To hedge against this risk, the firm may seek to buy the rupiah now and hold it till the payment is due. This will protect the U.S. company from any downside in USD/IDR (that is, a stronger rupiah) in the ensuing 30 days.

- **Speculation:** We have already seen that this is, by far, the most dominant activity in currency markets, with even retail players punting almost exclusively on currency movements when they trade online. By some estimates, speculation has accounted for more than 95% of all trading activity in foreign exchange markets in the last few years compared to about 20% of all foreign exchange trading activity in 1975. Speculation involves transactions undertaken for the sole purpose of making a profit from exchange rate fluctuations. Speculators tend to react to fast currency movements and follow market trends regardless of the long-term fundamental drivers.

Now that we know the basic reasons for spot transactions, we can introduce some important terms that are common in foreign exchange trading. These include:

- **Rollover:** This is a transaction designed to renew or extend spot deals. It is very common in foreign exchange markets because most traders are speculators and have no intention of taking delivery of the currency. The original delivery is extended and "exchanged" from the old spot delivery date to the current spot delivery date. There is often a carrying cost associated with rolling over a position, though sometimes traders can make money on a rollover. This is because the trader's profit/cost is determined by the difference in interest rates between the two currencies. The amount of the gain is determined by the interest rate differential between the two currencies, and fluctuates day-to-day with the movement of prices. The process of extending spot deals comprises what are also known in foreign exchange markets as "tomorrow-next procedures." For example if a spot transaction for the Japanese yen against the U.S. dollar was made on day one and was rolled over to day two, the cost to the buyer would be the difference in daily interest rates between of the U.S. and Japan multiplied by the amount of the transaction.

- **Buy/Sell Quotes and Pips:** There are always buying prices and selling prices for currencies in the foreign exchange market—the buy and sell quotes. In a currency pair, the sell quote is displayed on the left and is the price at which you can sell the base currency. It is also referred to as the bid price. The buy quote is displayed on the right and is the price at which you can buy the base currency. It is also referred to as the "ask" or "offer" price. For example, if the USD/SGD is quoted at 1.5500/1.5505, you can sell U.S. dollars for S$1.5500 each and you can buy U.S. dollars for S$1.5505. You often hear about prices moving "a few pips"—a pip (an acronym for Percentage in Point) is the smallest price increment a currency pair can make. Regardless of the fractional representation of the currency exchange rate, the pip is the smallest measure. For example, if the USD/SGD rises from 1.5500 to 1.5501, it has moved one pip. Or if the USD/JPY falls from 118.20 to 118.19, it has moved one pip. For traders, each pip represents a profit/loss value, and depends on the lot size, a standard amount of currency traded.

- **Margin Trading:** Foreign exchange trading is often conducted on the basis of margin trading. Margin trading allows foreign exchange market participants to trade large amounts of currencies with small deposits. For example, if a trader is required to pay a 5% margin deposit, to trade US$100,000, he only needs to place a deposit of US$5,000. The trader in this example is said to have a "gearing" of

20 times (US$5,000 × 20 = US$100,000). Margin trading contributes to the liquidity in the foreign exchange market and, when trading takes place in large amounts, it allows players to take better advantage of small price movements. But margin trading can be very risky, as illustrated by an advisory from the Commodity Futures Trading Commission (CFTC), the U.S. federal agency that regulates commodity futures and options markets within that country.

NOTE
WARNING: DON'T TRADE ON MARGIN UNLESS YOU UNDERSTAND WHAT IT MEANS

Margin trading can make you responsible for losses that greatly exceed the dollar amount you deposited. Many currency traders ask customers to give them money, which they sometimes refer to as "margin," often sums in the range of US$1,000 to US$5,000. However, those amounts, which are relatively small in the currency markets, actually control far larger dollar amounts of trading, a fact that often is poorly explained to customers. Don't trade on margin unless you fully understand what you are doing and are prepared to accept losses that exceed the margin amounts you paid.

Source: CFTC (Commodity Futures Trading Commission)

HOW SPOT TRANSACTIONS ARE CONDUCTED

A trader can contact a market maker to ask for a two-way quote for a particular currency when he wants to engage in a spot transaction. Previously this was done over the telephone on dedicated lines, but now electronic dealing systems are increasingly being used. These dealing systems have streamlined the process of trading in foreign exchange and made them accessible to more users, including retail players. There are many trading platforms offered by different companies that facilitate electronic trading but the basic elements are usually the same. Indeed, the trading services offered by online foreign exchange brokers can't really differ too much from each other because the core activity of participants is to buy or sell a currency. Therefore, these systems must be simple to use in order to attract a big customer base.

Typically, online trading services offer 24-hour access and also provide customers with comprehensive market information and a high level of execution. Many of the online trading platform providers advertise that their prices are real-time and competitive. The displayed prices are also advertised as being instantly executable so that traders can buy or sell the currencies instantly. A trading platform that continually rejects market orders because the transaction could not be executed at the price set by the customer will not survive for long.

An example of an simple online trading platform is online broker FXCM's FX Trading Station. (Note that FXCM has since upgraded its trading platform—it now offers Trading Station II. A video tour of the station is available at www.fxcm.com/software-preview.jsp.) FXCM's executives say an average of 2,900,000 currency trading orders are placed via its platform each month. A brief look at some of the functions offered by this system may be useful to the reader, but it should be reiterated that there is a plethora of trading platforms in the Internet space that offer similar online trading services.

CASE STUDY: FXCM'S TRADING STATION

The graphics below show some screenshots from FXCM's FX Trading Station:

Menu Bar

Clicking on the seven lighter buttons to the left opens dialogue boxes that facilitate the purchase or sale of currencies. FXCM says its "Quote" button has been disabled because all quotes appearing in the dealing rates window of its FX Trading Station are executable at the market price displayed and there is no need to request a quote from the market maker. The "Stop/Limit" button allows the user to set parameters to reduce his losses if his currency trade goes in the opposite direction to what he expects or to take profit if the currency has reached his profit target. The "Report" function allows the customer to view his account status and activity on a daily, weekly, monthly, or yearly basis. The three darker buttons to the right include the value-added services that online foreign exchange brokers offer, such as research, trading room, and chatroom facilities. FXCM says the trading room facility gives customers access to "professional trading tools similar to those used by institutional trading desks."

Placing a market order

Section of Dealing Rates Window

Market Order Dialogue Box

To place an order, the customer will click on the price where he would like to buy/sell the currency pair in the dealing rates window. This will bring up the market order dialogue box. These are shown in the two graphics above. Once the customer clicks "OK," FXCM says it will make every effort to fill the trade at the price requested. If the order is requested but the price has moved already, the customer will get a message saying that the market price has moved for him, so that he can decide on his next trading move. FXCM's FX Trading Station has an "Open Positions" window which shows the information a customer may need, including the open price and a real-time profit/loss calculation on the position in terms of both pips and dollars.

Source: *FXCM*

TRADERS' TALK

While electronic trading is becoming increasingly popular, foreign exchange players continue to call each other to make trades. It's unlikely that phone calls will be completely replaced, just as ATMs can't fully replace bank tellers. It is similar to online equity traders who maintain relationships with brokers to get an on-the-ground feel for the market. In the foreign exchange markets of today, placing orders through the phone applies more to the bigger players who deal with larger amounts, and who want direct confirmation of their trades from market makers. As such, it is still useful to outline a typical interaction between two traders engaging in a foreign exchange transaction. This is described below:

- Dealer A wants quotes from market maker B at which he can buy or sell 20 million Singapore dollars. He asks B for rates on **"spot dollar-sing on 20 dollars"** or perhaps **"I would like a price on 20 lots of dollar-sing."**

- B would reply **"dollar-sing is 1.5340-50,"** or just **"40-50"** if it's understood that the prefix is 1.53. Note that 1.5340 is the bid price and 1.5350 is the ask price. It means that B is willing to buy 20 million Singapore dollars at the rate of 1.5340 per U.S. dollar and sell at 1.5350.

- This bid-ask quote will be provided quickly by B and A has to respond promptly. The market maker may change or withdraw his quote at any time provided he says **"Change"** or **"Off"** before the quote has been accepted by A.

- When he hears the quotes, A will either agree to buy or sell by saying **"I buy"** or **"I sell"** and B replies by saying something like **"Done."** For example, A could say **"I buy 20 lots of dollar-sing at 1.5350."** Or A may also say **"Pass"** or **"Nothing done"** on the quote and perhaps look for another quote from another market maker he deals with. Or he may go back to B at a later time.

- Typically, there is no negotiation of the rate between the two traders.

- Once the deal is done, A and B each completes a record of the trade called a "ticket" with the currencies traded, the rate, the name and the city of the counterparties.

- The two tickets, formerly written on paper but now usually produced electronically, are promptly transmitted to the back offices of the two dealers for confirmation and payment.

NOTE
HOW TO RESOLVE TRADE-RELATED PROBLEMS

Disputes in foreign exchange trading may arise over misunderstandings or errors by either a trader or a broker. Whenever a trade is aborted, managers and traders must recognize that it may be impossible for the broker to find another counterparty at the original price. Managers should ensure that their staff understand that it is inappropriate to force a broker to accept a transaction in which a counterparty has withdrawn its interest before the trade could be consummated—a practice known as "stuffing."

Disputes, however, are inevitable, and management should establish clear policies and procedures for resolution at the senior management level with a transparent audit trail. For example, in many markets difference cheques are exchanged. Informal dispute resolution practices that sometimes develop in the market can be inconsistent with sound business practices. Care must be taken that informal dispute resolutions are achieved through good faith, arm's-length negotiation. Differences should routinely be referred to senior management for resolution, a process that effectively shifts the dispute from the trading level to the institution. In addition, maintaining records of trades conducted through automated dealing systems or executed over the telephone can aid in resolving disputed transactions.

Traders should not renege on a transaction, claiming credit line constraints, in an effort to "settle" a personal dispute. Instead, senior management should be made aware of a problem so that both counterparties may act to address and solve the issues. In all cases and at all times, traders should maintain professionalism, confidentiality, and proper language in telephone and electronic conversations with traders at other institutions.

Source: Guidelines for Foreign Exchange Trading Activities, Foreign Exchange Committee, New York Federal Reserve Board, July 2004

However as in any kind of business, disputes or disagreements between traders do occur in foreign exchange trading. In July 2004, the Foreign Exchange Committee of the New York Federal Reserve Board offered some guidelines for the foreign exchange trade which are outlined in the panel "How To Resolve Trade-Related Problems." In the context of our example above, A would represent the trader and B the broker.

TYPES OF ORDERS IN FOREIGN EXCHANGE MARKETS

It is important to remember that in any spot contract, there are a few variables that need to be agreed upon. They are:

- The currencies to be bought and sold. In every contract there are two currencies—the one that is bought and the one that is sold

- The amount of currency to be bought or sold

- The date at which the contract matures

- The rate at which the exchange of currencies will occur

There are several different types of orders in the foreign exchange market, which get ever more sophisticated as technology progresses. Some of the more common order types are given below and demonstrated in terms of a EUR/USD transaction.

- **Market Order:** An order at the current market price. If the current price of EUR/USD is 1.3100, a trader's market order will be executed at that price.

- **Entry Order:** This type of order is executed when the price touches a pre-specified level. It remains in effect until cancelled by the customer. For example, if the EUR/USD is currently at 1.3100, the entry order could be placed at 1.3090. Thus, the trader expects the currency pair to fall and is waiting to pick it up at 1.3090.

- **Stop-Entry Order:** An order to buy above or sell below the market at a pre-specified level, on the basis that the price will continue in the same direction from that point. This sort of order is placed when a trader is not sure if a currency pair will rise but once it breaks above a certain level, the trader expects the pair to rise further. For example, say the current price of EUR/USD is 1.3100. The trader expects a further gain in the pair if it rises above 1.3110. So, he places a stop-entry order above 1.3110, to ride on the anticipated further gains.

- **Limit Order:** An order to take profit at a pre-specified level. For example, if a trader buys EUR/USD at 1.3100 and has a profit target of 15 pips, then a limit order would be set 15 pips above 1.3100, or at 1.3115.

- **Stop-Loss Order:** An order to limit losses at a pre-specified level. For example, if a trader buys EUR/USD at 1.3100 and is prepared to lose 15 pips, then he would place a stop-loss order at 15 pips below

1.3100 or 1.3085. The stop-loss order acts as a safety net for his trade, controlling his losses.

- **OCO Order:** One Cancels the Other. Two orders whose outcome relies on the other—if one is executed, the other is cancelled. This is a particularly useful order type in that it allows traders to execute specific trading strategies based on technical analysis—without having to watch the market pip by pip.

EXAMPLE
A SIMPLE FOREIGN EXCHANGE TRANSACTION

Now we have explained the basics of spot transactions, let's look at the mechanics of transactions including profit/loss scenarios:

1. Assume a retail trader has a trading account of 10,000 Singapore dollars with a 5% margin deposit—the trader can therefore trade up to 200,000 Singapore dollars.

2. USD/SGD is currently quoted at 1.6500–1.6505 and he places a market order to buy 100,000 U.S. dollars at 1.6500, expecting the USD to rise against the SGD. At the same time, the trader places a stop-loss order at 1.6480, 20 pips below his market order price and a limit order at 1.6550, 50 pips above the order price.

3. The notional value of this trade is 165,000 Singapore dollars (100,000 U.S. dollars multiplied by 1.6500). As his margin depositis 5%, he will need to deposit 8,250 Singapore dollars to take up the position. If the USD strengthens against the SGD as expected and the limit order is reached at 1.6550, the position is closed.

4. Ignoring any related costs, the trader has made a profit of 50 pips on the position. For this trade, each pip gain represents a profit of 10 Singapore dollars. So, the total profit is 500 Singapore dollars. This represents a return of 500/8,250 or 6.1% on this particular trade.

5. If the USD/SGD falls instead of rising, his stop-loss order will kick in at 1.6480. When that happens the trader would have lost 200 Singapore dollars on the trade (20 pips multiplied by S$10 per pip), but the stop-loss order allows him to exit the position.

CROSS RATES

Spot transactions also involve cross currencies—two currencies, neither of which is the U.S. dollar. Major traded crosses include EUR/JPY, EUR/GBP, and AUD/JPY. For example, trade in the AUD/JPY cross is influenced by "Uridashi" bonds issued to Japanese investors in Australia. These are bonds in the currency of the issuer. Maturing Uridashi bonds will put downward pressure on the AUD as Japanese investors may want to convert the Australian dollars they receive to yen, to repatriate their funds. Apart from bond issuance such as uridashis in Australia and New Zealand, as well as yen-denominated "Samurai" bonds issued by non-Japanese companies in Japan, demand for different types of crosses is also growing as companies engage in more international trade. For example, a Japanese company doing business in South Korea may need

EXAMPLE
CALCULATING CROSS RATES

Say, the bid-ask spread between the Australian dollar and the U.S. dollar (AUD/USD) is 0.7500–0.7505, while the NZD/USD bid-ask spread is 0.6850–0.6854. What is the bid-ask spread for the cross rate AUD/NZD?

Determining the AUD/NZD bid:

1. Buy the USD by selling AUD at 0.7500 bid price for AUD/USD

2. Then sell USD to buy NZD at 0.6854 ask price for NZD/USD

3. Thus, the bid for the cross rate is 0.7500 AUD/USD/0.6854 NZD/USD = 1.0943 AUD/NZD

Determining the AUD/NZD ask:

1. Buy the USD by selling NZD at 0.6850 bid price for NZD/USD

2. Then sell USD to buy AUD at 0.7505 ask price for AUD/USD

3. Thus, the ask for the cross rate is 0.7505 AUD/USD/0.6850 NZD/USD = 1.0956 AUD/NZD

So, the bid-ask price for AUD/NZD is **1.0943–1.0956.** Note that the bid-ask spreads are wider for the cross than you will find for major currency pairs like EUR/USD. This is usually an indication that trading volumes are not as high for this type of transaction.

to conduct spot transactions for the JPY/KRW cross. Indeed, the Bank of Korea keeps a close watch on JPY/KRW as it doesn't want the won to strengthen too much relative to the yen. This may negatively affect the competitiveness of South Korea's exports against Japan's exports. Cross rates are calculated from the currencies of each of the two countries and a third country, usually the U.S. Therefore, the JPY/KRW is calculated from the USD/JPY and USD/KRW, and the AUD/NZD is calculated from AUD/USD and NZD/USD.

FORWARD CONTRACTS

We have already noted that forward contracts are over-the-counter agreements by counterparties to exchange a specified amount of different currencies at some future date, with the exchange rate being set at the time the contract is entered into. With a forward contract, a price is established on the trade date, but cash changes hands only on the settlement date. Here is an example of a forward transaction:

CASE STUDY: HOW FORWARDS ARE USED BY A COMPANY

A Malaysian infrastructure construction company, KL Transport Corporation, has just won a contract to build a stretch of road in India. The contract is signed for 10,000,000 Indian rupees, all of which will be paid after the completion of the work. This amount is consistent with KL Transport's expectation of gaining a minimum revenue of 1,000,000 Malaysian ringgit at the exchange rate of 0.10 ringgit per rupee from the project.

However, since the exchange rate could fluctuate and end with a possible depreciation of the rupee (which would reduce the company's revenue), KL Transport enters into a forward agreement with First State Bank of India to fix the exchange rate at 0.10 ringgit per rupee. The forward contract is a legal agreement, and constitutes an obligation on both parties involved. So, when the Malaysian company gets paid for its work, its ringgit revenues from the project will be based on 0.10 ringgit per rupee because of its deal with the bank.

The bank may have to find a counterparty for this transaction—either a party which wants to hedge against the appreciation of 10,000,000 rupees expiring at the same time or a party that wishes to speculate on an upward trend in rupees. If the bank itself plays the counterparty, then it bears the risk itself. By entering into a forward contract with maturity set around the time KL Transport expects to complete the project, it is guaranteed an exchange rate of 0.10 ringgit per rupee in the future irrespective of what happens to the spot rupee exchange rate. If the rupee were to depreciate during the period, KL Transport would be protected. However, if the rupee were to appreciate, then the Malaysian company would have to forego this favorable movement. In this case, the bank will profit from the deal. Even though this favorable movement represents a potential "loss" for KL Transport, it will proceed with the hedging since it knows an exchange rate of 0.10 ringgit per rupee is consistent with the revenue it expects from the project. The forward contract deal brings a degree of certainty to the financial position of KL Transport and it can focus on performing the important task at hand, which is building the road for its Indian client.

As indicated, KL Transport Corporation gets some peace of mind with its forward contract. By locking in future rates and the subsequent revenue stream, the Malaysian company is also able to make financial decisions on other projects more easily. It doesn't have to worry about fluctuations in the exchange rate over the course of its project in India as it is protected against any sharp depreciation of the Indian rupee against the Malaysian ringgit. And even if the rupee were to sharply appreciate, it can possibly reduce the implied losses from its forward contract by taking the risk of entering into another currency contract with a long position on the Indian rupee.

It must be noted that in a forward contract, each party has to be able to trust that the other party will hold to its side of the contract, because the two counterparties are exposed to each other's ability and willingness to perform the contract. There is a credit risk associated with each forward contract, which must be controlled. Often, this risk is controlled by banks, which act as intermediaries, giving reassurances about their clients. If its client fails to fulfil the forward contract, the bank assumes the obligation.

NON-DELIVERABLE FORWARDS

Another financial instrument that has quickly gained in importance in currency markets is the non-deliverable forward (NDF). Offered by banks, NDFs are forward contracts on non-convertible currencies or thinly traded currencies—these are currencies used for domestic transactions and not freely traded in currency markets, usually due to government restrictions (see Figure 7.1). NDFs are quoted against USD and settled in U.S. dollars.

Figure 7.1 — Examples of currencies where NDFs can be executed

Asia	Latin America
Chinese renminbi (CNY)	Argentine peso (ARS)
Indian rupee (INR)	Brazilian real (BRL)
Philippine peso (PHP)	Chilean peso (CLP)
South Korean won (KRW)	Colombian peso (COP)
Taiwan dollar (TWD)	Venezuelan bolivar (VEB)

Source: *Standard Chartered Bank*

There is no movement of the principal amounts of the two currencies contracted. The only movement is the settlement amount representing the difference between the contracted NDF rate and prevailing spot rate. So, NDFs are regarded as non-cash products, which are off a company's balance sheet. Furthermore, as the principal sums do not move, NDFs possess much lower counterparty risk.

The more active banks quote NDFs from between one month to one year. NDFs allow international companies and investors to hedge exchange rate exposure in countries like China and Taiwan without dealing in the underlying currency (in this case, the CNY and TWD respectively). Demand for NDFs arises principally out of regulatory and liquidity issues relating to the underlying currency. The Chinese Renminbi is a great example of a currency that is traded in the NDF market. With so much foreign investment reaching the mainland's shores these days, corporations and investors need to address risks associated with their exposure to the Chinese currency. As China doesn't have a free capital market yet, companies and investors turn to USD/CNY NDFs to mitigate risks. Since no Renminbi changes hands, their trading activity in USD/CNY NDFs doesn't have a direct impact on China's domestic market.

You will recall that the forward rate is the rate at which both parties execute the future currency exchange. For traditional forward contracts, this rate is based solely on the interest rate differential between both currencies and is derived so as to eliminate any arbitrage opportunities that may exist. This rule does not necessarily hold true for NDFs. The NDF market as a whole is somewhat illiquid and there may be restrictions on the notional size and maturity of the contracts. As such, NDF forward rates are not entirely based on interest rate differentials as forward contracts are with highly liquid and easily convertible currencies such as the Japanese yen or the Australian dollar. The NDF market tends to be more demand-and-supply driven. The following article shows how spot rates and non-deliverable forward rates relate to each other for the USD/CNY.

CURRENCY FUTURES
Currency futures were first created at the Chicago Mercantile Exchange (CME) in 1972, the year after President Nixon abandoned the gold standard.

NEWS CLIP
CHINA YUAN WEAKENS IN FORWARDS, FOCUS ON SPOT MARKET

The Chinese yuan weakened a touch in offshore forwards on Thursday, taking its cue from the spot market despite signs that Beijing may allow a speedier yuan appreciation.

In an article on its website on Wednesday, the official Xinhua news agency said the central bank would continue to pursue structural adjustment policies, including greater yuan flexibility. Dealers said the report suggested a pick-up in the pace of yuan gains, but a weakening in the currency on the spot foreign exchange market on Thursday meant offshore investors would be cautious for now.

China's central bank set the yuan's mid-point at 7.9762 per dollar on Thursday, up from Wednesday's close at 7.9713. "The (dollar/yuan) fixing was higher than yesterday so the reaction in NDFs to news overnight is not as great as expected," said a trader in Hong Kong. "They have said there is more possibility of the yuan strengthening but to my understanding, more possibility isn't equal to more appreciation."

One-month non-deliverable forwards (NDFs), offshore financial instruments used by foreign investors to bet on the future value of the yuan, priced the yuan at 7.9480 per dollar compared with 7.9470 late on Wednesday. The six-month contract moved to 7.8360 yuan per dollar, the weakest in about a week and down from 7.8340 on Wednesday. One-year NDFs priced the yuan at 7.7130 per dollar, also the weakest level in a week. It factors in about a 3.4% appreciation in the yuan.

The spot yuan has strengthened about 1.7% since it was revalued in July 2005.

"From the reports last night, you can tell there appears to be a consensus at the policy making level to allow faster appreciation of the currency," said Qing Wang, a senior currency strategist at Bank of America. "If that takes place, of course the NDF market will adjust accordingly. It depends on how the spot market moves from here."

Pressure inside and outside China for speedier yuan appreciation has intensified in the past two weeks, partly to try to cool booming growth in China's economy.

Beijing has ruled out another one-time revaluation of the currency, but some analysts say a widening of the yuan's trading band against the dollar now looks more likely. "This latest news supports our core view that China will widen the USD–CNY trading band from 0.3% daily to between 0.5%–1.0% in coming weeks," ABN AMRO senior currency strategist Shahab Jalinoos said in a note.

Source: "China yuan weakens in forwards, focus on spot market," *Reuters*, August 4, 2006

In a document entitled *The Birth of FX Futures*, CME chairman emeritus Leo Melamed writes that he asked the economist, Milton Friedman, in November 1971 whether he would consider doing an analysis on FX futures. They agreed that for a fee of US$7,500, Friedman would write a feasibility study on "The need for a futures market in currency." Submitted to the CME in December 1971, Professor Friedman's paper gave the concept of currency futures academic credibility. The CME was emboldened by this endorsement and set up trading in FX futures. This is what the CME says about that development:

> Until 1971, world currencies had been pegged to an international gold standard, but that year the gold standard was abolished and currency values were allowed to float. Leaders of CME recognized that a currency whose value was determined by market forces had become a commodity like any other, and therefore futures could be traded on it. There was (and still is) an enormous forward market for currency trading, but until then there were no exchange-traded, standardized futures on currencies. As with futures on agricultural commodities, currency futures offered an opportunity to hedge against risks in price changes, as well as to profit from changes in values. That year, CME formed the International Monetary Market (IMM), initially a separate exchange closely linked to CME, and hosted its first futures trades on foreign currencies.

The notion of trading futures on currencies was highly controversial. But the concept garnered credibility from the support of economist Milton Friedman, who pronounced that the IMM would "enable the world to operate more smoothly and effectively." Friedman's view proved correct, and now currency futures have become an integral part of international finance.

Unlike a forward contract, a currency futures contract is an agreement between two parties made through an organized exchange—in this case, a futures exchange. Investors use these futures contracts to hedge against foreign exchange risk. They can also be used to speculate on rising or falling exchange rates. The parties that trade on the exchange can trade for themselves or for their customers. There are specific rules and regulations that set the terms of the contract and the procedures for trading. The contract is for a specific amount of a specific currency to be delivered at a specific time determined by the exchange.

There is another key difference between forward and futures contracts. Intermediate gains or losses are posted each day during the life of the futures contract. This feature is known as *marking to market*. The intermediate gains or losses are given by the difference between today's futures price and yesterday's futures price. Every futures contract must be uniquely specified in order to be a tradeable instrument. Since all terms are determined in a currency futures contract, it can then be traded freely with other parties. So, traders can buy or sell futures contracts at will before their maturity date.

Settlement for futures contracts can occur over a range of dates while forward contracts typically only possess one settlement date. The futures exchange is the ultimate counterparty for all currency futures trades, so the only credit risk is the creditworthiness of the exchange. Once a trade is completed, the transaction is passed to the exchange's clearing house. Buyers and sellers of futures contracts have agreements with this clearing house. No credit intermediary is needed, but performance bonds, also called margins, are deposited to show that parties can honour their agreements to buy contracts. Note that futures margins are not collateral for loans, such as margins for foreign exchange spot trading, but good faith deposits demonstrating the ability and willingness of players to meet their contractual obligations.

For any given futures contract, brokers provide clients with its specifications, such as the contract sizes, time increments, trading hours, pricing limits, and other relevant information. This is an example of what a specification sheet might look like for euro FX futures:

Figure 7.2 — Specification Sheet from the Chicago Mercantile Exchange

FUTURES	OPTIONS
Ticker Symbol	Clearing = EC; Ticker = EC; GLOBEX = 6E; AON = LIG; (100 Threshold) &
Sample Quote	U.S. dollars per euro. Sample quote = 1.0922.
Contract Size	125,000 euro
Minimum Price Fluctuation (Tick)	Floor: Regular - 0.0001 = $12.50; Calendar Spread - 0.00005 = $6.25; All or None - 0.00005 = $6.25 GLOBEX®: Regular - 0.0001 = $12.50; Calendar Spread - 0.00005 = $6.25

Price Limit	Floor: No limits
	GLOBEX®: No limits
Contract Month Listings	Six months in the March Quarterly Cycle. Mar, Jun, Sep, Dec.
Trading Hours	Floor: 7.20 a.m. - 2.00 p.m. LTD(9.16 a.m.)^
	GLOBEX®: Mon/Thurs 5.00 p.m. - 4.00 p.m.
	Sun & Hol 5.00 p.m. - 4.00 p.m.
Last Trading Day	Trading ceases at 9.16 a.m. Central Time on the second business day immediately preceding the third Wednesday of the contract month (usually Monday).
Final Settlement Rule	Final settlement price is determined by the Trading Floor Pit Committee. Contract is physically delivered.
Position Limits/ Accountability	A person owing or controlling more than 10,000 contracts net long or net short in all contract months combined will provide, upon request, information regarding the nature of the position, trading strategy, and hedging information. For options, the option position accountability rule applies.
Trading Venue	Floor, GLOBEX®

In the specification sheet in Figure 7.2, the **ticker symbol** identifies the instrument on the CME. The **sample quote** is an indication of current bids and offers in the market of a particular contract. The **contract size** is the eligible size of a commodity that can be traded by the futures contract, which is fixed by the exchange. The **price limit** is the maximum daily price fluctuation on a futures contract during one session, as determined by the exchange. The setting of a price limit helps to contain any excessive volatility in the contract. The **contract month/year listings** are the month and year in which a given contract become deliverable if it is not liquidated or offset before the date specified for termination. The **last trading day** is the day on which trading ceases in a contract. **GLOBEX®** is CME's electronic trading application, while **floor** refers to where the futures can also be traded in the exchange. A floor trader is an individual who is registered to execute trades on the floor. **Six months in the March Quarterly Cycle** refers to how many contract month listings there are starting from the March quarter. **Position limits/accountability** spells out the limit that the exchange imposes on the number of positions that one person or entity can hold in a contract, while accountability makes it clear what the exchange can ask a person or entity, that is over the limit, to do.

CURRENCY OPTIONS

Another popular foreign exchange instrument is the currency option. It is a contract that grants the holder the right, but not the obligation, to buy or sell a currency at a (1) specified exchange rate during a (2) specified period of time. The buyer of a "Call Option" or "Call" has the right, but not the obligation to purchase the currency. In other words, he has the right to "call" the currency at the agreed rate, the "strike price". The buyer pays a fee (called a premium) for this call right. In "Put Option" or "Put" the seller ("writer") gives the buyers the right but not the obligation to sell a currency or other product to the writer (seller) of the option at a certain time for a certain price (the strike price). The writer (seller) has the obligation to purchase the currency or asset at that strike price, if the buyer decides to exercise the option. It is important to note that the writer of the option is agreeing to buy the currency if the buyer wants to exercise the option. The buyer pays the writer a fee (the "premium") for that right.

Currency options have gained acceptance as important tools in managing foreign exchange risk. They are used to offset the risks of unexpected movements in the foreign exchange market and effectively limit a trader's losses to the cost of purchasing the option. A currency option is no different from stock or commodity options except that the underlying asset is foreign exchange. In a currency option, one currency is bought and another sold. For example, an option to buy U.S. dollars for Japanese yen is a USD call and JPY put. Conversely, an option to sell USD for JPY is a USD put and a JPY call. Options basics like intrinsic value and time value, strike price and expiration period all apply to currency options and help in determining their pricing. Figure 7.3 gives an example of an option in USD/JPY:

Figure 7.3 — USD CALL/ JPY PUT

Face amount	: US$50,000,000
Option	: yen put
Option expiry	: 30 days
Strike	: 117.00
Exercise	: European

In this option, the expectation is that the JPY will fall against the USD from the current spot rate of 115. It would have been written when the USD/JPY currency pair was below the 117 level. Since it is a European option it can only be exercised at the end of the 30 days as stipulated in the terms of the contract. It would be profitable if the USD/JPY is lower than 117 at the end of 30 days. Then it is likely that the owner of the option will exercise it. Note that any premium quoted for a particular option during its life span reflects a consensus of its current value, which comprises both its intrinsic value and time value.

NOTE
THE GREEK OPTION MEASURES

Various measures, names after letters of the Greek alphabet, are used to measure risk in options.

- **Delta** measures the sensitivity to changes in the price of the underlying asset. It is the ratio between the change in the price of the underlying currency to the corresponding change in the option price. Positive delta means that the option position will rise in value if the currency rises and drop in value of the currency falls. Negative delta means that the option position will rise in value if the currency falls and drop in value if the currency rises.

- **Gamma** measures the rate of change in the delta. It is important because it indicates how a portfolio will react to large shifts in price.

- **Vega** measures the change in option prices when there is a change in volatility. It is the amount that the price of an option changes compared to a 1% change in volatility.

- **Theta** measures the decline rate in the value of an option as a result of the passage of time. It is the "time decay" on the value of an option. All things being equal as time passes an option will lose value as it nears maturity.

- **Rho** measures the sensitivity of an option to a change in interest rates.

- **Intrinsic Value:** Intrinsic value is the difference between the spot price and the strike or exercise price. A put option will have intrinsic value only when the spot price is below the strike price, as shown in Figure 7.3. A call option will have intrinsic value only when the spot price is above the strike price. Options which have positive intrinsic values are said to be "in-the-money."

- **Time Value:** When the price of a call or put option is more than its intrinsic value, it is because of its time value. Typically, time value is determined by five variables:

    - Spot or underlying price
    - Expected volatility of the underlying currency

- Exercise price
- Time to expiration
- Difference in the risk-free rate of interest that can be earned by the two currencies

Volatility is viewed as the most important factor among those listed above. It is a measure of movements in the price of the underlying currency. A high volatility increases the risk of the option and the uncertainty about future currency price movements, but also increases the probability that the option is in-the-money at expiration. Therefore, an increase in volatility causes an increase in the option price of both types—call and put options.

Volatilities are so important that option prices are typically quoted in units of implied volatility. The convention for converting volatilities to prices is the Garman–Kohlhagen option pricing formula, devised by Mark Garman and Steven Kohlhagen in 1983. Their work extended the Black–Scholes model, the first formalized pricing model for options. That model was devised by Fischer Black and Myron Scholes in 1973, initially to price European-style options on equities. It makes a number of assumptions, which include the ability to hedge continuously and also that price returns are normally distributed. Garman and Kohlhagen extended this model to cope with the presence of two interest rates—one for each currency. The original Black–Scholes concepts, like delta, gamma, theta, and vega, have become the basic vocabulary of option risk management.

TYPES OF CURRENCY OPTIONS

Typically, "plain vanilla" currency options refer to the standard puts and calls with a definitive structure, such as the USD call/JPY put in Figure 7.3. "Exotic" currency options may have a change in one or all of the standard features, and are often tailored to a specific investor's needs. Most exotic options are combinations of the following basic types of options:

- **Knock-Out Options:** These are like standard options except that they cease to exist if the underlying currency reaches a pre-determined level during the life of the option.

- **Knock-In Options:** These options are the reverse of knock-out options as they don't come into existence until the underlying currency reaches a certain pre-determined level. When this happens, a call or put option comes life and takes on all the usual characteristics associated with them.

- **Average Rate Options:** These options have their strike prices determined by an averaging process of the exchange rate, for example, the rate at the beginning of every month. The strike rate for the option is set at the end of the year at the average rate and used to calculate the value of the option.

NOTE
OPTIONS COMBINATIONS AND STRATEGIES

Combinations of options are used among professionals for many purposes, including taking directional views on currencies —anticipating that a particular currency will move up or down—or volatility views on currencies—anticipating that a particular exchange rate will vary by more or by less than the market expects. Among the options combinations that are currently most widely used by traders in the over-the-counter market are the following:

- **Straddle:** A straddle consists of one put and one call with the same expiration date, face amount, and strike price. The strike price is usually set at the forward rate, or at-the-money forward, where the delta is about 0.50. A long straddle gains if there is higher than forecast volatility, regardless of which of the two currencies in the pair goes up and which goes down—and any potential loss is limited to the cost of the two premiums. By the same token, a short straddle gains if there is less than expected volatility, and the potential gain is limited to the premiums. Thus, a trader buys volatility by buying a straddle, and sells volatility by selling a straddle. Straddles account for the largest volume of transactions in interbank trading.

- **Strangle:** A strangle differs from a straddle in that it consists of a put and a call at different strike prices, both of which are out-of-the-money, rather than at-the-money. Often the strike prices are set at 0.25 delta. It is a less aggressive position than the straddle—a long strangle costs less to buy, but it requires a higher volatility (relative to market expectations of volatility) to be profitable.

- **Risk Reversal:** A risk reversal is a directional play, rather than a volatility play. A dealer exchanges an out-of-the-money (OTM) put for an OTM call (or vice versa) with a counterparty. Since the OTM put and the OTM call will usually be of different values, the dealer pays or receives a premium for making the exchange. The dealer will quote the implied volatility differential at which he is prepared to a make the exchange.

Source: "Main Instruments: Over-the-Counter Market—Currency Options," New York Federal Reserve Board

- **Basket Options:** These options have all the characteristics of a standard option, except that the strike price is based on the weighted value of the component currencies, calculated in the buyer's base currency. The buyer stipulates the maturity of the option, the foreign currency amounts which make up the basket, and the strike price, which is expressed in units of the base currency.

FOREIGN EXCHANGE SWAPS

A foreign exchange swap is another over-the-counter, short-term derivative instrument. In foreign exchange swaps, one currency is swapped for another for a period of time, and then swapped back, creating an exchange and re-exchange—foreign exchange swaps don't provide a stream of interest payments like interest rate swaps.

Also, they are structurally different from currency swaps. Typically, currency swaps involve three exchanges between the two counterparties: they will exchange equal initial principal amounts of two currencies at the spot exchange rate; then exchange a stream of fixed or floating interest rate payments in their swapped currencies for the agreed period of the swap; and finally re-exchange the principal amount at maturity at the initial spot exchange rate. In contrast, each foreign exchange swap has two separate legs settling on two different value dates, despite being recorded in trading volume data as a single transaction. The two counterparties involved in a swap agree to exchange two currencies at a particular rate on one date—called the "near date"—and to reverse payments, typically on another specified subsequent date—called the "far date." In practice, a foreign exchange swap is the combination of a spot and forward transaction. Thus, foreign exchange swaps can be priced easily, based on available forward rates and, generally, satisfy the interest rate parity condition. The BIS triennial survey of 2004 showed that foreign exchange swaps comprise the most heavily traded product in currency markets.

Foreign exchange swaps come in different maturities, with the most common being those that mature inside of a week, but there are swaps with maturities of one week, one month, or three months. Foreign exchange swaps are most useful for those who have large amounts of one currency and need liquidity in another currency. For example, if a Singapore company enters a joint venture in Indonesia and needs Indonesian rupiah to cover the start-up costs of the venture for a period of time, it can change Singapore dollars to Indonesian rupiah and simultaneously exchange forward Indonesian rupiah to Singapore dollars. Consequently, it creates liquidity in Indonesian rupiah for itself, without having to borrow in the currency.

THE COST OF A FOREIGN EXCHANGE SWAP

In general, the cost of a foreign exchange swap is determined by the interest rate differential between the two swapped currencies. Arbitrage and the principle of interest rate parity, mentioned earlier in the book, will

EXAMPLE
THE MECHANICS OF A FOREIGN EXCHANGE SWAP

Say a company has EUR500,000 in currency, sitting in a bank account in Europe, invested at short-term rates. It has a funding requirement of US$450,000 for three months in the U.S. and wants to use its euro funds to meet the requirement. If it does not want to take any foreign exchange risk on the transaction, it can use a foreign exchange swap. This allows the company to use what it has in one currency to fund obligations in a different currency, without incurring foreign exchange risk. Therefore, foreign exchange swaps are useful management tools for companies that have assets and liabilities in different currencies.

In the foreign exchange swap transaction, the company agrees to sell the euros to the bank at the spot rate (USD/EUR) of 0.90. A full exchange of funds takes place on the near date and the company will deliver EUR500,000 to the bank. In return, the bank will deliver US$450,000 to the company on the near date. At the same time, the company would agree to buy back the euros and send back the U.S. dollars in three months' time at a spot price of 0.90, adjusted for forward points of minus 0.0045, for a forward price of 0.8955.

In this case, on the far date the bank would return the EUR500,000 to the company and the latter will send the bank US$447,750.

The forward points adjustment is easily explained and calculated. In this case, assume the prevailing interest rate in the eurozone is 5% and in the U.S. is 3%. By entering into the foreign exchange swap with the bank, the company is giving the bank the use of a currency which it could invest at 5%. In return the bank is giving the company the use of U.S. dollars which it can only invest at 3%. The purpose of the forward points adjustment is to equalize this interest rate differential and compensate the company for "giving up" or "receiving" the higher interest-bearing currency.

The forward points are easy to calculate and a simple method is outlined below:

Near Date

- On the near date the bank receives EUR500,000 and pays the company US$450,000.

- US$450,000 divided by EUR500,000 = Spot exchange rate of 0.9000

- In the three month period, the bank could earn 5% interest on the EUR500,000 for three months = EUR6,250

- In the three month period, the company could earn 3% interest on the US$450,000 for three months = US$3,375

- At the end of the period, the bank would have EUR506,250 while the company would have US$453,375

Far Date

- US$453,375 divided by EUR506,250 = Exchange Rate of 0.8955

- The bank returns the EUR500,000 to the company at the agreed upon rate of 0.8955 and the company sends the bank US$447,750

Note that the US$447,750 that the company sends back to the bank represents a US$2,250 "gain" on the transaction. This is simply the monetized difference between the interest rates in the two countries. Two percent earnings on EUR500,000 for three months translated back to U.S. dollars is US$2,250.

Source: "Foreign Exchange Swap Transaction," Allied Irish Bank

operate to make the cost of a foreign exchange swap equal to the foreign exchange value of the interest rate differential between the two currencies for the period of the swap. The cost of a foreign exchange swap is measured by swap points, or the foreign exchange equivalent of the interest rate differential between two currencies for the period. The difference between the amounts of interest that can be earned on the two currencies during the period of the swap can be calculated. For the period of the swap, the counterparty who holds the currency that pays the higher interest rate will pay the points, neutralizing the interest rate differential and equalizing the return on the two currencies. The counterparty who holds the currency that pays the lower interest will earn, or receive, the points.

The foreign exchange swap is a very flexible and convenient instrument that is used for a variety of funding, hedging, position management, speculative, and other purposes.

Foreign exchange swaps are also used by central banks as monetary policy tools. The motivation for central banks to undertake a swap is to either affect domestic liquidity or to manage foreign exchange reserves. Using an example from the Reserve Bank of New Zealand, this is how central banks can utilise foreign exchange swaps in their monetary operations:

EXAMPLE
CENTRAL BANK USE OF FOREIGN EXCHANGE SWAPS

Foreign exchange swaps allow the central bank to inject or withdraw New Zealand dollars (NZD) on specified dates. Foreign exchange swaps have two "legs" (or sides) to the transaction. When the bank injects cash, the first leg will involve selling NZD for another currency (usually USD) on a given day at a given exchange rate (e.g. 0.6850). The second or maturing leg of the transaction is when the NZD is bought back at a future date at a predetermined exchange rate (e.g. 0.6800). In this instance, the 0.0050 difference in the exchange rates between the first and second legs is called the forward points. These reflect the differential between New Zealand and U.S. interest rates. In this example, the bank invests the U.S. dollars received in the first leg for the same term as the foreign exchange swap. By performing a specific calculation using the U.S. deposit interest rate and the 0.0050 interest rate differential, it is possible to calculate a New Zealand interest rate return for the bank.

Source: Jan Frazer, "Liquidity management in the New Zealand banking system," Reserve Bank of New Zealand, Vol. 67(4).

 SUMMARY

Foreign exchange trading is often conducted on the basis of margin trading. Margin trading allows foreign exchange market participants to trade large amounts of currencies with small deposits. The main products being used in the foreign exchange markets include spot contracts, forwards, options and swaps. Spot transactions are single outright transactions involving the exchange of two currencies in currency pairs. They have several key uses which are:

- clearing transactions
- arbitrage
- hedging
- speculation

A trader can contact a market maker to ask for a two-way quote for a particular currency when he wants to engage in a spot transaction. Previously this was done over the telephone on dedicated lines, but now electronic dealing systems are increasingly being used. These dealing systems have streamlined the process of trading in foreign exchange and made them accessible to more users, including retail players. There are several types of orders for spot transactions through which traders execute their trading strategies. These include limit orders and stop-loss orders. Spot transactions also involve cross currencies, which usually refer to two currencies that are traded which do not involve the U.S. dollar. Elsewhere, forward contracts are over-the-counter agreements by counterparties to exchange a specified amount of different currencies at some future date, with the exchange rate being set at the time the contract is entered into. Non-deliverable forwards (NDFs) are also popular in foreign exchange markets because it allows traders to bet on currencies with trading restrictions like the Chinese yuan. A currency futures contract is similar to a forward contract except that it is an agreement between two parties made through an organized exchange. Another popular foreign exchange instrument is the currency option. They have gained acceptance as important tools in managing foreign exchange risk. Finally, foreign exchange swaps are very flexible and convenient instrument that are used for a variety of funding, hedging, position management, speculation, and other purposes.

QUICK QUIZ

1. Name three key functions of foreign exchange spot transactions.

2. What is meant by a rollover in spot transactions? Is there any cost associated with rollovers?

3. The USD/JPY currently trades at 118.20, while the EUR/USD trades at 1.3202. Where will a 10-pip upward move for USD/JPY take the currency pair? Where would a downward move of 10 pips take the EUR/USD?

4. Why is it considered potentially dangerous to trade on margin in foreign exchange markets?

5. Name four types of orders in spot transactions.

6. Bid-ask spreads tend to be wider for cross rates. What does this normally reflect?

7. Why are volatilities important to options?

8. Explain the basic mechanics of a foreign exchange swap. What is the main attraction of such swaps to companies that do business outside their home countries?

HEDGE FUNDS AND FOREIGN EXCHANGE

HEDGE FUNDS: WHAT ARE THEY AND WHERE DID THEY COME FROM

Some dictionaries describe a hedge fund as: "An investment company that uses high-risk techniques, such as borrowing money and selling short, in an effort to make extraordinary capital gains." Mario Gabelli, a famous hedge fund manager once said: "Today, if asked to define a hedge fund, I suspect most folks would characterize it as a highly speculative vehicle for unwitting fat cats and careless financial institutions to lose their shirts." But that description is at odds with the original intent of hedge funds. If you stopped someone on the street and asked him what a "hedge" was, he would probably reply: "A row of closely planted shrubs" or "a bunch of low plants to form a fence or boundary." Another definition is a barrier to keep people in line or a means of protection or defense. This aspect of a protection or defense is why hedge funds were originated. The idea was to undertake securities transactions that reduced the risk of loss of an existing investment position by counterbalancing one transaction against another.

That is what Alfred Winslow Jones had in mind when launched the first hedge fund in 1949. While he was working on the editorial staff of Fortune magazine he did an article about investment funds in 1948 and decided he might try his hand at the profession. After raising $100,000 including $40,000 of his own money he started an investment program designed to minimize the risk of holding long-term stock positions by short selling other stocks. (Short selling involves borrowing stock from someone else and then selling it in the market in the expectation that the price will go down so that you are able to buy back the stock you sold at a lower price and return the borrowed stock and make a profit.) This was what is now referred to as the classic long/short equities model used by many hedge funds today. Jones also borrowed money against his stock holdings in order to leverage his positions and thus enhance his returns. Another important innovation introduced by Jones in 1952 was the conversion of his fund from a general partnership into a limited partnership with a 20%

incentive fee as compensation for the managing partner. Jones thus was the first money manager to combine four characteristics: (1) short selling, (2) use of leverage, (3) sharing of risk in a partnership with other investors and (4) compensation based on investment performance. The hedge fund was thus born. When Fortune magazine featured an article in 1966 which reported the obscure investment fund that outperformed every mutual fund on the market with double-digit returns in one year and high double-digits return over five years, hedge funds became popular and many hedge funds were formed. Unfortunately many funds did not follow Jones' strategy of stock picking and hedging but instead became involved in riskier long-term leverage strategies. Therefore in 1969–70 many funds had large losses and during the bear market of 1973–74 a number of hedge funds went bust. Then there was a quiet period in the industry until Institutional Investor magazine in 1986 featured the double-digit returns of Julian Robertson's Tiger Fund. Again investors flocked to the industry which now offered thousands of funds and many different strategies. During the early 1990s many money manager left the traditional mutual fund industry to start hedge funds. History repeated itself in the late 1990s and the early 2000s when a number of famous hedge funds such as Robertson's Tiger Fund failed. However since that time the hedge fund industry has continued to grow and some estimate its size to be in excess of $1 trillion.

TYPES OF HEDGE FUNDS

The "hedge" of hedge funds has lost its meaning since today a hedge fund can engage in any type of investing and thus has a great deal of freedom as compared to more strictly regulated mutual funds. In mid-2008 the Barclay Hedge Database had the following types of hedge funds in their system (see next page).

Included in those fund categories are funds that not only invest in stocks, bonds or commodities but also currencies. At that time the Barclay service reported on 131 currency funds and managed accounts by currency traders.

Here is a description of some of the more popular types of strategies:

- **Market Neutral (or Relative Value) Funds:** These funds attempt to obtain returns (profits) that have low or no correlation with the traditional equity, fixed income or currency markets by using quantitative techniques. The idea is to improve the risk/return structure of a portfolio of investments.

- **Event Driven Funds:** Managers of such funds use particular events such as corporate acquisitions, spin-offs and restructuring or impending country rating downgrades or upgrades to make profitable investments.

TYPES OF HEDGE FUNDS

HEDGE FUND TYPE	ASSETS US$ BILLION
Convertible Arbitrage	28.1
Distressed Securities	78.9
Emerging Markets	303.2
Equity Long Bias	213.3
Equity Long/Short	269.2
Equity Long-Only	76.5
Equity Market Neutral	60.2
Event Driven	153.4
Fixed Income	156.3
Macro	85.2
Merger Arbitrage	38.3
Multi-Strategy	232.8
Sector Specific	106.0
Others	37.8

Source: *Barclay Hedge Database (2008)*

- **Long/Short Funds:** This is a model where the managers make a decision as to what direction a stock, bond, currency or commodity will move to, then position themselves long or short according to which direction they think their investments will move-going long sector they think will go up and short those they think will go down. Many managers use such valuation measures as price-to-book value ratios in their mathematical models to cull the winners from the losers.

- **Tactical Trading:** This strategy involves making a investment decision based on the direction of market prices of currencies, commodities, equities, bonds, etc. with some managers taking a "systematic" approach where they may follow a particular trend based on technical analysis while other managers may take "discretionary" approach relying on both fundamental valuation measures and technical analysis.

THE DISMAL SCIENCE: THE SEARCH FOR BETTER ECONOMIC POLICY

There had been many years of success, of rapid growth fueled by the money of international investors anxious to get in on a good thing. But then, with startling suddenness, things went sour. The leader admitted that some bad investments had been made and that even good investments had been financed with too much debt and too little equity. But much of the problem, he insisted, was other people's fault: Investors who pulled out their money at the first whiff of difficulty, forcing a sudden financial restructuring that aggravated the losses; hedge funds that, seeing his weakness, speculated against him. And so, to the shock of many, he suddenly changed the rules, imposing new restrictions on the ability of short-term investors to withdraw funds. "If we had been smart," he declared, "we would have tied up these guys for a long, long time when we were kings of the world rather than excrement."

No, this isn't another article about Malaysia and its fiery prime minister. The individual in question is Julian Robertson, manager of—yes—a hedge fund, Tiger Management, until recently the largest such fund in the world. In its heyday in the summer of 1998, Tiger had more than $20 billion under management, considerably more than George Soros' Quantum Fund, and was reputed to be even more aggressive than Quantum in making plays against troubled economies. Notably, Tiger was perhaps the biggest player in the yen "carry trade"—borrowing yen and investing the proceeds in dollars—and its short position in the yen put it in a position to benefit from troubles throughout Asia. But when the yen abruptly strengthened in the last few months of 1998, Tiger lost heavily—more than $2 billion on one day in October—and investors began pulling out. The losses continued in 1999—from January to the end of September Tiger lost 23 percent, compared with a gain of 5 percent for the average S&P 500 stock. By the end of September, between losses and withdrawals, Tiger was down to a mere $8 billion under management. And a furious Robertson, blaming flighty European investors for aggravating the problem, announced that henceforth the privilege of quarterly withdrawals would be revoked.

Source: Tiger's Tale The Leverage That Moved The World. By Paul Krugman. Posted Thursday, Nov. 4, 1999, at 3:30 AM ET

NEWS CLIP
LTCM, A HEDGE FUND "ABOVE SUSPICION"

So for the past year, governments in Asia and elsewhere have been politely told to put their house in order, make their systems more transparent and subject to the laws of the market. Above all, they must stop propping up failing banks or enterprises on the pretext of some connection with a crony or his hangers-on.

This argument may have lost some of its edge since the rescue of the flagship hedge fund, Long Term Capital Management (LTCM), on September 23, 1998. That was the day when William J. McDonough, president of the Federal Reserve Bank of New York, called on the cream of the international financial establishment to refloat the fund which was virtually bankrupt. And, in only a few hours, 15 or so American and European institutions (including three French banks) came up with US$3.5 billion in return for a 90% share in the fund and a promise that a supervisory board would be established.

The banks have played a double game in their dealings with LTCM. Many financial establishments and even state bodies, including the Chinese and Italian central banks, put money into it. The banks offered LTCM credit facilities that gave it a degree of leverage (the difference between the expected profit on an operation and the cost of financing it) that promised spectacular returns. They also served to offset its financial transactions. And, better still, many leading figures such as the chairmen of Merrill Lynch and Paine Webber, David Komansky and Donald Marron, put their own money into it.

The banks' staggering lack of curiosity about the fund's activities is particularly disturbing in view of the astronomical sums involved. At the beginning of the year, LTCM had capital of US$4.8 billion, a portfolio of US$200 billion (borrowing capacity in terms of leverage) and derivatives with a notional value of US$1,250 billion.

But the banks had put their faith in the fund's pedigree and reputation. The founder, John Meriwether, was a legendary trader who, after a spectacular career, had left Salomon Brothers following a scandal over the purchase of U.S. Treasury bonds. This had not tarnished his reputation or dented his confidence. Asked whether he believed in efficient markets, he replied: "I MAKE them efficient." Moreover, the fund's principal shareholders included two eminent experts in the "science" of risk, Myron Scholes and Robert Merton, who had been awarded the Nobel prize for economics in 1997 for their work on derivatives, and a dazzling array of professors of finance, young doctors of mathematics and physics and other "rocket scientists" capable of inventing extremely complex, daring and profitable financial schemes.

The fund's operations were conducted in absolute secrecy. Investors who asked questions were told to take their money somewhere else. Nevertheless, despite the minimum initial payment of US$10 million frozen for three years, there was a rush to invest and the results appeared to be well up to expectations. After taking 2% for "administrative expenses" and 25% of the profits, the fund was able to offer its shareholders returns of 42.8% in 1995, 40.8% in 1996, and "only" 17.1% in 1997 (the year of the Asian financial crisis). But in September, after mistakenly gambling on a convergence in interest rates, it found itself on the verge of bankruptcy.

Although he had no supervisory authority over the institution, Fed chief McDonough considered the rescue justified because a sudden and disorderly retreat from LTCM's positions would have posed unacceptable risks to the American economy. And in fact, in a climate of general panic, creditors would have had to get the best price they could for the US$200 billion portfolio. The Fed stresses that it was not really a rescue because no public funds were involved. It swears it had no intention of helping wealthy speculators out of a hole and vows that the shareholders will not emerge unscathed. The LTCM spokesman, on the other hand, thanked the firms that had contributed funds and added "the boys are very happy today. They're in better financial shape than ever over the long run."

The supervisory board has assigned some of its best derivatives experts to monitor the management of the fund, but the latest news is that the patient is still bleeding despite the injection of new blood. Two weeks after the rescue, the fund is rumored to have lost a further $200 million.

Source: Ibrahim Warde, "LTCM, a hedge fund above suspicion," *Le Monde Diplomatique*, November 1998

HEDGE FUNDS, CURRENCY MARKETS, AND CENTRAL BANKS

Concern regarding the activities of hedge funds and their impact on currencies has been the focus of central banks around the world. There have been a number of instances where hedge funds have had a big impact on currency movements and have made an enormous amount of money from currency speculation.

Black Wednesday

Probably the most famous example of currency speculation benefitting hedge funds was the success George Soros had in speculating on the pound sterling. On September 16, 1992, known as Black Wednesday, he sold US$10 billion worth of pounds short. Since the Bank of England did not want to raise interest rates on the pound in line with the interest rates of currencies in the European Exchange Rate Mechanism (ERM), and also refused to float the currency, a crisis was imminent, which Soros recognized. The Bank of England was finally forced to take its currency out of the ERM and devalue the pound sterling. According to reports, Soros earned an estimated US$1.1 billion on that trade and became famous for being "the man who broke the Bank of England."

NEWS CLIP
REVISITING BLACK WEDNESDAY

Black Wednesday, the day that sterling was forced out of the Exchange Rate Mechanism, twisted the old parameters of party politics out of all recognition. Until then, in the impressionistic way that most people view the parties, the Tories were seen as uncaring but competent, Labour as cuddly but inept. September 16, 1992 altered that equation utterly. From that date, the Tories ceased to be the hard-faced hommes d'affaires whom you would trust in a crisis. For the next 15 years, they were seen as uncaring and incompetent. Much of the political fall-out was, of course, merited. John Major had identified himself utterly with ERM membership: Indeed, he had called for it in his maiden speech in 1979. During the 23 months of membership, he kept insisting that leaving would be "the devaluer's option, the inflationary option". In fact, leaving the system was the beginning of the prosperity that Britain has enjoyed ever since: Inflation, interest rates and unemployment fell immediately, and Britain began the longest period of continuous growth in its history. Many voters drew the understandable conclusion that the Major government had been prepared to inflict a recession on the country rather than own up to a mistake. The notion that we "joined at the wrong rate", which suddenly came into vogue after the event, is in any case demonstrably false. The idea that 3 DM to the pound was too high a rate is hard to reconcile with it having been too low a rate two years before; or, for that matter, with the pound having recovered this level by 1998. The plain fact is that there is no permanently right rate. The funny thing is that their arguments for abandoning the pound today are exactly the same as their arguments for joining the ERM in the 1980s. Then, as now, euro-enthusiasts claimed that it would boost business. In fact, more than 100,000 firms went bankrupt during our 23 months of membership. Then, as now, they promised that it would create jobs. In fact, unemployment doubled to just under 3 million. Then, as now, they claimed that it would bring lower interest rates. But interest rates were in double figures for most of our time in the system despite inflation at barely three per cent and 1.75 million homes were overtaken by negative equity.

Then, as now, they assured us that it would bring stability. In the event, our trade-weighted exchange rate was less stable during membership than before or since. If these people had been employed as the forecasters in the private sector, they would be out of a job. But, because pro-Europeanism is regarded in media circles as evidence of re-spectability, the same clods who got it all so wrong last time are allowed to trot out the same discredited arguments. Will we never learn?

Source: Telegraph.co.uk, September 16, 2007

The Asian Financial Crisis

The Asian financial crisis that started in the summer of 1997 is also known at the "East Asian financial crises" and the "IMF crisis." It began in Thailand when the Thai central bank was forced to devalue the baht after massive efforts to defend it in the face of speculative attacks. The baht had been semi-pegged to the U.S. dollar and Thailand was running a current account deficit, making it vulnerable to such an attack. The government and the private sector had borrowed U.S. dollars extensively. Most damaging was the central bank's repeated public assertions that they would not allow a devaluation of the baht. This encouraged private Thai businesses to borrow U.S. dollars, which had lower interest rates than baht loans. The central bank thus set the country up for a disaster with businesses earning baht but having loans in U.S. dollars. When the baht was suddenly devalued, those U.S. dollar loans increased dramatically in baht terms. The crisis spread throughout Asia, the effects being falling currencies, stocks, and asset prices, combined with an incredible increase in private debt.

During the Asian currency crisis a number of Asian currencies crashed. The Philippine peso fell to a low of pesos 51.5 to US$1 by the end of 2000 from a 1994 high of about 24.2 pesos, a decline of 53%. (Please note that we say that the currency "fell to a low" because while previously one US$ could only purchase 24.2 pesos, later one dollar could purchase 51.5 pesos, so the pesos fell in value versus the US$.) The Thai baht fell from a high of baht 22.5 per US$1 in June of 1997 to a low of baht 55.9 by January of

1998, a drop of 60%. The South Korean won fell from a high of won 756 per US$ in July of 1995 to a low of 1960 by December of 1997, a 61% drop. Holders of Malaysian ringgit lost 48% in US$ terms when the ringgit went from 2.44 per US$1 in June of 1995 to a low of 4.66 by January of 1998. The Indonesian rupiah had the worst crash of all when it moved from rupiah 2130 to US$1 in January of 1995 to a low of 16,595 by June of 1998.

Hedge funds were active in the markets during each of these currency fluctuations and were able to profit from the dramatic changes in currency values taking place. Of course, there was a great deal of trend–following behavior with event driven funds and tactical traders playing their role in attempting to take advantage of the panic conditions in a number of countries.

Figure 8.1 — Crises-hit currencies in the 1990s

To US$	Low	Date	High	Date	% Drop from High to Low
Indonesian rupiah	16595	06/98	2130	01/95	-87%
South Korean won	1960	12/97	756	07/95	-61%
Thai baht	55.9	01/98	22.5	06/97	-60%
Philippines peso	51.5	10/00	24.2	12/94	-53%
Malaysian ringgit	4.66	01/98	2.44	06/95	-48%
British pounds	1.42	02/93	2	09/92	-29%

Periods for The Asian Countries are from Dec 1994 to Dec 2000 while that for U.K. is from Dec 1989 to Dec 1995

Figure 8.2 — Protestors against the IMF measures in 1997–98

Source: AFP Photo

Figure 8.3 — British pound

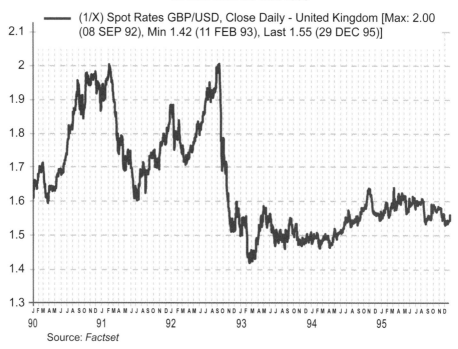

29 Dec 1989–29 Dec 1995

(1/X) Spot Rates GBP/USD, Close Daily - United Kingdom [Max: 2.00 (08 SEP 92), Min 1.42 (11 FEB 93), Last 1.55 (29 DEC 95)]

Source: Factset

Figure 8.4 — Indonesian rupiah

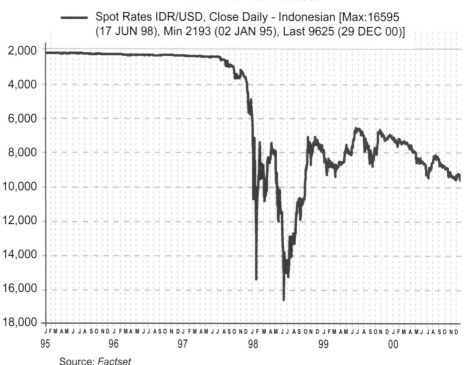

30 Dec 1994–29 Dec 2000

Spot Rates IDR/USD, Close Daily - Indonesian [Max:16595 (17 JUN 98), Min 2193 (02 JAN 95), Last 9625 (29 DEC 00)]

Source: Factset

Figure 8.5 — South Korean won

30 Dec 1994–29 Dec 2000

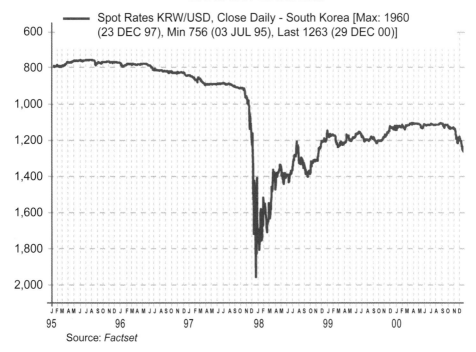

Source: *Factset*

Figure 8.6 — Thai baht

30 Dec 1994–29 Dec 2000

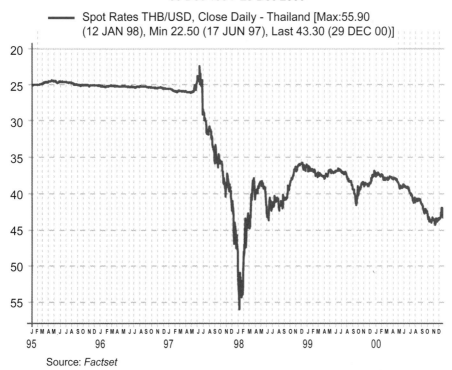

Source: *Factset*

Figure 8.7 — Philippines peso

30 Dec 1994–29 Dec 2000

Spot Rates PHP/USD, Close Daily - Philippines [Max: 51.50 (30 OCT 00), Min 24.20 (30 DEC 94), Last 49.90 (29 DEC 00)]

Source: *Factset*

Figure 8.8 — Malaysian ringgit

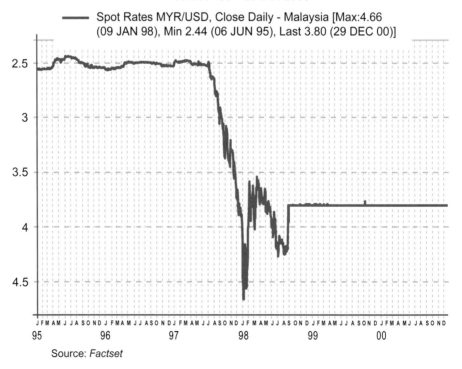

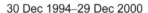

30 Dec 1994–29 Dec 2000

Spot Rates MYR/USD, Close Daily - Malaysia [Max:4.66 (09 JAN 98), Min 2.44 (06 JUN 95), Last 3.80 (29 DEC 00)]

Source: *Factset*

In Hong Kong, the Hong Kong Monetary Authority (HKMA) recognized that speculators were attempting to take advantage of the currency board system. This system was where overnight rates were automatically increased, in proportion to the sales of the local currency, in order to maintain the U.S. dollar peg. But those interest rate increases hit the stock market and speculators profited by short-selling shares. Financial Secretary Donald Tsang declared war on the speculators by buying up massive amounts of Hang Seng Index component shares. The HKMA spent US$15 billion to buy shares in various companies, in some cases becoming the largest shareholder. In 2001, after the Hong Kong stock market recovered, the HKMA started selling those shares and made a profit of US$4 billion.

At the start of 1997, the Malaysian ringgit was trading above 2.50 to the U.S. dollar but within days of the Thai baht devaluation, the ringgit

Figure 8.9 — Changing currency during the Asian financial crisis

Source: AFP Photo

was hit by speculators and fell to 3.80 per U.S. dollar. Capital controls were adopted and aid offered by the IMF was refused. Prime Minister Mahathir accused hedge funds of manipulating the Malaysian ringgit. At a World Bank–IMF meeting in Hong Kong, the Malaysian Prime Minister said: "I am saying that currency trading is unnecessary, unproductive, and totally immoral. It should be stopped."

From country to country, the fallout of the crisis took various forms. The International Monetary Fund (IMF) initiated a US$40 billion program to stabilize the currencies of the worst-hit countries—South Korea, Thailand, and Indonesia. Japan was in a deep recession and had a banking system with large amounts of bad debt. The U.S. purchased US$2 billion worth of Japanese yen to prevent a disastrous slide of that currency. Indonesia's President Suharto, who had led the country for 30 years, was forced to resign in 1998 after widespread rioting due to sharp price rises as a result of the rupiah's devaluation. In the Philippines, growth dropped to virtually zero in 1998 and economic growth in Asia generally slowed.

The development of the Asian crisis is an example of how the interplay of currency rates and interest rates can result in massive speculative swings. When borrowers of U.S. dollars were unable to pay back their loans, the rush to sell assets resulted in a collapse of the value of real estate and that led lenders to panic and accelerate the withdrawal of credit. As those creditors withdrew their money by converting local currencies into U.S. dollars, there was a massive flood of local currencies onto the market, further pushing down exchange rates. In order to prevent further currency depreciation, governments lifted interest rates and used their U.S. dollars to buy local currencies. But the high interest rates damaged their economies and the selling of U.S. dollars resulted in a near-emptying of their foreign reserve holdings, making them even more vulnerable to speculative attack.

At the time of the Asian currency crisis, then Malaysian Prime Minister Mahathir Mohamad accused George Soros of ruining Malaysia's economy with "massive currency speculation." There have also been allegations that hedge funds in general were a significant factor in causing the crisis. In July 1997, at the 30th ASEAN Ministerial Meeting held in Subang Jaya, Malaysia, the ministers issued a joint declaration expressing serious concern. But finance ministers of these same countries, who had attended the 3rd APEC finance ministers meeting in Kyoto, Japan in March 1996, had failed to double the amounts available under the "General Agreement to Borrow" and the "Emergency Finance Mechanism" which would have built capacity to prevent currency manipulation. The IMF created a series of bailout packages for the countries that were most badly hurt by the crisis, but those loan packages were tied to drastic economic reforms such as cutbacks on government spending to reduce deficits, allowing insolvent banks and other financial institutions to fail, and an aggressive program to raise interest rates. Of course, those measures only worsened the economic situation in the short term. In South Korea, there were demonstrations against the IMF with protesters holding banners such as, "IMF = I Am Fired." The rationale behind those measures was that confidence would be restored in the countries' fiscal solvency, bankrupt companies and banks that were careless in their lending practices would be penalized, and currency values would be protected. As a result of the IMF programs, the affected countries experienced economic crises as loans taken in U.S. dollars became much more expensive in local currencies. What followed were major currency devaluations, a high number of bankruptcies, rising unemployment, real estate crashes, and, of course, political and social unrest.

THE ETHICAL ISSUES OF CURRENCY SPECULATION

As a result of the Asian currency crisis, and many other such crises, there have been a number of studies designed to curb currency speculation. In the 1960s when the gold standard was still in force, Nobel Prize-winning economist James Tobin suggested the imposition of a tax on each currency transaction so as to discourage speculation. Tobin estimated that such a tax could yield billions of dollars every year, which could be channeled to address the world's food, health, and environmental problems. This so-called "Tobin Tax" would act to deter short-term transactions because it would make rapid movement of large sums between countries more expensive.

But the consensus view of economists is that financial markets work best if transaction costs are minimized, and a tax on currency transactions, along the lines that Tobin proposed, is a non-starter. Instead it is likely that more regional and community currencies could emerge as people search for ways to distance their regions and communities from the vagaries of speculation in foreign exchange markets. The former chief executive officer of Citibank, Walter Wriston, once said that currency speculation was "a kind of global plebiscite on the monetary and fiscal policies of governments." A plebiscite is a direct vote of the people of a nation on a matter of national importance. However, some critics say that currency speculation makes a mockery of this as the only matters of "national importance" to speculators are their profits. And they can only maximize their profits by destabilizing economies. As the economist, Bernard Lietaer, said: "Volatility creates profitability. The worst thing that can happen to a currency speculator is when nothing happens."

 SUMMARY

The influence of hedge funds on foreign exchange markets and the direction of exchange rates is a very important driver of exchange rates. While interbank players may be said to form the major force in foreign exchange markets, hedge funds can be described as their leading edge, embracing the latest technological, product and service innovations to garner the best returns for the portfolios that they manage. They can arguably be viewed as a conduit between the past and the future of foreign exchange markets. The hedge fund industry can be traced back to Alfred Winslow Jones who founded the first hedge fund in 1949. This fund took both long and short positions in shares so that it could gain whether share prices rose or fell. The hedge funds of today use both short selling and leveraged trading techniques. They typically charge management as well as incentive fees. The annual management fee, based on the year's net asset value, usually varies between one to three per cent while the incentive fee usually accounts for 15 to 25% of the net profits of the fund. Hedge funds are typically unregulated. The issue of regulation is a major talking point within and outside the hedge fund industry, which gets more heated whenever there's a collapse like Long-Term Capital Management in 1998 or Amaranth Advisors in 2006. The nature of the aftermaths of these two scandals needs to be noted as it gives us an insight to how the hedge fund industry has developed in recent years. Concern regarding the activities of hedge funds and their impact on currencies continues to be the focus of central banks around the world.

 QUICK QUIZ

1. Who founded the first hedge fund? What were the financial securities that were the focus of that hedge fund?

2. Which hedge fund collapsed raising questions about the roles of other financial institutions that had been putting money into it?

3. Who became famous as "the man who broke the Bank of England"?

4. Where did the Asian Financial Crisis of 1997 start?

5. Which countries were viewed as the three worst-hit in the Asian Financial Crisis?

REVIEW OF THE PAST AND LOOKING TO THE FUTURE

FUTURE

We started the book by showing how trade originally functioned without money in the form of coins and paper. Instead, many different forms of currency were used such as cattle, cowrie shells, beads, and jade. We discussed the popularity of barter trade, starting some time during the Neolithic period, and how it was eventually superseded by transactions involving coins and paper money. A key motivation for this shift was that people had to find mediums of exchange that were easier to transport and more widely accepted. We showed you where and when coins first appeared, tracing their origins back to a place in modern-day Turkey called Lydia. We also indicated why coins became popular, what they were made of and backed by. Then, we discussed the origins of paper money in China at around 800 AD and tracked the development of paper money in Europe in the centuries that followed. But we also pointed out that the early history of money is still cloudy with new views about the origins of money regularly being put forward by historians.

Next, we looked at the origins of modern-day financial centers starting with the humble coffee houses of London where people of all commercial persuasions would meet and information would be exchanged on areas of commerce, finance and shipping. We showed how the early information lists supplied by publicans helped to develop a thirst for more such information. We looked at the East India Company, one of the longest-surviving companies of all time. This helped us track the expansion of global trade from the seventeenth century. It is said that without this company, there would have been no British empire. We discussed the different standards against which money was backed through the ages like silver and gold and how the gold standard was abandoned by U.S. President Nixon in 1971. That precipitated the collapse of the Bretton Woods agreement. The development of foreign exchange markets as we know them today quickly followed. The advent of foreign exchange markets in the 1970s led to the development of interbank markets, which remain the foundation of foreign exchange trading. Interbank markets kicked off in the 1980s when large commercial banks began viewing foreign exchange trading as a business in itself. Rather than just buying and selling currencies for their customers as a standard banking service, they started to trade on their own account with other commercial banks. The number of participants in interbank markets has expanded from just the large commercial banks to other financial institutions such as finance companies, investment banks and central banks.

THE PRESENT

We have seen how electronic communication capabilities such as those provided by Reuters and EBS, followed by the internet, have helped trading volumes in the foreign exchange market soar. We also described services such as prime brokerage and "white-labelling" that are growing in these markets amid intense competition between the different liquidity providers to capture more market share in foreign exchange trading. We discussed why exchange rates are of significant concern to governments, as well as the role of central banks in foreign exchange markets. This was displayed with an inside look at the operations of the Bank of Japan. Like other central banks around the world, the BOJ has said that its mission is to lay the foundation for sound economic growth by maintaining price stability and ensuring the stability of the financial system.

As the interbank markets grew, a concurrent development was the growth of global portfolio investment that has resulted in even more new players trading in foreign exchange markets. Organisations such as insurance companies, pension funds, mutual funds and hedge funds entered the world of foreign exchange trading. Meanwhile, the growth of international trade and capital flows has resulted in more companies participating in foreign exchange markets. We discussed the main goals of corporations when they participate in foreign exchange trading, showing some simple examples of how exchange rates can have an impact on the operations of importers, exporters and other companies engaging in cross-border activity.

We also described the exposure to foreign exchange that consumers face on a daily basis—sometimes directly when they travel to different countries and often indirectly such as when they use or consume an imported product, which could be as simple as an apple or an orange. Amid the development of international trade and communications, foreign exchange markets have become more accessible to retail players and speculators.

Painting a broader picture of the foreign exchange market as it stands today, we also looked into how the international monetary system developed, discussing key organisations that support the system such as the IMF and WTO. The Federal Reserve Bank of New York describes the international monetary system as "the legal and institutional framework—the laws, rules, customs, instruments, and organisations—within which the foreign exchange market operates". As we have noted earlier, such a system has developed to have a stabilising influence on global currencies which, in turn, helps to foster economic cooperation between countries and facilitate international trade.

We have traced how global trade developed in the years that followed Bretton Woods and how bilateral free trade agreements have become popular in recent years as barriers to trade across borders are continuously torn down. Against these developments, factors such as a country's balance of payment and inflation give us an idea about which direction currencies flow within the international monetary system. The current account and trade deficits or surpluses of countries and the differences in inflation rates between countries allow us to ascertain the demand and supply for their currencies, which ultimately have an impact on exchange rates. We introduced the different kinds of currency regimes encompassing fixed rate systems and floating rate systems and their various hybrids. It should be reiterated that governments choose currency regimes that best suit their prevailing political and economic needs—there is still no one system that is used by all governments.

CHANGE AND GROWTH

We also examined the introduction of the euro. Indeed, as we mentioned, in some societies it is rare to see a new currency born, but in others new currencies are commonplace. Brazil and Argentina, for example, have had a number of currencies in the last 50 years. The creation of the euro was highly significant as it represented one of the largest monetary changeovers the world has ever seen. The euro is now regarded as the world's second most important currency, after the U.S. dollar. The creation of the euro saw disparate and nationalistic European countries come together to form a group dedicated to economic cooperation, fueled by a common currency. The development of the euro is also an opportunity to show what forms the basis for the creation of any currency and the roles that governments, central banks and other interest groups play.

We also looked at how the international monetary system has been pressured in recent years, with the classic example of the Argentine peso crisis in the 1990s and early 2000s.

After setting the backdrop for the global foreign exchange landscape, we finally introduced you to currencies themselves. Recall that foreign exchange trading volumes are now collated once every three years by the Bank for International Settlements. Its triennial survey for 2004 showed the staggering extent of foreign exchange trading—then at $1.9 trillion a day (BIS's latest survey, released late last year, shows trading volumes had hit US$ 3.2 trillion by April 2007.) Growth has been driven by hedge funds, central banks and other investors, adding to the liquidity already provided by commercial and investment banks. It should be stressed that the most important component of daily trading volume is speculative activity—this usually relates to global capital seeking the most profitable return in the shortest period of time. It is estimated that 95% of foreign exchange transactions are speculative. More than 40% of trades last less than two days, while about 80% of trades last less than one week—this means that 40% of currency trades are reversed in less than two days and 80% are reversed in less than a week.

We also described the major attractions of the foreign exchange market to participants. These include: (1) high liquidity levels, (2) high accessibility for many different types of participants and (3) efficiency. We introduced the different types of currencies traded. The U.S. dollar (USD), the euro (EUR), the British pound (GBP) and the Japanese yen (JPY) continue to be the four most important currencies in the world and account for the dominant share of foreign exchange trading. We looked at the factors that influence their exchange rates against each other and against other currencies of the world, as well as the financial linkages among economies including foreign exchange rates, interest rates, and foreign direct investment. We discussed the importance of power purchasing parities as well as interest rate parities to show how exchange rates will tend to find levels that best reflect the differentials in purchasing power and interest rates. We also delved into the notion that currencies have become an asset class in themselves.

CURRENCIES AS AN INVESTMENT

A number of studies have noted the attractiveness of currencies compared to bonds and stocks in investors' search for yield. Some experts say that interest in currencies as an asset class was reinforced by disappointing yields in stock and bond markets and investors are now using various exchange rate models to trade in currencies. We have delved deeper by looking at some of the more popular models.

The concept of uncovered interest rate parities was introduced. Recall that according to uncovered interest parity, the difference in interest rates between the two countries simply reflects the rate at which investors expect the high interest-rate currency to depreciate against the low interest-rate currency. When this depreciation occurs, investors who borrowed a given amount in the low interest-rate currency and then lent it in the high interest-rate currency will find that their return is worth less. Indeed, the uncovered interest parity condition implies that investors should expect to receive no profits, as they should expect the return from lending in the high interest-rate currency to ultimately be worth as much as the cost of borrowing in the low interest-rate currency. In practice, however, investors in international financial markets do seem able to make profits through such strategies. In fact, market participants and commentators have often cited the "carry trade" as the source of several recent exchange rate swings.

Finally, in the previous chapter, we looked at the main products that are being used in today's foreign exchange markets, including spot contracts, forwards, options and swaps. We also showed how dealers might conduct a spot transaction and the various types of orders that are executed in foreign exchange markets.

It should be reiterated that consumers' uses of currency help add a rich, vibrant layer to the global foreign exchange market. But consumers do not set exchange rates between currencies. They instead respond to exchange rates, which pass down to them through agents such as banks and moneychangers that influence currency rates. Of course, the supply and demand for currencies originate with the users of those currencies, the consumers, but the many intermediaries such as central banks, foreign exchange traders, and others, influence the ultimate fixing of exchange rates.

NEW TRENDS

What are the new trends that foreign exchange markets might see in the years to come? Well, something big is already happening and we have alluded to it earlier in this book—the development of digital money. Nowadays, money is largely electronic, with checking and savings account balances essentially entries in the computers of banks. The bulk of financial transactions are electronic. Indeed, the US$3.2 trillion average daily trading volume in foreign exchange markets is likely to be totally electronic. So, the question now is not if, but "How long will it be before the numerous, and usually small, transactions that still require cash and checks become electronic?"

Only a small fraction of trading volumes in foreign exchange markets is used to finance cross-border trade of goods and services. Most of it is used to trade in securities like shares, government bonds, corporate bonds, foreign exchange options, currency futures and derivatives, and increasingly, to gamble on foreign exchange markets themselves. A growing number of people and organizations are unhappy with this state of affairs as the scope for profitable investment in production has not kept pace with the accumulation of capital. They say that, in effect, money is churned to make more money, skipping the intermediary stage of producing useful goods and services. David Korten, author of the book *The Post-Corporate World: Life After Capitalism*, said that ordinary people are victims of the war of money against life. The consequences of this are rapid depletion of real wealth and concentration of money in the hands of a few. He wrote: Driven by a single-minded dedication to generating ever greater profits for the benefit of their investors, global corporations and financial institutions have turned their economic power into political power. They now dominate the decision processes of governments and are rewriting the rules of world commerce through international trade and investment agreements to allow themselves to expand their profits without regard to the social and environmental consequences borne by the larger society.

Bernard Lietaer, author of the 2001 book *The Future of Money: Creating New Wealth, Work and a Wiser World*, said that people have forgotten that they created money, which is now instead leading them around. A former banker but now based at the University of California, Berkeley, Lietaer said that it is time to design a money system that takes people towards sustainability and community. He wrote: Your money's value is determined by a global casino of unprecedented proportions: $2 trillion are traded per day in foreign exchange markets, 100 times more than the trading volume of all the stock markets of the world combined. Only two percent of these foreign exchange transactions relate to the "real" economy reflecting movements of real goods and services in the world, and 98% are purely speculative. This global casino is triggering the foreign exchange crises which shook Mexico

OPINION
ELECTRONIC MONEY

Electronic transactions are less expensive and increasingly becoming more convenient than those with cash or checks. For large institutions such as corporations and governments, this provides strong inducements for eliminating paper, and we will see an acceleration of the already rapid move towards business-to-business electronic commerce. However, the factors of cost and convenience are not likely by themselves to induce individuals to switch quickly. People are not faced with a choice between electronic money and the huge stones of Yap that weigh tons. Cash, checks, and credit cards work well. The advantages of electronic banking are not compelling for individuals, and the inertia of ingrained habits is great. As an example, tens of millions of passbook savings accounts still exist, although banks have been trying to eliminate them to reduce costs. The only way to get people to change quickly is to either compel them to do so, or offer them substantial inducements. Compulsion occurs when governments or corporations require Social Security or payroll checks to be handled by electronic funds transfers. Inducements to change can come either as lower costs, or as greater convenience (as in the rapid acceptance of electronic devices for paying for road and tunnel tolls). Therefore the speed with which cash and checks are displaced in transactions by individuals will depend largely on the actions by large institutions and how they are accepted by society, and are thus harder to predict.

Source: Andrew M. Odlyzko, "The Future of Money," Digital Technology Center, University of Minnesota

in 1994–95, Asia in 1997 and Russia in 1998. These emergencies are the dislocation symptoms of the old Industrial Age money system. Unless some precautions are taken soon, there is at least a 50–50 chance that the next five to ten years will see a global money meltdown, the only plausible way for a global depression. Lietaer, who helped to design the single European currency system, is now one of the champions of alternative, community-based currencies. Community currencies are value-exchange systems used at the local level to replace, in part, currencies and barter systems. Because they can only be earned and spent locally, they encourage local economic initiatives and enhance community control over economic life. Over the past 20 years, more than a hundred community currency projects of varying forms have been launched across the U.S. and thousands have been tested worldwide.

NEWS CLIP
QQ: CHINA'S NEW COIN OF THE REALM?

China's fastest-rising currency is not the yuan. It's the QQ coin—online play money created by marketers to sell such things as virtual flowers for instant-message buddies, cell phone ring tones and magical swords for online games. In recent weeks, the QQ coin's real-world value has risen as much as 70%.

It's the most extreme case of a so-called virtual currency blurring the boundaries between the online and real worlds—and challenging legal limits. A Chinese Internet company called Tencent Holdings Ltd designed the payment system in 2002 to allow its 233 million regular registered users to shop for treats in its virtual world. Virtual currencies are in use in many countries—but nowhere have they taken root more deeply than in China. Selling virtual amusement to China's Internet community, the world's second-largest, is big business. Tencent, a company listed on the Hong Kong stock exchange and famous in China for its penguin mascot, retails QQ coins for one yuan (13 cents) each, and also awards them for free to top-scoring videogamers to keep them playing. QQ's virtual universe is a marketing tool too—used by the likes of Coca-Cola Co. for promotions.

According to one government estimate, the total volume of trading in virtual items in China last year was worth about US$900 million. About 45% of that went for items in the Tencent world. Then last year something happened that Tencent hadn't originally planned. Online game sites beyond Tencent started accepting QQ coins as payment. The coins appeal as a safer, more practical way to conduct small online purchases, because credit cards are not yet commonplace in China.

At informal online currency marketplaces, thousands of users helped turn the QQ coins back into cash by selling them at a discount that varies based on the laws of supply and demand. Traders began jumping into the QQ coin market as an opportunity to make a quick yuan off of currency speculation. State-run media reported that some online shoppers began using QQ coins to buy real-world items such as CDs and makeup. So-called QQ Girls started accepting the coins as payment for intimate private chats online. Gamblers caught wind, too, and started using the currency to get around China's anti-gambling laws, converting wins in online mahjong and card games back into cash. Dozens of third-party trading posts sprouted up to ease transactions, turning the QQ coin into a kind of parallel currency.

Source: Geoffrey A. Fowler and Juying Qin, "QQ: China's New Coin of the Realm," *The Wall Street Journal*, March 30, 2007

NOTE
WHAT ARE COMMUNITY CURRENCIES?

Community currencies are meant to complement, not replace national currency systems. Small towns and cities are adopting community currencies to remind people to shop at community-based, owner-operated establishments, which keep the money in the community, unlike national chain stores. Community currencies also encourage those who lack opportunities in the formal economy, such as youth, senior citizens, and the unemployed, to contribute productively to local economic life, expanding the local economic base.

Conventional economic development strategies tend to look outside the community for new sources of investment capital. This approach discounts and often overlooks things that are valued and valuable to the local community. Community currencies enhance the value of and attention to locally—as opposed to nationally or globally—defined "supply and demand." One sociological study has shown that community currency movements are a response to high unemployment and poverty levels. Because a community currency gives unemployed and underemployed persons an opportunity to participate in the economy and serve the community, it promotes economic well-being and community-wide cooperation.

Moreover, because a community currency can only be used locally, the use of a successful community currency limits capital flight. Money earned in the region is spent in the region. The use of a local currency is also likely to generate increased services for the underserved. For example, with the aid of a local-currency grant, unemployed persons can earn money, in the form of a local currency, for assisting the elderly with shopping and other errands. Most of the existing community currency programs emphasize the non-economic benefits the currency offers in terms of community empowerment and self-reliance. These programs generate "social capital" that the formal economy cannot, and they enhance community life.

Source: Michiana Community Currency Initiative

APPENDIX:
ISO CURRENCY CODES

CODE	COUNTRY	
AED	United Arab Emirates	Dirham
AFN	Afghanistan	Afghani
ALL	Albania	Lek
AMD	Armenia	Dram
ANG	Netherlands Antilles	Guilder (also called Florin)
AOA	Angola	Kwanza
ARS	Argentina	Peso
AUD	Australia	Dollar
AWG	Aruba	Guilder (also called Florin)
AZN	Azerbaijan	New Manat
BAM	Bosnia and Herzegovina	Convertible Mark
BBD	Barbados	Dollar
BDT	Bangladesh	Taka
BGN	Bulgaria	Lev
BHD	Bahrain	Dinar
BIF	Burundi	Franc
BMD	Bermuda	Dollar
BND	Brunei Darussalam	Dollar
BOB	Bolivia	Boliviano
BRL	Brazil	Real
BSD	Bahamas	Dollar
BTN	Bhutan	Ngultrum
BWP	Botswana	Pula
BYR	Belarus	Ruble
BZD	Belize	Dollar
CAD	Canada	Dollar
CDF	Democratic Republic of Congo	Franc
CHF	Switzerland	Franc
CLP	Chile	Peso
CNY	China	Renminbi
COP	Colombia	Peso

CRC	Costa Rica	Colon
CUP	Cuba	Peso
CVE	Cape Verde	Escudo
CZK	Czech Republic	Koruna
DJF	Djibouti	Franc
DKK	Denmark	Krone
DOP	Dominican Republic	Peso
DZD	Algeria	Dinar
EEK	Estonia	Kroon
EGP	Egypt	Pound
ERN	Eritrea	Nakfa
ETB	Ethiopia	Birr
EUR	Eurozone	Euro
FJD	Fiji	Dollar
FKP	Falkland Islands	Pound
GBP	United Kingdom	Pound
GEL	Georgia	Lari
GGP	Guernsey	Pound
GHC	Ghana	Cedi
GIP	Gibraltar	Pound
GMD	Gambia	Dalasi
GNF	Guinea	Franc
GTQ	Guatemala	Quetzal
GYD	Guyana	Dollar
HKD	Hong Kong	Dollar
HNL	Honduras	Lempira
HRK	Croatia	Kuna
HTG	Haiti	Gourde
HUF	Hungary	Forint
IDR	Indonesia	Rupiah
ILS	Israel	New Shekel
IMP	Isle of Man	Pound
INR	India	Rupee
IQD	Iraq	Dinar
IRR	Iran	Rial
ISK	Iceland	Krona
JEP	Jersey	Pound
JMD	Jamaica	Dollar
JOD	Jordan	Dinar
JPY	Japan	Yen
KES	Kenya	Shilling
KGS	Kyrgyzstan	Som
KHR	Cambodia	Riel
KMF	Comoros	Franc
KPW	North Korea	Won
KRW	South Korea	Won

KWD	Kuwait	Dinar
KYD	Cayman Islands	Dollar
KZT	Kazakhstan	Tenge
LAK	Laos	Kip
LBP	Lebanon	Pound
LKR	Sri Lanka	Rupee
LRD	Liberia	Dollar
LSL	Lesotho	Loti
LTL	Lithuania	Lita
LVL	Latvia	Lat
LYD	Libya	Dinar
MAD	Morocco	Dirham
MDL	Moldova	Leu
MGA	Madagascar	Ariary
MKD	Macedonia	Denar
MMK	Myanmar (Burma)	Kyat
MNT	Mongolia	Tugrik
MOP	Macao	Pataca
MRO	Mauritania	Ouguiya
MUR	Mauritius	Rupee
MVR	Maldives	Rufiyaa
MWK	Malawi	Kwacha
MXN	Mexico	Peso
MYR	Malaysia	Ringgit
MZN	Mozambique	Metical
NAD	Namibia	Dollar
NGN	Nigeria	Naira
NIO	Nicaragua	Cordoba
NOK	Norway	Krone
NPR	Nepal	Rupee
NZD	New Zealand	Dollar
OMR	Oman	Rial
PAB	Panama	Balboa
PEN	Peru	Nuevo Sol
PGK	Papua New Guinea	Kina
PHP	The Philippines	Peso
PKR	Pakistan	Rupee
PLN	Poland	Zloty
PYG	Paraguay	Guarani
QAR	Qatar	Rial
RON	Romania	New Leu
RSD	Serbia	Dinar
RUB	Russia	Ruble
RWF	Rwanda	Franc
SAR	Saudi Arabia	Riyal
SBD	Solomon Islands	Dollar

SCR	Seychelles	Rupee
SDG	Sudan	Pound
SEK	Sweden	Krona
SGD	Singapore	Dollar
SHP	Saint Helena	Pound
SKK	Slovakia	Koruna
SLL	Sierra Leone	Leone
SOS	Somalia	Shilling
SRD	Suriname	Dollar
STD	Sao Tome and Principe	Dobra
SYP	Syria	Pound
SZL	Swaziland	Lilangeni
THB	Thailand	Baht
TJS	Tajikistan	Somoni
TMM	Turkmenistan	Manat
TND	Tunisia	Dinar
TOP	Tonga	Pa'anga
TRY	Turkey	New Lira
TTD	Trinidad and Tobago	Dollar
TWD	Taiwan	New Dollar
TZS	Tanzania	Shilling
UAH	Ukraine	Hryvnia
UGX	Uganda	Shilling
USD	United States of America	Dollar
UYU	Uruguay	Peso
UZS	Uzbekistan	Som
VEF	Venezuela	Bolívar Fuerte
VND	Vietnam	Dong
VUV	Vanuatu	Vatu
WST	Samoa	Tala
XDR	International Monetary Fund (IMF)	Special Drawing Rights
YER	Yemen	Rial
ZAR	South Africa	Rand
ZMK	Zambia	Kwacha
ZWN	Zimbabwe	Dollar

QUICK QUIZ ANSWERS

CHAPTER 1

1. The Neolithic period
2. In barter trade, A must want what B has, and B must simultaneously want what A has.
3. Cowrie shells
4. Medium of exchange; measure of value; store of value
5. Lydia
6. More than a millennium
7. The Precious Note of the Great Ming was issued in one denomination only. This was commercially inconvenient and the Note lost value.
8. The temple of Shamash

CHAPTER 2

1. Sir Thomas Gresham; Gresham's Law (bad money drives good money out of monetary systems).
2. Coffee houses
3. Opium
4. Thaler
5. Mexico
6. 1821
7. U.S. dollar
8. Smithsonian Agreement

CHAPTER 3

1. Pigeons
2. Market makers contribute to liquidity and price stability in the short term, and provide useful price information.
3. It allows them to outsource their currency pricing to banks which have larger liquidity bases.

4. Any five from: importing or exporting goods; buying assets; participating in joint venture projects; buying or selling stocks or bonds; opening foreign retail outlets; capacity expansions; goodwill payments; international payroll payments; charitable activities; legal proceedings; receiving and paying royalties; receiving and paying rent.
5. Maintain price stability; ensure the stability of Japan's financial system
6. Equities and long-term debt investments in developed markets
7. A few days only
8. To pay for their children's education in overseas universities; to pay for care in a foreign hospital; to remit money home if they are working overseas; to buy a wristwatch on an auction site on the internet; to deliver a present to a friend who's getting married in another country.

CHAPTER 4

1. International Monetary Fund, World Trade Organization, World Bank
2. They were devised to address the potential for inadequate reserves of gold and U.S. dollars.
3. Any five from: AFTA; ASEAN; CAN; CARICOM; CACM; CER; CIS; COMESA; EU; MERCOSUR; MSG; NAFTA.
4. Any three from: higher price levels; higher GDP; higher interest rates; lower trade barriers; higher exchange rates.
5. Full convertibility is in place when countries allow transactions in both their current and capital accounts.
6. Low inflation; low interest rates; sound state finances; stable exchange rate
7. Greece
8. The Argentine peso and the U.S. dollar were set at one-to-one parity.
9. The answer will depend on your nationality.

CHAPTER 5

1. Every three years
2. 95%
3. In a carry trade, an investor borrows in a low interest rate currency and, with these funds, takes a long position (buys) in a higher interest-rate currency, betting that the exchange rate will not change so as to offset the interest rate differential between the two currencies.
4. Any five from: 24-hour market; high liquidity; easy entry; simple trading conditions; neutral conditions; high leverage; low transaction costs; tight bid-ask spreads; real-time quotes and instant execution.
5. Participants can typically leverage their positions to as much as 100 times the cash they put up. Risks are commensurate with higher leverage there is a risk of losing a lot of money if a leveraged bet goes wrong.

6. Money that is issued on the authority, or fiat, of a government but not tied in value to a precious commodity. Each country has control over the supply and production of its own currency.
7. The U.S. dollar, the euro, the Japanese yen and the U.K. pound sterling
8. They are growing in importance because investors are constantly searching for new sources of yield to enhance their portfolios.

CHAPTER 6

1. Any four from: local economic data releases; foreign economic data releases; the raising or lowering of interest rates by central banks; public comment on monetary policy by central banks; the expectation of public comment on monetary policy by central banks; political developments; natural disasters; changes in commodity prices.
2. Hurricanes Katrina and Rita had a negative impact on the U.S. dollar because investors were worried about their impact on U.S. economic growth.
3. Stock market rallies usually lift a local currency because it creates more demand for that currency in order to buy the stocks.
4. Exchange rates will adjust to equalize the relative purchasing power of currencies.
5. No, it wouldn't, as other exchange rate models have failed to improve on the results of the random walk model.
6. The forward rate of a country that has a lower interest rate will sell at a premium (forward premium) to its spot currency rate, while the country with a higher interest rate will sell at a discount (forward discount) to its spot currency rate.
7. Uncovered interest parity theorizes that investors should not be able to make profits from carry trade. The conundrum is that they do make profits.
8. Sterilized intervention allows a country to alter its debt composition without affecting its money supply.

CHAPTER 7

1. Any three from: clearing transactions; arbitrage; hedging; speculation.
2. Rollovers are transactions designed to renew or extend spot deals. There is often a carrying cost associated with rolling over a position, though sometimes traders can make money on a rollover.
3. 118.30; 1.3192
4. Margin trading can potentially see investors suffer losses that greatly exceed the amounts that they have deposited.
5. Any four from: market order; entry order; stop-entry order; limit order; stop-loss order; OCO order.
6. Lower liquidity

7. Option prices are typically quoted in units of implied volatility.
8. In foreign exchange swaps, one currency is swapped for another for a period of time, and then swapped back, creating an exchange and re-exchange. Foreign exchange swaps are most useful for those who have plenty of one currency and need liquidity in another currency.

CHAPTER 8

1. Alfred Winslow Jones; shares
2. Long-Term Capital Management
3. George Soros
4. Thailand
5. South Korea, Thailand, Indonesia

BIBLIOGRAPHY

Bank for International Settlements, "Triennial Central Bank Survey of Foreign Exchange and Derivatives Market Activity." (Online) Available at www.bis.org/publ/rpfx05t.pdf.

Bank of Japan, "Mission and Activities of the Bank of Japan." (Online) Available at http://www.boj.or.jp/en/type/exp/about/mission.htm.

British History Online, "The Royal Exchange." (Online) Available at http://www.british-history.ac.uk/report.aspx?compid=45060.

British Museum, "The Origins of Coinage." (Online) Available at http://www.britishmuseum.org/explore/themes/money/the_origins_of_coinage.aspx.

Dale, **Richard**, *The First Crash: Lessons from the South Sea Bubble*. Princeton: Princeton University Press, 2004.

Davies, **Glynn**, *A History of Money from Ancient Times to the Present Day*. Cardiff: University of Wales Press, 2002.

Evans, **Martin** and **Lyons**, **Richard**, "Frequently Asked Questions About the Micro Approach to FX." (Online) Available at http://faculty.haas.berkeley.edu/lyons/docs/.

Galati, **Gabriele** and **Melvin**, **Michael**, "Why has FX trading surged? Explaining the 2004 Triennial Survey." Bank *for International Settlements Quarterly Review*, December 2004.

Institute for International Monetary Affairs, "The Euro – Five Years On: Implications for Asia." (Online) Available at www.iima.or.jp/pdf/2004/occasional15.pdf.

Jeanne, **Olivier** and **Rose**, **Andrew K**, "Noise Trading and Exchange Rate Regimes." Reserve Bank of New Zealand Discussion Paper Series, Reserve Bank of New Zealand, 1999.

Kosrovi, **Zahra**, "Coins in Greek Literature." (Online) Available at http://oldmoney.vassar.edu/papers/greek_literature.html.

Lamy, **Pascal**, "Multilateral or Bilateral Trade Agreements: Which way to go?" Speech, January 2007. (Online) Available at www.wto.org/english/news_e/sppl_e/sppl53_e.htm.

Lietaer, **Bernard**, *The Future of Money: Creating New Wealth, Work and a Wiser World*. London: Random House, 2001.

Lillich, **Mike**, "New Book Traces History of Interest and Usury in Many Cultures." (Online) Available at www.purdue.edu/UNS/html4ever/2004/040907.Houkes.interest.html.

"Marco Polo and His Travels." (Online) Available at www.silk-road.com/artl/marcopolo.shtml.

Meese, **Richard** and **Rogoff**, **Kenneth**, "Empirical Exchange Rate Models of the Seventies: Do They Fit Out of Sample." *Journal of International Economics*, February, 1983.

Melamed, **Leo**, "The Birth of FX Futures." (Online) Available at www.cme.com/files/birthoffutures.pdf.

Mizrach, **Bruce** and **Neely**, **Christopher J**. "The Transition to Electronic Communications Networks in the Secondary Treasury Market." (Online) Available at http://research.stlouisfed.org/publications/review/06/11/Mizrach.pdf.

Moxham, **Roy**, *Tea: A History of Addiction, Exploitation and Empire*. New York: Carroll & Graf, 2003.

Mundell, **Robert**, "Uses and Abuses of Gresham's Law in the History of Money." (Online) Available at www.columbia.edu/~ram15/grash.html.

Neely, **Christopher J**, "An Analysis of Recent Studies of the Effect of Foreign Exchange Intervention." Working Paper. Federal Reserve Bank of St Louis, 2005.

Oberlechner, **Thomas**, *The Psychology of the Foreign Exchange Market*, Chichester. John Wiley & Sons, 2004.

President Franklin D Roosevelt's Message to Congress on the Bretton Woods Money and Banking Proposals. (Online) Available at www.ibiblio.org/pha/policy/1945/450212a.html.

Shamah, **Shani**, *A Foreign Exchange Primer*, Chichester. John Wiley & Sons, 2003.

Solomon, **Robert**, *The International Monetary System*, 1945–1981: *An Insider's View*, New York. Harper and Row, 1982.

Spiegel, **Mark M**, "Argentina's Currency Crisis: Lessons for Asia." (Online) Available at www.iadb.org/laeba/downloads/WP_2_2002_Spiegel.pdf.

Spiegel, **Mark M**, "Japanese Foreign Exchange Intervention." FRBSF Economic Letter. Federal Reserve Bank of San Francisco, December 2003.

Standage, **Tom**, *A History of the World in 6 Glasses*. New York: Walker & Company, 2006.

Tai, **Stephen**, "Chopmarks on 5 Mexican Silver Dollars Circulated in China." (Online) Available at www.charm.ru/coins/misc/chopmarks.shtml.

The Economist, "Paper Gains." (Online) Available at www.economist.com/diversions/millennium.

"Triumphs of London, 1675" (Online) Available at www.umich.edu/~ece/student_projects/coffee/TriumphsofLondon.html.

Tumpel-Gugerell, **Gertrude**, "Exchange rate moves in a global economy: A central banking perspective." Speech, December 2004. (Online) Available at http://www.ecb.int/press/key/date/2004/html/sp041203.en.html.

Von Glahn, **Richard**, *Fountain of Fortune: Money and Monetary Policy in China, 1000–1700*. Berkeley: University of California Press, 1996.

Weatherford, **Jack Mciver,** *The History of Money*, New York. Three Rivers Press, 1997.

GLOSSARY

Algorithmic trading
Algorithmic trading enables an investor to place an order to buy or sell a defined quantity of currency into a quantitative model that automatically generates the timing of orders and the size of orders based on goals specified by algorithmic parameters and constraints.

Balance of payments
The balance of payments accounts of a country record the payments and receipts of the residents of that country in their transactions with residents of other countries. Strictly defined, the balance of payments of a country is a way of measuring the flow of payments during a specific period of time (usually one year) between that country and all other countries. The calculation includes the country's exports and imports of good, services, and financial transfers so that all payments and liabilities to foreigners (the debits) and all payments and obligations received from foreigners (the credits) are used.

Barter
To trade by exchanging goods and services for other goods and services, not for money.

Bretton Woods agreement
An agreement signed at the Mount Washington Hotel in the ski resort town of Bretton Woods in 1944 that outlined rules and regulations for an international monetary system. It established a fixed exchange rate linked to the US dollar. It also created the International Monetary Fund and the precursor to the present-day World Bank.

Coin Hoard
A group of coins whose discovery makes it clear that the hoard was deliberately buried in a group.

Convertibility

Current account convertibility means that foreign exchange can be freely bought and sold provided its use is associated with international trade in goods and services. But under current account convertibility there still are restrictions when the intended use of the foreign exchange is to purchase foreign financial assets or to make equity investments. If convertibility is allowed for transactions in both the current and the capital accounts, we say there is full convertibility—this equates to free capital mobility.

Cross Rates

Cross rates usually refer to two currencies that are traded which do not involve the U.S. dollar.

Double coincidence of wants

In barter trade, one party must want what the other party has and the latter party must simultaneously want what the first party has.

Electronic money

Electronic money is a payment instrument whereby monetary value is electronically stored on a technical device in the possession of the customer. The amount of stored monetary value is decreased or increased, as appropriate, whenever the owner of the device uses it to make purchase, sale, loading or unloading transactions.

Entry Order

This type of order is executed when the price touches a pre-specified level. It remains in effect until cancelled by the customer.

European joint float

The European joint float, popularly called the "snake", was established in 1972 by West Germany, France, Italy, the Netherlands, Belgium and Luxembourg. It was an agreement between these countries to manage their currencies so that their exchange rates moved in tandem.

Federal funds rate

The federal funds rate is the interest rate on overnight loans between banks in the U.S. These loans are most often used by banks to satisfy their reserve requirements.

Fisher Effect

According to the Fisher Effect, nominal interest rates will adjust to expected inflation rates. On an international level, the Fisher Effect forecasts that the difference in nominal interest rates between two countries should be equal to the expected difference in inflation. Countries with higher expected inflation rates will therefore have higher nominal interest rates and countries with lower expected inflation rates will have lower nominal interest rates.

Foreign exchange swap

An over-the-counter short-term derivative instrument. Two parties exchange agreed-upon amounts of two currencies as a spot transaction, simultaneously agreeing to unwind the exchange at a future date, based on a rule that reflects both interest and principal payments. In practice, a foreign exchange swap is the combination of a spot and forward transaction.

Forward contracts

Over-the-counter agreements by counterparties to exchange a specified amount of different currencies at some future date, with the exchange rate being set at the time the contract is entered into. With a forward contract, a price is established on the trade date, but cash changes hands only on the settlement date.

Forward rates

Forward rates can be quoted in two ways—as an outright quote or as forward points. The outright quote is simply a bid-ask price similar to spot market quotes. The forward points are the amounts that need to be added to or subtracted from the spot rates. The forward premium or discount is typically the difference in short-term interest rates between the two countries.

Gresham's Law

Gresham's Law is a law about money in circulation and its basic premise is that bad money drives good money out of monetary systems.

Implied volatility

Implied volatility is the estimated volatility of a currency's price. It increases when markets are bearish on that currency and decreases when markets are bullish. This is simply because bearish markets are perceived as more risky than bullish markets.

Indentured loans

In the Middle Ages, indenture loans allowed the poor to borrow money for major expenses like paying for property or traveling. But lenders frequently abused the system and would inflate the debt or add new conditions to the loans, even after the debt was fully repaid.

Limit Order

An order to take profit at a pre-specified level.

Maastricht criteria

1. **Low inflation:** The rise of the price of daily food may not be higher than 1.5 percentage points above the inflation rate of the three EU countries with the lowest inflation.

2. **Low interest rates:** Interest on long-term government loans may not be higher than two percentage points above the interest rates of the three countries with the lowest interest rates.

3. **Sound state finances:** The budget deficit must either be lower than 3 percent of national income, or be falling and almost have reached 3 percent, or be of a transitory nature. The deficit must also be lower than 60 percent of national income, or be falling at a sufficient rate towards the 60 percent mark.

4. **Stable exchange rate:** The exchange rate must have stayed within the normal boundaries of the exchange rate mechanism of the EU countries—also called the EMS countries—for two years. The country must have been a member of this mechanism for the same period.

Market Maker

A market maker is a dealer who quotes buying and selling prices for one or more currencies to his customers, seeking to make a profit from the difference between the buying and selling prices. As in stock and commodities markets, market makers are viewed as useful to the functioning of currency markets. They contribute to liquidity and price stability in the short term, and provide useful price information.

Market Order

An order at the current market price.

Measure of value

Money is used to let people fairly assess the comparative worth of different goods and services.

Medium of exchange

Money is used so that goods and services can be exchanged easily.

Non-deliverable forwards

Offered by banks, non-deliverable forwards, or NDFs, are forward contracts on non-convertible currencies or thinly traded currencies—these are currencies mostly used for domestic transactions and not freely traded in currency markets, usually due to government restrictions on their use.

OCO Order

One Cancels the Other. Two orders whereby if one is executed, the other is cancelled.

Prime brokerage

Prime brokerage typically refers to an investment bank's package of services to clients, mostly hedge fund clients. The advantage of such a bundled service is that it centralises a number of tasks such as securities clearing, financing leverage, custody, securities lending, foreign exchange trading and a number of other services.

Random Walk model
The Random Walk model is based on an investment theory that says market prices follow a random path up and down, without any influence by past price movements, making it impossible to predict with any accuracy which direction the market will move at any point.

Smithsonian agreement
The Smithsonian agreement in late 1971 created a new dollar standard and was signed by the Group of Ten nations—Belgium, Canada, France, Germany, Italy, Japan, the Netherlands, Sweden, the UK and the US.

Special Drawing Rights
The International Monetary Fund was empowered in 1969 to issue Special Drawing Rights (SDRs), which members could add to their holdings of foreign currencies and gold held in their central banks. SDRs can be considered to be an artificial currency used by the IMF and is defined as a basket of national currencies.

Spot transactions
Single outright transactions involving the exchange of two currencies. Transactions are done at a rate agreed on the date of the contract for value or delivery (cash settlement) typically within two business days.

Stop-Entry Order
An order to buy above or sell below the market at a pre-specified level, on the view that the price will continue in the same direction from that point. For example, this sort of order is placed when a trader is not sure if a currency pair will rise but once it breaks above a certain level, the trader expects the pair to rise further.

Stop-Loss Order
An order to limit losses at a pre-specified level.

Store of value
Money can be reliably saved and used at a later date with predictability.

Term structure of interest rates
The term structure of interest rates is typically defined as a yield curve displaying the relationship between spot rates of zero-coupon securities and their terms to maturity. The yield curve allows investors to ascertain expectations of interest rates at different time intervals into the future.

Uncovered interest rate parity
The uncovered interest parity condition contends that the difference in interest rates between the two countries simply reflects the rate at which investors expect the high-interest-rate currency to depreciate against the low- interest-rate currency.

White Labelling
White labeling allows smaller banks and financial institutions to outsource their currency pricing to providers with large liquidity bases like major global banks. They can thus offer their own clients a broader array of foreign exchange services, without the costs of independently developing those services.

INDEX

A

Alfred Winslow Jones, 165, 179, 196
Algorithmic trading, 47, 51, 52, 201
Amaranth Advisors, 180
Arbitrage, 129-131, 138, 150, 159, 162, 167, 195
Argentina crisis, 92, 96-98, 134, 199
Aristotle, 5, 14, 15
Asian Financial Crisis, 93, 94, 97, 101, 170, 172, 180
Asset class, 103, 113, 114, 116, 184
Athenian drachma, 29

B

Balance of payments, 27, 40, 42, 78, 84, 85, 201
Bank for International Settlements, 59, 101, 115, 116, 183, 197
Bank of England, 13, 60, 171, 180
Bank of Korea, 124, 148
Bank of Japan, 57, 58, 59, 73, 182, 197
Barter, 1-6, 19, 20, 38, 181, 186, 193, 201, 202
Bid-ask spreads, 48, 50, 107, 147, 163, 194
Big Mac index, 127, 128
Bill of exchange, 11

BIS, 45, 59, 101-105, 111, 112, 129, 159, 183, 197
Black-Scholes model, 157
Black Wednesday, 171
Bretton Woods agreement, 40, 42, 44, 75, 99, 181, 201
British Empire, 25, 26, 28, 44, 181
British Museum, 7, 8, 197
Buy/Sell quotes, 139

C

Carry trade, 104, 116, 133, 134, 168, 184, 194, 195
Central bank, 13, 41-43, 47, 57, 59, 61, 72, 79-92, 96, 97, 101, 108, 109, 115-119, 121, 124, 131, 132, 134-136, 151, 161, 162, 169, 170, 172, 180, 182, 183, 185, 195, 197, 199, 205
Chinese warlords, 33
Clearing transactions, 137, 162, 195
Coffee houses, 21-25, 44, 181, 193
Commodity Futures Trading Commission, 108, 140
Community currencies, 179, 186, 188
Convertibility, 6, 88, 89, 97, 100, 194, 202
Copper coins, 27, 28,
Cowrie shell, 3, 4, 181, 193

P

Paper money, 1, 6, 8-14, 19, 20, 31, 34, 43, 181
Percentage in Point, 139
Pips, 139, 142, 145, 146, 163
Plato, 5, 14
Portability, 6, 34
Portfolio Balance model, 124, 136
Precious Note of the Great Ming, 193
Prime brokerage, 51, 52, 54, 72, 182, 204
Purchasing Power Parity model, 136

R

Raleigh, Sir Walter 25
Random Walk model, 126, 129, 136, 195, 205
Reuters, 45-47, 51, 67, 72, 152, 182
Risk reversal, 158
Rollover, 139, 163, 195
Roosevelt, Franklin Delano 37, 75, 78
Royal Exchange, 21-23, 44, 197

S

Shang dynasty, 4
Silk Road, 3, 10, 198
Silver, 5, 7-12, 14, 22, 25-35, 43, 44, 47, 75, 109, 110, 181, 199
Silver coin, 8, 27, 29-32
Silver content, 8, 22, 29
Smithsonian agreement, 41, 42, 193, 205
snake, 42, 202
Song dynasty, 8, 9, 10, 19
Soros, George, 60, 168, 171, 178, 196
Speculation, 27, 39, 40, 75, 121, 138, 162, 163, 170, 171, 178, 179, 187, 195
Spot transactions, 102, 137, 139, 140, 146-148, 162, 163, 205

Stability of value, 6
Staters, 8
Starbucks, 21
Straddle, 158
Strangle, 158
Stockholm Banco, 12, 13
Store of value, 1, 6, 34, 193, 205
Striking of coins, 8
Sveriges Riksbank, 13

T

Tang dynasty, 8-10, 19
Tea, 9, 25-27, 44, 69, 198
Term structure of interest rates, 205
Time value, 155, 156
Thalers, 30
The Great Depression, 36-38
Tobin Tax, 179
Traders' talk, 143
Trading platforms, 49, 51-53, 66, 67, 138, 140, 141
Treaty of Bogue, 28
Treaty of Nanjing, 28

U

U.S. Coinage Act, 30
U.S. Department of Treasury, 61, 64, 65
Uncovered interest rate parity, 206
United Nations Conference on Trade and Development, 87
Uruguay round, 79

V

Volatility, 61, 63, 108, 111, 118, 154, 156-158, 179, 196, 203

W

White labeling, 206
World Bank, 70, 77, 78, 178, 194, 201
World Trade Organisation, 77-80, 82,
    83, 99, 102, 182, 194, 198

Y

Yuan dynasty, 10

Other titles in the series

Mark Mobius
Masterclass Series

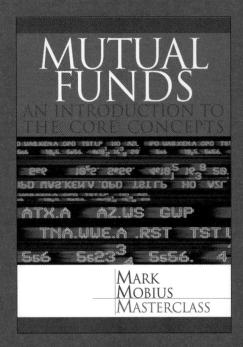

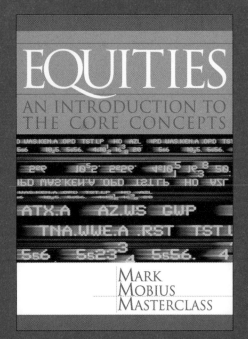

9780470821435 • 250 pages

Mutual Funds: An Introduction to the Core Concepts gives an in-depth understanding of mutual fund structure, the benefits of owning funds, how to build a portfolio of mutual funds and how to evaluate its performance.

Highlights of the book include detailed coverage of:
- The history of mutual funds
- Different types of funds, including open and closed-end, equity, bond and money market funds
- The structure of mutual funds
- Techniques for selecting the right types of funds
- Strategies for buying and selling funds
- The latest industry trends and growth drivers
- How to determine a fund's risk and investment style
- How to calculate return on investments and evaluate fund costs

9780470821442 • 250 pages

Equities: An Introduction to the Core Concepts offers a comprehensive guide on the rewards of equity ownership that will help investors make informed equity investments decisions.

Highlights of the book include detailed coverage of:
- The history of equities
- Different types of risks including volatility risk, political risk, currency risk, company risk, transactional risk, and liquidity risk.
- Techniques in selecting the right mix of equities
- Understanding corporate behavior
- Different types of shares and their various characteristics
- Transferability and negotiability of equities
- Analysis of financial statements

WILEY

Now you know.

wiley.com